The
WORLD'S
BIGGEST
DOERS

The Story of the Lions

ROBERT J. CASEY

and

W. A. S. DOUGLAS

Wilcox & Follett Co.   CHICAGO

NEW YORK   TORONTO   MEXICO CITY

Editor: ARTHUR BROGUE

Book Design by Stanford W. Williamson

PRINTED IN U.S.A.

Melvin Jones, Founder and Secretary-General of The
International Association of Lions Clubs

DEDICATION

To all Lions everywhere for their unceasing efforts "to create and foster a spirit of 'generous consideration' among the peoples of the world through a study of the problems of international relationships."

CONTENTS

Chapter		Page
1	THE ODD GENESIS OF AN IDEA	1
2	THE NEW ORDER	10
3	GRASS ROOTS	19
4	THE OLD MONARCH	28
5	OFF-STAGE NOISES	39
6	DIVIDENDS IN DEMOCRACY	46
7	ACCORDING TO THE CODE	56
8	THE WHY OF IT	63
9	GROWING PAINS	74
10	HOME OFFICE	85
11	PENNY WATCHING	91
12	LIONS IN PRINT	99
13	ROAR! YOU LIONS!	110
14	INCREASE AND MULTIPLY	116
15	HAPPY BIRTHDAY	127
16	EATIN' MEETIN'	140
17	FUN WITH FINES	148
18	THE WORLD'S BIGGEST DOERS	156
19	KIND HEARTS	169

vii

Chapter   *Page*

20   INTO EVERYTHING   177
21   "WHAT'S GOOD FOR BUSINESS—"   193
22   NOR FLOOD NOR DROUGHT NOR BOMBS   204
23   LIONS AND THE UNITED NATIONS   211
24   LIONS INTERNATIONAL CITY   229
25   DEMONSTRATION OF THE JONES LAW   236

     APPENDIX   245
         Past Presidents of Lions International   247
         Lions Clubs Abroad   253
         The Extension of Lionism   257
         Annual Conventions of The International
             Association of Lions Clubs   258
     INDEX   299

The WORLD'S BIGGEST DOERS

SERVICE CLUB

"These things really form the foundation of our Association—the name, the symbols, The Lions Code of Ethics, The Lions Clubs' Objects, its slogan, its colors, and lapel button . . . and on these things, the Association began to build."

—MELVIN JONES

1

THE ODD GENESIS OF AN IDEA

MARCH, 1913, is memorable for many things, such as—for instance—the inauguration of Woodrow Wilson to the presidency of the United States, the Dayton flood, the death of J. Pierpont Morgan, Sr., and some trouble with Mexico over the foreign policies of Huerta. Less well publicized, but very likely of more importance to hundreds of thousands of people scattered across the world, is the fact that during that month Melvin Jones, a Chicago insurance man, was invited to luncheon by one William Towne.

Why he accepted the invitation is a point not quite clear to anybody, probably including Mr. Jones himself. As a typical successful businessman of his period, he was accustomed to look upon his midday meal as an annoying interruption. He conceivably gave it no rating as an occasion for relaxation, good-fellowship, and friendly intercourse. He no doubt would have sensed mental unbalance in anybody who seriously suggested it as a public benefaction. Nevertheless he joined Mr. Towne at a weekly meeting of a luncheon club known as "The Business Circle" and he began to wonder why such organizations couldn't be put to some practical use. He answered the question for himself in 1917 with the formation of The International Association of Lions Clubs.

It is difficult for anyone acquainted with America since the turn of the century to realize that there wasn't any such thing as the modern service club before 1917, and that such organizations did not become a real force in urban life until the twenties. True, there were associations in something of the same pattern meeting regularly to promote a community of interest. There were civic-betterment societies and religious societies and secret societies and trade guilds and social coteries and business fraternities, and corporations, syndicates, and trusts—just as now. There were clubs designed to band together the followers of every conceivable sport or enthusiasm or political principle from dog racing to free silver. There were theater clubs and traveling men's clubs and, of course, luncheon clubs. There were even a few societies whose policy was the assistance of members by other members. But the concern of any of these associations and sodalities for anyone outside the membership roster was extremely nebulous.

Nobody talked of service, except in so far as the word applied to the waiters on that March day when Mr. Jones sat down with The Business Circle in the old Boston Oyster House in Chicago's loop. The organization had been in existence since 1909 and at one time had a membership of 200. The list was down to thirty-nine in 1913, and only seventeen were on hand when Mr. Towne introduced his guest. Some of those present, Mr. Jones remembers, were important men in the community: Edward Hines and E. C. Hooker, both in the lumber business; D. S. Sattler, an undertaker; E. C. North, a contractor; and Charles Stevens of the stationery firm of Stevens & Maloney. There were others, now recalled vaguely as successful manufacturers, merchants, and professional men, who had the marks of upstanding citizens, much the same sort of members as those who have subsequently given the service club its stature and strength. A few who remained in the organization were obviously bound together by long acquaintance and mutual respect but a newcomer could not help noticing that they all seemed to be sitting on the edges of their chairs.

The Business Circle, like other sodalities of its period, had been assembled on a "help-one-another" basis. But Jones was quick to detect that the dues as of March, 1913, were going to other organizations where virtue was less of its own reward. Some of those with whom he broke bread for the first time at the Boston Oyster House and sundry alumni to whom his curiosity led him afterward, admitted that they had transferred their affiliations because of "better connections." One organization, for instance, had been boasting of international affiliations for the past few years. Another was enrolling hundreds of neophytes on a promise of broader interests and activities. Jones didn't know much about clubs, but it seemed to him that at the moment one differed from another only to the extent of its good intentions.

All of this, at the moment, was a matter of no particular concern to him. Melvin Jones was probably the last man in the world anybody would have picked out as a

crusader, reformer, uplifter, or organizer. He had none
of the earmarks of that character whom the satirists of a
nearing future were to refer to as a "joiner." He was gregarious. He liked people. He made friends easily and
kept them. But it is significant that until he was brought
to the table of The Business Circle by Mr. Towne he had
never been a member of a club. Neither had he ever been
active in politics—if that makes any difference.

Melvin Jones was born on January 13, 1880, at Fort
Thomas, Arizona, where his father, Captain John Calvin
Jones, was commanding a troop of Scouts under Major
General Miles. His earliest memories were a weird mix-
ture of horse opera and sudden death. Horses and bugles
and blue-clad troopers—gaunt, frightened settlers—painted
Indians—ghostly wagon trains afloat in dust. The life of
the southwest frontier as he remembers it now had all
the improbable trappings of a class B movie—too real in
all its details to meet the standards of a modern movie
producer. One of the realest people in his life has been
Captain Hertig, whom he never saw. Hertig was killed
on Cibicu Creek the year young Melvin was born. But
no one seemed to talk about anyone else during the years
of the Apache wars until Geronimo was captured and
Captain Jones moved on to a new station in the North.
Yet, these early experiences made a vivid and lasting impression on Jones's memory; they had a bearing on his
life's philosophies and from them he gained poise, equilib-
rium, and understanding—qualities which were to prove
so useful to him later in life.

Melvin Jones stopped for a time between the Gila
River and Chicago at St. Louis and Quincy, Illinois, where
he went to school. He had no taste for the army. There

Members of the old Business Circle, circa 1917, con-
gregating around lion's statue in front of Chicago
Art Institute to celebrate the change of the club's name
to the Lions Club

Mrs. Melvin Jones in 1925, relaxing between rounds in the finals of the National Women's Open Golf Tournament, at Pinehurst, North Carolina, where she won the title.

was little about his enforced connection with it that he cared to remember. Nor was he much interested in business. When, in his twenties, he moved on to Chicago, he was not certain whether he would make a career of music or the law. He was a good law student, and for many years he enjoyed local celebrity as a tenor. But in the end he tore up the schedule he had prepared for himself and went into the offices of Johnson & Higgins, insurance brokers. In 1913 he was head of his own agency and doing well—well enough, at any rate, to be invited to membership in "The Business Circle."

The Circle, after the fashion of groups of its sort, then and since, had made "classification by occupation" the basis of its membership. So far as Jones's occupation was concerned he had no competition. The insurance man who had preceded him had gone to join some organization offering a better contact. But the new member had attended only one or two meetings before he discovered that what one did for a living was a matter of deep interest to one's associates.

There was the case of Brother Charles Stevens of Stevens & Maloney, for instance. He was a stationer, of course, but he was also a printer, and held two classifications. Some of the members, having nothing else to do, made it their business to find out why he held two classifications and just what he intended to call himself. Mr. Stevens, who got the inference that his fellow club members were looking on him as a sort of Jekyll and Hyde, began to absent himself from meetings, and, considering the size of the turnout that was sitting down to the weekly chop at the Boston Oyster House, it is hardly remarkable that he was missed.

Most of the conversation during several meetings was devoted to what some members looked upon as Stevens' "defection." Jones listened with growing incredulity, and presently forgot that he was not only a new member of The Circle, but the newest member. "I don't see anything complicated about it," he said. "He doesn't want more than anyone else and he's confused. I could straighten him out on the matter in a minute."

So Jones was promptly given the assignment to call on Mr. Stevens and so rose out of a neophyte's obscurity.

It is not a matter of record whether Stevens came back as a printer or a dealer in paper and ink. Nobody paid much attention to that phase of the episode. The interest of the membership was in Melvin Jones, who had been able to convince him that he ought to come back in any category. It was obvious that Mr. Jones had a talent for finagling, if you care to put it that way, or diplomacy, that might some day be useful.

Out of such trivia spring great associations of men— powerful coalitions with millions of members.

At that moment it is unlikely that Melvin Jones was listening to any off-stage calls of destiny. He had listened to the blandishments of William Towne and had joined The Business Circle without any idea at all that he might be changing the whole course of his life. Such clubs as The Circle, to his notion, weren't the nuclei of vast national institutions. They were just agencies through which a man had a chance to meet people of his own kind —a whole lot of people.

Nor did it seem extraordinary to him that he had been able to placate the ruffled Mr. Stevens. That sort of business was just another form of salesmanship. And sales-

manship was just the routine of providing something that
somebody needed. But once the misunderstood brother
had been brought back, the other brothers seemed to rate
the job as a great feat of diplomacy; and whether he
wanted to or not, the newcomer found himself talking
up in the meetings.

None of the matters up for discussion at The Circle
luncheons were ever very serious, as he remembers them.
With no particular policy except to eat an occasional chop
in concert, the clubs of the period couldn't be concerned
with much except such purely domestic details as "How
do we get some dinner music and speakers?" and "Where
do we eat next week?" It is difficult to figure out how a
couple of dozen business men could get up a blood pressure over a prospective change in menu or meeting place
or time of assembly. But somehow they managed it, and
in such discussions Jones took no part. It is of record,
however, that he did show his disapproval of The Business
Circle's desultory adjournment from May to October.

"If we can't stand the sight of one another for six
months of the year," he mentioned at one of the meetings,
"then I can't see any reason why we should be clubby
for the other six. It doesn't seem to me to make any difference whether we meet on Wednesdays or Mondays.
But it does make a difference whether we meet at all
or not."

The older members, probably miffed by the young
upstart's criticism, tabled his proposal for a year-round
schedule of meetings. But it became obvious that they
had listened to him. As a sort of dare, they elected him
secretary when the new club year began on January 1,
1914.

He accepted the honor, wondering what he had let himself in for. He took the membership roster with him when he went back to his office and put in the rest of the afternoon telephoning to his friends around town. On January 10, he was formally inducted into his new job. He closed his speech of acceptance on an optimistic note. Better days were ahead, he told the eighteen or nineteen brothers who had come to listen to him. The Business Circle was just about to go places—watch our smoke. The next meeting would be held on January 17 at the Planters Hotel in Chicago and, after the accepted formula, he hoped for a big turnout and plenty of enthusiasm.

He wasn't so enthusiastic himself. He had talked up the prospects of the new day so continuously that he had come to believe in it himself, but he wasn't sure that anybody had listened to him. He was well grounded in the philosophy of brotherhood. He was in total agreement with the American principles of personal liberty and individual rights, but he was also aware of the instincts of mutuality that had led mankind to live in communities. But he likewise knew that most men don't act without reason. And when you got right down to it he was asking them to join an organization that certainly didn't offer much. Maybe somebody would come to his meeting. Maybe not. If all the invitees had stayed away simultaneously he would have been entirely prepared.

So it came about that when the president dropped the gavel to call the brothers to order at the Planters Hotel on January 17, he was probably the most astounded man in the room, although there were plenty of runners-up. The attendance, for the first time in half a dozen years, had hit a total of seventy-five. When this record was maintained at the next meeting, it became obvious that something new had been added to The Circle's methods of organization.

Like many another man who has taken on a job because he wanted to show that it could be done, Melvin Jones suddenly found himself up to his elbows in work that he could never have foreseen. The Circle's membership began to increase and as it did, so did the secretary's correspondence. Telephone calls from the brothers, chiefly on matters of personal concern, became a constant and insistent part of the Jones Insurance Company's normal business day. Save for the club luncheons, the secretary's meals became sketchy and irregular. His working hours began to embrace most of the time he was awake. But when he stopped one day to ask himself why he had taken on all this gratuitous burden, it suddenly occurred to him that he was having the time of his life.

"You're working yourself to death for somebody else without pay," his wife pointed out realistically. And then he enunciated the principle that in later years more than anything else was to make the Association of Lions Clubs the greatest organization of its sort that the world had even seen.

"I'm finding out," he said, "that you don't get very far until you start doing something for somebody else. And I'm beginning to believe it might help some of these clubs, like The Circle, to take that to heart."

2

THE NEW ORDER

MELVIN JONES has never been much interested in partisan politics. In the beginning he was apathetic, because the proponent of one school of American political philosophy so closely resembled another. Later, as principal pacifier in a group of a thousand varied interests, he had little use for such dynamite as election arguments. But no one who has followed his career for more than a few weeks would hint that he lacked understanding of political techniques—anybody's political techniques.

He, himself, was a long time realizing this. He thought his success in reviving The Business Circle was due to "salesmanship," which—in turn—was motivated by friendly concern and a ready sympathy. Well, some call it salesmanship and some don't, but that is about all Jim Farley had.

Jones carried his sympathy into the offices of The Circle's leading absentees, some of whom he found to be

lukewarm, some nourishing vague grudges, some hostile.
He found out that before he could hope to ask them
back into the fold, he must first find out why they were
staying away. To do that he must first establish himself
in their confidence—and when he had done that, he sel-
dom needed to go further. He got the prodigals to return
and new members to join virtually for the asking. And
he learned a lot about what we then called luncheon
classification clubs just by listening to a considerable body
of his friends and customers who thought them all non-
sense. Occasionally he answered, sometimes he argued.
But mostly he sat quietly and listened, for quite a lot of
the adverse criticism seemed to be an echoing of his own
thoughts.

The club idea was well on its way, but in 1914 nobody
was quite prepared to say what course it was to take or
where it was going to go. The weekly meeting to partake
of lamb and peas and pie had become a sort of established
ritual. In cities which the advertising men used to call
"the hundred-thousand group," there were literally thousands of luncheon clubs, something like The Circle as
Jones found it in 1913—well established and displaying
some signs of permanence. Some were alive and vigorous
and given to youthful horseplay. Some were merely alive.
But all of them, including a percentage that outwardly
seemed pretty moribund, were guaranteed a certain lon-
gevity by one characteristic of the American male which
he probably will be the last to admit, his ingrained habit
of waiting to be called for his meals.

Whatever else might be said of joining a luncheon
classification club, the member knew that one day a week
at least his noonday meal would be waiting for him in a

certain set place at a certain set time. And thereafter his
attendance was quite likely to be regular, unless he
changed his place of business or took his patronage to
some other club.

Basically, there was nothing startlingly new in the
luncheon classification club as it first sprang up among
the office buildings. It wasn't such a far cry from the
Fourth of July Picnic, or the church social, or the First
Ward Marching Club's Annual Clambake and Chowder
Festival. But as it acquired some social status in the nation's
business districts, it began to develop possibilities which a
few practical psychologists, Jones included, were quick
to recognize.

Even today, with most of the tricks laid bare for all
to see, it is still something of a job to get any half dozen
businessmen together to discuss a cause or project or, for
that matter, to do anything else. Because of the male's
natural shyness or habitual boredom or whatever it is,
he has to be lured into contact with his fellow man—a
fact which was recognized by the tax collectors of Babylon
as well as the lobbyists and fund raisers of another country
and another era. We'll give a big banquet—good food
and plenty of it, good entertainment, relaxation, merriment—-and then! The technique was three or four thousand years old; it was still unbettered in 1914—but it
certainly was being subjected to some new tests and new
applications. Men were answering the mess call as of old
—not every leap year or every Labor Day, but every
week. And as yet no worthy cause had benefited by this
phenomenon. No promoter of the public good had so
far seized upon his opportunity.

Somebody has explained the phenomenon of the luncheon classification club's growth in the United States with the suggestion that all men are lonesome. And while that may be oversimplification, it probably comes close enough to the truth of the matter to merit repetition. Men joined the clubs that preceded the big international organization just to meet other men, some of whom they scarcely knew. Aside from this brief social contact, the club of that period had nothing at all to offer. Not until later was there any attempt to put friendship or club-brotherhood to any practical use. And the "Jones Law" that there is no progress without service was not recognized until a long time after that.

Associations for mutual helpfulness were no newer at the turn of the century than associations for the sharing of midday meals. There is record of a group called "The Civil Club" assembled in London in 1669, frankly announcing that "members should give preference to one another in their respective callings." It is significant that some club activity took much the same direction in the United States two hundred and fifty years later, and even more significant that public criticism in 1669 caused the Civil Club to abandon personal interest in favor of "service above self." The sessions at the Mermaid Tavern and the impromptu meetings at the Old Cheshire Cheese were merely manifestations of the same urge that had produced the Civil Club, although they placed less emphasis on *self*. They provided fellowship, food, and drink—and an interchange of ideas between kindred minds. So did students' messes at a later date, and post-office lunchrooms and, until quite recently, the old Algonquin Hotel Round Table.

The luncheon classification club, as reborn in the early nineteen hundreds, was able to find itself more quickly

than had its various prototypes. With increasing congestion in the cities and the spread of adequate transportation,
these new organizations found no difficulty getting members—as witness The Business Circle's original two hundred. Their rapid increase caused the newspapers to recognize them as something of a social phenomenon. They
began to make news. And as publicity added to their
attraction, they got more members.

The expansion for a time followed the pattern of a
snowball rolling downhill. Whatever the club, no matter
how large or small, it shared in the importance of the
general movement. The individual member, who may have
joined merely because somebody else asked him to, suddenly found himself rejoicing in his organization's improved social status. Yesterday he may have been John
Doe, Mortician, Call Me "Joe." But today he was "John
Doe, the civic leader, active in the work of The Business
Circle or of the Town Planners or of the Uptown Boost-
ers."

Somebody has said that the development of these
clubs—the broadening of their ideas as well as the length-
ening of their membership rolls—closely follows the graph
of the population movement from the rural districts to
the cities in the early part of the century. It is set forth
that small-town neighborliness—"folksiness"—camarade-
rie, or whatever you choose to call it, was one feature of
rural life that could not be transferred to the metropolitan
districts. It remained back in farm homes or in the offices
clustering about Courthouse Square, and the new city
dwellers missed it.

Of course all this goes back to the proposition that the
luncheon classification club's popularity stemmed princi-

pally from man's loneliness. But there were some concomitant factors. As the clubs reached mature growth they
offered the newcomers not only comradeship but also
prestige. Membership committees with plenty of material
to select from were getting more and more particular about
entrance requirements. And the button of a well-publi-
cized organization became an outward sign of success
when you displayed it on a visit to the old home town.

The association of *Likes* in a vast and bewildering
world of *Unlikes* is a basic instinct. In other fields of human endeavor it has brought about the formation of re-.
ligious sects, the New York 400, the American Medical
Association, the Redheaded Men's League, the Iowa Society of California, and the Guild of Former Pipe-Organ
Pumpers.

By the very speed of their growth and the complexity
of their demands, the great cities of the United States in
the 1900's were all composed of loose confederations of
total strangers. More or less, they are the same today.
Not all of the new city folk were transplanted small-
towners, yearning for the more demonstrative democracy
of the corn belt. Nobody has ever suggested that the forward march of luncheon classification clubs was a sort of
vicarious back-to-the-farm movement. There were large
native-born populations in the 1900's. There were also
hegiras into the cities from industrial areas that could
never be classed as rural, and lesser migrations between
cities. The result was, of course, that nobody knew his
next-door neighbor any more intimately than he does
today. Whatever else the early club had to offer, it gave
the bewildered neophyte a chance to talk to somebody and
listen to the unfamiliar echoes of his own voice.

Melvin Jones was thirty-three years old when he went over to the Boston Oyster House with William Towne "to meet a few of the boys." He was perhaps a year older when he began to sense a trend in the luncheon classification clubs that he could not explain and vaguely began to contemplate them as a factor in the life of the whole civilized world. He was perhaps thirty-seven when his "part-time labors" on behalf of The Business Circle had virtually pushed the insurance business out of his office. Looking at him now as he is nearing seventy, with the record of an incredible job of organization behind him, you wonder how he could have been content in any career not closely identified with service clubs in general and the Lions in particular. It is an academic discussion, of course. For Jones recognized his métier at once and never looked back.

Some wags in his Association have charged him with devoting his time to the organization of the Lions because he was "the first golf widower on record." The basis for the quip is the fact that Rose Amanda Freeman Jones was a successful golfer—so good that she began to gather up cups and titles in 1916, and continued to be one of the country's top performers well into the twenties, but her husband denies that her spectacular career influenced his own, one way or another. As a matter of fact, old-timers in the organization recall how, as another unpaid worker, she toiled day and night over paper work that was something more than an incidental factor in bringing The International Association of Lions Clubs into being.

Without going out of Chicago, without knowing anything of the operation of other clubs, Jones became convinced during his first months as secretary of The Business

Circle that the purely local club with a limited membership would presently be hard put to carry enough weight in the community to justify its own existence. To carry out his philosophy of progress through service, it was apparent that an association must have a sizeable, though well-selected, membership and numerous far-reaching contacts. It was still too early to discuss details for a possible grouping of kindred spirits all over the world. But he knew that an organization such as the one he envisioned would have to have some such feature. Other organizers, apparently, had sensed it too. For presently the news columns were filled with reports of meetings of civic, professional, and business groups, laying plans for some sort of society with international ramifications.

Jones brought this matter before The Circle. He had made some inquiries about the country, he said, and had come to the conclusion that whatever individual members might think about the purposes of the club it could not carry them out alone. It was not only desirable but also highly important to find means of affiliating The Circle with other congenial clubs.

At the end of the year, the board of directors of The Circle approved the plan to seek a national contact. Significantly, the board proposed no plan by which this contact was to be effected. It was the unanimous decision of the committee on ways and means that Melvin Jones should not be hampered in his work by outside advice or interference.

So Jones started out with what ideas he happened to have on hand. His fellow members began to refer facetiously to his insurance office as International Headquarters which, considering the nature of the work done in it, was not a bad title. The time Jones had left for his business of record became less and less as he and Mrs. Jones toiled far into the night, month after month, putting out what was virtually a campaign of direct-by-mail advertising. Correspondence went on and on and back and forth until it totaled hundreds of thousands of words. But it was the sort of interchange that would have discouraged anybody but Jones.

Nothing much came of it until 1917. This is the historic date that every good Lion has pasted in his hat.

3

GRASS ROOTS

For three years Jones was in correspondence with assorted unaffiliated clubs that had been established—many for a considerable time—in cities of all sizes from coast to coast. At insurance conventions and on what he wryly called vacation jaunts he made it a point to exchange views with men who were active in clubs in their own communities. As a visitor in a number of typical American cities, he had a chance to attend some club meetings and study the local techniques. He contrived to see at close range the workings of luncheon classification clubs throughout the country big enough and vital enough to get an occasional mention in the day's news. He analyzed them critically, made careful note of all that he considered efficient about their operation, and added to this what he thought would be of help in a national association. Eventually he rated them in his confidential notebook on a basis of debits and credits. In three years he had made slow progress toward forming an alliance between The Circle and even one coterie of kindred spirits. But he had learned quite a lot about clubs.

It had been his original idea to bring all the country's unaffiliated clubs into a loose confederation, each member group to operate locally under its original name and organization. But presently he found that sentiment among luncheon-club members favored, rather, a single association of clubs all with the same name and committed to one program and purpose.

The farther he traveled and the more profound his study of club methods the more he was convinced of the truth of the "Jones Law" and the relationship between progress and service. The purely commercial organizations, the little juntas of mutual back-scratchers, were, he thought, going the way of London's Civil Club two hundred and fifty years before.

"Any association that presumes to leadership in the community," he flatly informed The Circle, "will have to offer something more than business reciprocity among the members." He went on to comment on the crass commercialism of The Business Circle's name. It would have to be changed, he declared. And he said this so persistently during the three years of his search of national contacts that the members eventually agreed not only to change the name of The Circle but also its constitution, by-laws, and hopes for the future, should the occasion arise.

The occasion, as has been mentioned, arose on June 7, 1917. What happened then was the inception of what was later to be rated as the largest service-club organization in the world with a membership in 1949 of 381,426 in 7,427 clubs in twenty-six countries on five continents.

At the invitation of Jones, in his capacity of secretary of The Business Circle, twenty delegates representing some twenty-seven clubs met that June day with The Circle for noon luncheon in the East Room of Chicago's Hotel LaSalle. Acceptances had been received from the twenty as far back as two months previously to a proposition that they get together to discuss plans for the promotion of the status of the clubs they represented from local or regional to national or possibly international. Some of the delegates came prepared to abandon the identity of their local organizations and to unite under a central directorate with a single name. What Jones foresaw, however, was the probability that every delegate would fight to preserve the name of his own club by transferring it to the central organization. And he gave considerable thought to a compromise name before he went into the meeting.

He wasn't prepared to waste any sentiment over the name of The Circle. He was quite willing to let it go without a mention. In a sort of preliminary caucus he went over the matter with his fellow members and once more got their agreement to accept a title more in keeping with the purposes and objectives of a worth-while association.

Lion Charles B. Clemens recalls the general trend of Jones's strategy. (Clemens was vice-president of The Circle at the time.)

"It was one day just before one of the last Circle luncheon meetings before June 7," he says. "He cornered me for a cloakroom session.

" 'Charlie,' Jones said to me, 'what do you think of chucking the name Circle for the name Lions?'

" 'Well, I don't know,' I objected. 'Lions have fleas, and they scratch.'

" 'Circles crochet and knit,' he came back. 'Which would you rather do—have fleas and scratch or crochet and knit?'

" 'You win,' I said, 'I'll take the fleas and scratch.'

" 'Fine! Are you with me in this?'

"I said I was.

" 'All right,' Jones said.

"I went out to my chicken croquettes and from where I sat, I saw Mel take Joe Trienens and Bill Livingston and Edwin J. Raber and about twenty others into the little room, one by one, and as they came out, I could picture each one as thinking he was the one who would help put it over."

A mass of detail work kept Jones from carrying on a personal lobby among the visiting delegates on the day of the organization meeting. But this phase of his reception program wasn't neglected. He deputized Maury Blink (better known to Lions as the man who later drew up the final design for the organization's emblem) to make a canvass of the voting visitors and deliver a short sales talk to each. Blink's report was encouraging. As Jones had foreseen, each delegate wanted the new central organization to take the name of the club or association he represented. But the name Lions was the unanimous second choice. That may explain, to some extent at least, the great calm with which Jones addressed The Business Circle luncheon preceding the conference and to which all the delegates had been invited.

"For months," he began, "The Business Circle has been in correspondence with clubs operating in many cities under various names, hoping to effect an institutional organization. Today we meet for that purpose. Each club must be liberal; must give as well as take; perhaps give up its present name and take another."

And then, in a magnificent gesture, in the technique if not in the scope of America's offer at the disarmament conference some years later, he gave his all.

"We, The Business Circle, are proud to be the first to sacrifice our cherished name for the good of all."

Jones knew his oratorical nuances, just as he knew his timing. The meeting had been started off on a lofty plane and lyrically he held it there. "The rose by any other name" was given brief attention. And then—

"The lover thinks not of the loved one's name but of her," he said. "And the poet writes:

Thy name, thy name;
I told the rose thy name.
It blushed and stirred; its petals trembled in ecstasy.
I called thy name aloud
And lo! the bird burst into song within the thick-
*   leaved tree.*

I spake it when the dawn was gray and cold,
And straight from out the east up shot the sun!
I spake it to the night;
The clouds that rolled above dispersed;
The stars came one by one.

.   .   .   .

And if before the gates of Heaven I stand,
And can of my own worth no entrance win,

I think that then if I should breathe thy name,
The eternal doors would stir and let me in.

If I should breathe thy name,
  Thy name, thy name.

"Recently," he said, "I looked on the wreck of what had been a large plant. The owner had built a wonderful institution. Then came mismanagement, then drink, then suicide. And towering above this waste was the story of fifty years in two words—the owner's name.

"Gentlemen, back of your name you must have an international organization, and back of that organization, men!"

Immediately following Jones's speech, Edwin J. Raber and W. J. Livingston moved the adoption of the following resolution:

". . . that the directors of The Business Circle of Chicago . . have full power to make and complete all arrangements for affiliation and any act they do in the premises shall be the act of this club and binding thereon."

F. M. Hallenbeck, then president of The Business Circle, put the motion to a vote and it was unanimously carried.

With the consent of the members, President Hallenbeck then appointed D. S. Sattler as the acting delegate to represent The Business Circle at the conference which was to follow. In his capacity as acting chairman of the conference, Hallenbeck appointed Melvin Jones to act as secretary of the conference. He urged all delegates to assemble promptly; asked the Board of Directors of The Business Circle to remain in the hotel; and with the singing of "The Star-Spangled Banner," he adjourned the luncheon.

Strong groups were represented at the conference which followed the luncheon. There were the Optimists from Chicago and other cities, the Reciprocity Clubs, the Wheels, the Concord Club of Omaha, the Business and Professional Men's Association of St. Paul, the Cirgonians of Los Angeles, the Vortex of St. Louis and Detroit, and the Lions Clubs, an Indiana corporation.

Almost without exception, representatives from these clubs arose to make speeches in favor of adopting the name of their own organizations. But this oratory sounded like what it was, the effort of a convention delegate to do right by a favorite son. It was apparent that the name of the completed organization was going to be the second —or compromise—choice in the democratic American fashion. And there was never any doubt about what the compromise choice was going to be.

The off-stage conversations between the delegates and Jones, through Maury Blink, had given some direction to the search for a uniform name. In the informal discussion that followed the close of the keynote address, it was obvious that the name Lions was widely and seriously favored.

Blink's preliminary canvass of the vote had proved that the name Lions had a definite appeal to the imagination of a number of men already active in club work. "The lion stood for something," Jones later remarked, "not so much as a noble animal but rather as a symbol of great deeds and high accomplishment, in heraldry and mythology."

But still there were those present who hung tenaciously

to their own name. The Optimists arose again to urge all
the groups present to accept the name Optimist. However,
Gust Messing, representing the Business and Professional
Men's Association of St. Paul, called attention to the fact
that the purpose of the meeting was to form an international association of clubs not already in an international association, and the following motion was made
by E. N. Kearcher, of St. Louis:

> "That the representatives in session form an organiza-
> tion of the clubs not now in conflict with one another,
> details to be worked out, and a national name be
> adopted later, subject to the ratification by the club
> represented by the voting member."

When this motion was seconded and carried, the Optimists
withdrew from the meeting.

A further discussion of names ensued and an invitation
was formally extended to all those present to accept the
name "Lions." When no one seemed too displeased, an
agreement was made to call a meeting within 90 days
(subject to prior ratification of the clubs), at which
officers and directors were to be elected, a new charter
was to be applied for, new objects and ethics were to be
agreed upon, and a constitution was to be adopted.

With the heavy business out of the way, Joseph
Trienens was then called upon to furnish cigars for the
group. It seems that Joe had been detained in attending
one of the recent meetings of the Board of Directors of
The Business Circle because of the birth of a grand-
daughter, and this information was conveyed to the Board
during its session. The Board had immediately dispatched
to Joe the following telegram:

"Congratulations of Business Circle upon happy event. We hope baby, mother, and grandpa are doing nicely. We await cigars." When Joe put in an appearance at the conference he swore that he had already supplied cigars three different times to the Board as a result of this one blessed event, and that the demands which had been made upon him had therefore been fully met, but nevertheless he would present cigars to all who were present. And he did.

The conference adjourned with the reading of the Business Man's Prayer, by W. J. Power:

"Teach me that sixty minutes make an hour, sixteen ounces one pound, and one hundred cents one dollar. Help me to live so that I can lie down at night with a clear conscience, without a gun under my pillow and unhaunted by the faces of those to whom I have brought pain.

"Grant that I may earn my meal ticket on the square and that in earning it I may not stick the gaff where it does not belong. Deafen me to the jingle of tainted money and the rustle of unholy skirts. Blind me to the faults of the other fellow, but reveal to me mine own.

"Guide me so that each night when I look across the table at my wife, who has been a blessing to me, I will have nothing to conceal. Keep me young enough to laugh with my children.

"And when comes the smell of flowers and the tread of soft steps and the crunching of wheels out in front, make the ceremony short and the epitaph simple: 'Here Lies a Man!' "

4

THE OLD MONARCH

So the Lions had become Lions instinctively and automatically without trying to explain to themselves why they were doing it. One who comes to a study of the phenomenon years afterward is surprised to discover that it was by no means entirely due to the hypnotism of Melvin Jones.

There is something hereditary about the veneration of the lion as a symbol of all the noble virtues. Man, since his first days on earth, had been a deep respecter of the lion family, and an atavistic instinct of awe for the old monarch remains with the human race in an age and locality where such animals have become almost mythical.

Considering the admiration with which man had regarded the lion since the time when the pair of them were fighting for the supremacy of the jungle, it is not remarkable that the chivalry of the middle ages made lion symbolism and legend into the outward signs of a cult.

The likeness of the lion—or what was meant to be his likeness—was in greater demand than any other heraldic device on the shields of the elect.

The crests of the Lacys, Marshals, Fitzalans, Montforts, Percys, Talbots, and other noble, not to say royal, families depicted lions in assorted attitudes—passant, couchant, salient, rampant. Richard III who was called lionhearted because, it was said, he acquired a lion's courage by eating its heart, carried a banner which showed a lion rampant, touching the ground with one foot and clawing the air in rage.

Among the ancients, as man carried his awe of the lion up through strange new civilizations, the original animal got so completely covered with strange honors as to be almost unrecognizable. Two Egyptian deities, the god Shu and the goddess Sekhet, were depicted with lions' heads. The Assyrians used the lion symbol to indicate the all-consuming power of fire. Both the Assyrians and the Greeks worked the lion's massive physique into their architecture. The lion, somewhat distorted but still recognizable, went as far afield as the sculpture of China where, as in the West, he typified majesty.

In Christian art, the lion became the symbol of Christ as the Lion of Judah, sometimes bearing the cruciform nimbus. He is the pictorial sign of St. Jerome, St. Mark the Evangelist, and the Prophet Daniel.

In recent years the lion has been largely separated from his legendary status. Biological science has found out a lot of things about him in a close association denied to his early biographers. Moving pictures taken by such investigators as Carl Akeley and Martin Johnson have occasionally shown old Leo doing things entirely out of character.

On the other hand, such modern associates of the lion as Frank Buck and Clyde Beatty testify that many leonine attributes continue to command their respect.

The late Cy de Vry, long-time director of Chicago's Lincoln Park Zoo, knew all that modern investigation had to tell him about lions, but he continued to talk of them in the language of heraldry.

"I have been with lions for forty years," he told a Lions Club thirty years ago. "You cannot find a truer friend, one with cleaner habits or a more staunch defender of his rights. I do not know who named your organization, but you have the best name of them all."

Melvin Jones, who certainly made a study of the subject before he campaigned for the adoption of the name by the organization convention, says that it was mainly because of the symbolism surrounding the lion, not only hundreds of years ago, but right now, that the noble beast was the unanimous selection of the delegates. Men aren't too credulous about the lion's mythical qualities, and whether—viewed strictly as a jungle animal—he is brave or cravenhearted, wise or stupid, kindly or vicious, makes no difference. As a symbol he is the embodiment of the virtues. "After all," a New York Lion named Frank Lord once observed, "no man can be a Lion and act like a lamb, and it is especially impossible for you to be a Lion and act like a jackass." And every Lion who heard him knew exactly what he meant.

"In 2200 B.C.," Mr. Jones is fond of saying, "David had his 'lion-faced' warriors. In 1161 B.C. the Philistines answered the challenge of Samson: 'What is sweeter than honey? and what is stronger than a lion?' (Judges 14:18). The expression 'courage of a lion' goes back to 3000 B.C.

So there we have courage and strength, two of the four official symbols of Lionism.

"The third symbol is activity. A lion is always busy, always ready for action. Even when he lies down, it is said, he is nearly in a position to spring."

Martin Johnson confirmed this point.

"A lion will charge from a distance of more than two hundred yards when in open country," he wrote. "He may come at a trot during the early part of his charge, but he soon breaks out into a gallop that outspeeds a fast horse. I am told by men who have taken the time that the charging lion can cover the last hundred yards in about three seconds. [Theodore] Roosevelt observed that a horse standing a hundred yards from a lion will be overtaken before it can get to its full gallop."*

But for Jones, the chief attractiveness of the lion as an emblem is in the fourth symbolic quality traditionally credited to him.

"The lion stands for fidelity," Jones says. "In ancient art and mythology, one lion usually stood for strength, two for fidelity. The second usage springs from the belief that once a lion had chosen his mate, he never chose another."

In that, you hear the echo of his voice in the formative period of the organization, when he was trying to promote a consciousness of a loyalty less mercenary than the back-scratching that had made the luncheon-classification-club movement a target for Nathan, Mencken, and Sinclair Lewis. Loyalty all through the years has been his principal text—a text on which he has expounded with all the fervor

*Lion: African Adventure with the King of Beasts, G. P. Putnam's Sons, 1929.

of Androcles, that other expert on the sterling qualities
of lions.

The official magazine of Lionism handed down an in-
terpretation of the Association's name in the issue of January, 1931:

"Our name was not selected at random, neither was
it a coined name. From time immemorial, the lion has been
the symbol of all that was good, and because of the symbolism the name was chosen. Four outstanding qualities—
Courage, Strength, Activity, and Fidelity—had largely to
do with the adoption of the name. The last mentioned
of these qualities, Fidelity, has a deep and peculiar significance for all Lions. The lion has been a symbol of
Fidelity through the ages and among all the nations, ancient and modern. It stands for loyalty to a friend, loyalty
to a principle, loyalty to a duty, loyalty to a trust."

SLOGAN AND EMBLEM

Once the founding fathers had agreed to take the
lion's name, the selection of club colors was simple—what
could they have been save the tawny gold of the lion's
coat and the purple of his royal heritage!

"To Lions," runs the story that has grown up with
the organization, "purple stands for loyalty to country,
loyalty to friends, and loyalty to one's self and one's own
integrity of mind and heart. Gold signifies purity in life,
sincerity of purpose, liberality in judgments, and generosity in mind, heart, and purse toward one's fellow men.

"To Lions, the combination of purple and gold sym-
bolizes co-operation and education, enlightenment and
entertainment and recreation."

A slogan to fit the name and colors came somewhat later. Its selection was simplified by the use of an acrostic: Liberty, Intelligence, Our Nation's Safety.

Membership approval of these matters came quickly and with virtually no dissension. The choice of an emblem, however, was something else again. Three years of directors' meetings, conferences with manufacturing jewelers and draughtsmen, and endless wrangles with critical brothers produced a continuous roar that justified the Association's proud name. It wasn't until 1920 that the design as it now appears on lapel badges and letterheads was finally adopted.

The emblem, as you are continuously looking at it in trains, busses, offices, hotel lobbies, and virtually everywhere else, consists of a gold letter "L" on a circular purple field. Bordering this is a circular gold area with two conventionalized lion profiles at either side and facing away from the center. The word "Lions" appears at the top and "International" at the bottom.

The sponsors of the successful design were careful to point out, "the mouths of the lions are left open to receive jewels as some members may wish pins set with diamonds."

It is a plain, decent emblem without any confusion of ornament—effective because of its simplicity. You might wonder why so basic and uncomplicated a design should not have been in production two or three weeks after the constitution was adopted. And so it might have been had it not been for the volunteer services of unsung Cellinis filled with notions about a sort of new heraldry. Presently every man who had anything at all to do with the selection of the emblem became his own designer and none could see any good at all in a sketch submitted by anybody else. For the first couple of years any committee that had anything to do with the matter could work out no better plan than to appoint a new committee to supersede previous committees that failed to survive delusions of talent and good advice.

The final argument seems to have been between members who wanted a conventionalized alphabetical design and those who favored something like the Rosa Bonheur portrait of "The Monarch." The present design is something of a compromise and in that as in most things pertaining to Lions, you may find the hand of the ubiquitous Melvin Jones.

The Lions' Board of Directors, meeting in Oklahoma City on January 13, 1920, had tossed out the proposal of the latest committee and showed some favor toward a design submitted by the governing board of the Oklahoma City Lions Club. The Directors, apparently tired of it all, followed the usual routine, bundled up all the suggestions that had been given them and passed the mess to yet another committee. Jones went back to Chicago, opened up the filing cabinet and pulled out a couple of hundred designs and suggestions. With these and a pair of scissors and a paste pot he began to put together something of his own.

Obviously, he thought, there would have to be an "L" somewhere on the emblem. Also there would have to be some representation of a lion. There would have to be a chain or circle symbolic of union. And the word "International" ought to appear somewhere in the ensemble. Painstakingly, he cut these items out of the discarded sketches and pasted them together in a rough jigsaw puzzle that didn't quite fit. At this point he sent out a call for Maurice Blink, a commercial artist, and probably the only Lion in the country who hadn't bothered the numerous committees with designs of his own.

"Can you fix up something like this?" inquired Jones. "I mean something combining these elements?"

"Sure," answered Lion Blink. "When do you want it?"

The artist came back in a couple of days with three sketches. One of them, virtually identical with the emblem as it appears today, Jones laid before his fellow committee members, saying, "It represents a lion facing both past and future—proud of the past and confident of the future, looking in all directions to do a service." They approved it. At their next meeting in Chicago, April 12, 1920, the Directors underscored their approval by empowering Jones to lay in an emergency supply of lapel buttons.

LION HUNT

Failure to distinguish between the symbolic lion of song and the nonsymbolic lion of jungle and zoo has in the past given the members many an acute and actual pain. A war has almost erased—but not quite—the time back in 1939 when some bright Hollywood press agent set out to find an understudy for the M.G.M. lion. Quite without malice aforethought—just as one lion fancier to another—the Metro-Goldwyn-Mayer company invited The International Association of Lions Clubs to join the safari. The purpose of this interesting and no doubt important hunt was to get a livelier animal to act as trade-mark in the titles of M.G.M. pictures. Old Leo, who had been yawning in this role for many years, was showing signs of senil-

ity. So the M.G.M. publicity department announced that
there would be a contest. Anybody with a lion of the right
qualifications could send it in and maybe get a prize. The
rules stipulated that the entrant was to be a male cub of
American birth and African strain and under eight months
old. The lion didn't have to be submitted in person—not
at first. The judges' preliminary studies could be made
from photographs.

It became apparent within a few days after the announcement that nearly every Lions Club in the country
had at least one live lion mascot. Those that didn't own
lions borrowed some. The judges toiled for weeks under
an avalanche of photographs before they finally decided
on nine finalists. These honored cubs were escorted—
in person with all expenses paid—to the International
Convention of Lions Clubs held that year at Pittsburgh.

The contest was won by "Cubby," representing the
Kalamazoo Lions Club. The sponsors of Ajax (named for
Ajax Baird) and Leo of Binghamton and Rocky of Little
Rock were somewhat critical of the decision. They said,
libelously, that Cubby was a "runt without personality or
voice." But anyway, Clyde Beatty, chief judge, hung the
ribbon around Cubby's neck and awarded him $300 prize
money and the title "Leo Junior," which never seems to
have been of much use to him.

Secretary-General Melvin Jones followed Cubby's
progress as far as the New York World's Fair, where
before multitudes of people and many famous movie stars
he was given a coronation that he didn't like. He was
then flown directly to the M.G.M. studios in Hollywood
to take up his assigned tasks. But about then, Jones had
to worry about other lions—in fact, two of them.

Mel Chico, his namesake (Melvin of Chicago), was only a temporary embarrassment. A mannerly little lion as lion manners go, his failure to win a prize for the Chicago Central Lions Club needn't have worried him much—and didn't. He wasn't much trouble and he could always go back to Lincoln Park Zoo, where he had been born. As a matter of fact he did go there without any entourage of press agents such as the one that had accompanied him to Pittsburgh. He behaved himself and eventually got into a circus, which is considered a pretty successful career for a nonsymbolic lion.

"Jack Garner," however, was a different problem. Mel Chico and the other contestants were Jones's responsibility only because he was generally considered responsible for lower-case lions as well as the other kind. But "Jack Garner," who was named in honor of the then Vice-President of the United States by some of his enthusiastic admirers, notably Colonel W. G. Higgins of San Antonio and Gene Germany of Dallas, had been presented to Melvin Jones as his very own. Thus "Jack Garner" became a definite responsibility of Jones's.

When "Jack Garner" checked in at the William Penn Hotel in Pittsburgh, he was definitely annoyed. He had had an uncomfortable trip in a crate with some rough corners which the plaudits of his accompanying clacque had made no smoother. His face was scratched and his hair mussed.

He didn't seem to recognize Jones. Or if he did, he wasn't showing any enthusiasm. He didn't like his hotel accommodations either. The pictures on the walls were something he found particularly objectionable. As many a more inhibited hotel guest has been tempted to do,

"Jack Garner" smashed to bits a fine chromo of a sticky little girl with a basket of kittens and another of moonlight in Venice. It took the firm hand of a male nurse named Beatty to quiet him down. And by that time, it was obvious that he wasn't going to win any prize.

Even at the 1939 (pre-red point) price of raw meat, Jones hesitated to introduce this agile kitten into his family. His home then as now was in Flossmoor—one of Chicago's more sedate suburbs. He tried to give the animal away, but the people who are fond of lion cubs—except academically—are very few and generally well supplied. Jones recalls with feigned bitterness how Edgar Elbert, then District Governor of the Lions in Illinois, avoided receiving "Jack Garner" as a surprise present by leaving on a fishing trip just at the wrong time.

Finally the resourceful Secretary-General got the cub admitted to the animal hospital at Lincoln Park Zoo for the treatment of his sundry wounds. One of the staff, who thought maybe people had been misjudging "Jack Garner," called one day to ask that he be allowed to remain in the zoo.

"I hate to part with him, of course," said Jones, "but . . . "

Then he sighed a deep sigh.

"He's all right now," he observes. "He's turned into the very nicest kind of lion—but of course during the past few weeks they haven't stuck him into hotels or movie contests."

5

OFF-STAGE NOISES

JONES'S LAW ("You can't get very far without doing something for somebody else") had been a long time an unproved theory before the great merger of 1917. But once the International Association of Lions Clubs was an accomplished fact, it was subjected to some fairly severe tests.

The birth pangs of Lionism had hardly ceased before it became apparent that here was a newcomer with an entirely new personality and purpose and, as it turned out, an entirely new destiny. The Lions acknowledge a debt of heirship to their predecessors in the luncheon-club field, both from those groups which later affiliated with them and from those who went a separate way.

"The Lions were very fortunate," says Melvin Jones, "in that they had the experiences of all other similar organizations from which to build and from whose experiences they could profit."

The basic pattern of service clubs as they are known today was not established at the time Jones began to lay the groundwork for his organization. Up to that time, other groups had followed a familiar routine. They had been organized in response to an urge for fellowship, and they were operating on the "classification" basis of member selection—which is to say they were picking representatives from each business, industry, or profession—one to a "class." This had been the usual custom since the first businessmen's lunch club decided to branch out.

Individually the members were people of importance in their own towns. Collectively they had a greater opportunity for promoting the public weal. But they seem to have been slow to realize their own strength. Although they soon began to call themselves "service" clubs, it was a long time before they did much for humanity at large except to send occasional committees to wait on the mayor.

But these other groups had not yet heard of Jones's Law, and it was up to the Lions to lead the way in the service field.

The Lions were men who had reached a position in life with a deep feeling and sense of responsibility to help others, and being alive to the social and economic needs of the day, they favored an organization through which the co-operation of its members could meet these needs. That is why the Lions sought not only the membership of the business and professional men, as was the custom of the period, but sought also the membership of clergymen, educators, and others having to do with community life.

So the Lions confess to no breach of modesty when they point to some of the improvements that they can fairly claim were contributed to the club pattern by Lionism.

Credit for the development of standards superior to the phony golden-rule slogans of the "you-plug-for-me-and-I'll-plug-for-you" type has been given mainly to the simple fact that superior standards were set up in the first place. It is also true that they were drummed in. It is further true that a favorable "climate" was created for them when the Lions adopted rules designed democratically to broaden their base of membership. Jones's Law may not have been immediately evident in all of this, but it was there.

The Lions' departure from the trodden ways of the luncheon classification clubs, and the ups and downs that accompanied their assimilation by Lionism, reveal aspects of the service-club movement that escaped the attention of such snipers at conformity as Sinclair Lewis. His satire of the American small businessman, mainstay of the service clubs, appeared in 1922. Two years later Henry Mencken and George Jean Nathan founded *The American Mercury* as an arena for the same sort of Babbitt-heckling. At the same time, George Bernard Shaw was bellowing insults at the American joiner that could be heard distinctly all the way from London. In 1927, André Siegfried, another critic from overseas, derided the "twaddle of 'service,'" as the term was popularly understood in this country, calling it "the doctrine of an optimistic pharisee trying to reconcile success with justice."

He wrote: "One has to smile when the stodgy businessman proudly declares that 'service' to the community is his one and only passion, while he draws up a wonderful balance sheet. . . . He hopes by conscientious service to keep his customers and sell them again next year. Baedecker, that great philosopher, advised giving good tips, 'but only if you intend to return.' "*

These were the years when no periodical with any pretension to literacy was without its monthly controversy over Babbitt and all his works. *Forum* drew blood and pained protests from some organizations when an article by Bruce Bliven appeared in the issue of December, 1928.

All of this may have been bitter but beneficial medicine. The Lions can point to evidence of their own right thinking and acting before the days when Nathan and Mencken were the self-appointed diagnosticians of what ailed most of us. But one may be permitted to speculate on what effect, if any, the Babbitt-baiting had, particularly on groups that most resented it. Before becoming too involved in such speculation, however, it may be well to recall that the vinegary editors of the old *Mercury* may never have meant a word they said about the service clubs. They may have been fooling all along for sweet publicity's sake.

In 1923, when the pair were getting ready to launch their magazine and with it some monthly barbs at "service and such," Nathan wrote to Mencken in mock despair concerning another of their joint efforts:

"The newspaper reviews of 'The American Credo' are beginning to come in by the basketful. A *tragidrame!* They are so far all extremely favorable. This will kill the book. We sit ourselves down and compose a tome that studiously insults every American institution and every American that we don't like, and here we find that the whole caboodle of newspapers hops on the beer keg

*America Comes of Age, Harcourt Brace, 1927.

and agrees with us completely. As I have been fearing, this will mark the beginning of the end. . . . I have a feeling that the newspaper boys and girls, seized with a sudden astuteness, are doing the thing deliberately."[*]

The Lions, however, seem never to have been directly in the line of fire of the monthly barrage from Baltimore. Melvin Jones explains:

"They couldn't fairly blast our Objects, our Code, and the way we are trying to live up to them." The evidence is not contradictable.

Article II, section F, of the constitution adopted by The International Association of Lions Clubs several years before the appearance of either "Babbitt" or *The American Mercury* stipulates that a purpose of the Association shall be to "encourage efficiency and promote high ethical standards, *provided that no club shall hold out as one of its objects financial benefits to its members.*"

By-laws governing local clubs implement this ruling from on high by providing that:

"No officer of this club shall use it as a means of furthering personal, political, or other aspirations."

And, significantly, these rules were promulgated when the typical approach of the service club to the prospective member was too frequently like this one:

"To become a member of the .... Club costs but $25. Not to become a member may cost you hundreds—yes, thousands—of dollars. Suppose you are earning an income of $250 to $500 a month. Then suppose that the practical instruction, the personal and business help, and the intelligent co-operation rendered by the club adds only twenty per cent additional each month

[*] Isaac Goldberg, *The Man Mencken*, Simon and Schuster, 1925.

to your salary or income. Under such circumstances by
not becoming a member you would lose each month more
than the full cost of membership."*

"The Lions Club is not and does not pretend to be a
Chamber of Commerce or a purely commercial organization," Judge Calvin T. Cothan said at a Lions convention
in Little Rock in 1920. "It co-operates with and does
much of the work that would otherwise have to be done
by such organizations, but it does not duplicate their work.

"It is a commercial organization and something more,
something higher and better. It believes with Holy Writ
that this life is something more than meat, that there are
other questions worthy of consideration besides the purely
material.

"The Lions Club does not take the place of any other
club; it does not imitate any other club or organization.
It has a niche and a spirit peculiarly its own. It gives its
full and hearty co-operation with all clubs, the Chamber
of Commerce, and other civic and commercial organizations, and takes an active part in all movements in the
community which seek to promote any betterment, civic
or industrial or educational. And it gives its hearty endorsement to any plans looking toward the elimination
of class distinction. . . . If I should attempt to define
Lionism in one word, it would be 'Service.'

"It serves by inculcating certain ideals and principles
and by translating these ideals and principles into action.
. . . A man cannot subscribe to the Lions Code of Ethics
and honestly try to live up to it without improving himself and his associates and at the same time greatly bene-
fiting his community."

*The Cosmopolitan Idea.

THE LITTLE THINGS

"You don't get anywhere without doing something for somebody else," was the theory of Melvin Jones. And application of that theory was what made the Lions a different sort of club from all others. As Judge Cothan said, it was not a Chamber of Commerce or a political junta. On the other hand, with plenty of volunteer man-power and sufficient funds, the Lions Clubs became an important factor in cutting red tape and getting quick action in emergencies.

In a thousand ways, they made their influence felt—aiding the blind with guide dogs and the semiblind with artificial eyes, providing mechanical arms and legs for the crippled, helping a neighbor to rebuild a house destroyed by fire, supporting children's wards in hospitals, equipping playgrounds, and giving practical encouragement to local music societies. A world justifiably skeptical of good deeds as they get into the rotogravure has come to realize that the Lions' routine of helpfulness has no liaison with the newsreels or the press agents. It goes on and on, always unsung and only meagerly honored save by the ones it benefits.

In 1948, at the Gold Discovery Days Pageant, in Custer, South Dakota, the Lions Club entered a float in the opening parade. As one might have expected, it was a live lion in a suitable conveyance. The sign on the chariot, however, gave the exhibit a peculiar aptness.

"This," announced the banner in large letters, "is the only LION in this neighborhood who doesn't work."

6

DIVIDENDS IN DEMOCRACY

IN the twenties, the nation, prodded by depression and war and a suspicion that *laissez faire* wasn't the whole answer, groped toward new goals of social and economic democracy. That the Lions moved in the same direction may be one explanation of why, though later starters than some in the club movement, they have outdistanced the field in the matter of issuing charters and acquiring new members.

Three questions of policy in which the Lions chose a liberal course, turned out to be the best possible promotion for the organization. Bravest of these was the creation of the "associate member" classification. "Associate members," says the constitution, "are partners or associates of active members." Recognition of them as a membership classification on a par with their seniors, the active members, lets down barriers of stodginess and snobbery behind which some organizations have preferred to seclude themselves.

Instead of accepting only the ranking member of a firm, the Lions have made the up-and-coming fellows feel at home. Toward this end they have also instituted a "father-son classification" which, without in any way affecting the occupational apportionment of membership, welcomes either a member's son or his father into the Lions fellowship. Father and son decide between themselves which shall be the active and which the associate member if they are in the same line of business. The status of the other member of the club in the same occupational classification is undisturbed by the father-son arrangement. One doesn't have to be an Einstein to figure out the connection between this departure from hallowed precedent of similar organizations and the soaring membership of the Lions.

Another factor contributing to the Lions' growth has been the decision of the Directors to grant charters to clubs in towns of less than 5,000 population. The third element was the Directors' decision, confirmed by constitutional amendment, to permit more than one Lions Club to a city.

Adherence to these policies gave the Lions a character with an especial appeal to young men. And an accident of timing made an unusually large supply of youthful prospects available at precisely the time when The International Association of Lions Clubs was beginning to pick up momentum.

Melvin Jones's analysis of why the Lions moved into the lead within so short a space of years is in part:

"In the first place the Lions were fortunate enough to be surrounded by a group of men with high ideals that could appeal to a large group of young men who were just then returning from the front with a world-wide vision;

a group of young men, active, energetic, enthusiastic—
the doers of the earth."

In its beginnings, the service-club movement received
its impetus from the fact that it was adapted to big-city
living. But this is no longer true in the case of the Lions
Clubs. Even the big city clubs of Lions International now
have their agricultural committees that maintain liaison
with the surrounding rural area. In towns in the heart
of the farm districts where the "farmer" classification is
well represented, the agricultural committee of the local
Lions Club tackles problems of soil conservation and
animal husbandry, pest abatement, and rural fire protection.

The Board of Directors of the International Association, in session in Chicago in 1922, became involved in a
discussion of a constitutional provision dating back to 1919
which barred the chartering of clubs in cities of less than
10,000 population. The debate was closed and the Directors
were about to go on record with a vote upholding the provision when an Assistant Secretary of the Association burst
into the meeting with a rare old "halt-I-forbid-the-banns"
effect. He was waving a sheaf of checks, thirty in all,
which had just arrived from a small but progressive community in Oklahoma.

"We can't let these fellows down," he urged. "That
District Governor over there will be disappointed if we
do!"

A. V. Davenport, Tulsa insurance man and cattleman,
who was on the Board, agreed. "I hope," he said, "the
whole matter will be tabled."

The matter was tabled, and the Board then agreed
that any club in a town that would subscribe to the Lions
Club Objects and Ethics and could meet the financial and

other obligations of a Lions Club would be issued a charter.

The present Lions International constitution makes no mention whatever of population restrictions. So it has come about that applications for Lions Club charters will be entertained by the Board of Directors from any community where the applicants are willing and able to abide by the rules of the International Association.

Minimum charter membership also was tempered to the size of the town. In 1923, the Board ruled that twenty members were a sufficient nucleus in municipalities of less than 10,000 inhabitants. The sliding scale then runs from a requirement of twenty-five members in towns of 10,000 to 20,000, up to fifty members in cities of over 60,000. In 1928, Crook (pop. 225), Colorado, was bragging of itself as the world's smallest town with the most active service club.

It follows that in many such towns the classification of one active and one associate member from each type of business has had to be liberally interpreted. Some places where there are Lions, clubs may have butchers and bakers but no candlestick makers. In such cases, it has been considered to the best interests of the club to accept an additional butcher or baker to make up the deficit.

The original process of selecting members has developed with the years into a fine art. The list of suggested Lions Club classifications has been expanded to just under 1,000 occupations, giving the make-up of the membership an elasticity undreamed of by the inaugurators of the custom of picking members according to the business they were in.

It may readily be seen how such a policy has operated against monopolistic practice and contributed something

toward realism and modesty. One does not get a chance
to feel himself one of the elect, for instance, by being the
only cheesemonger in town invited to join the weekly
luncheon club.

Some occupations have been divided and subdivided to
a highly imaginative degree. The packing industry, for
instance, includes meat packing and shipping, canned
meats, packing-house by-products, and just plain packing.
Under cotton, the list takes in batting, goods, waste,
thread, and just cotton, not to mention cotton seed and
cotton-oil milling. Interior decorating and interior furnishing and decorating occupy separate niches. Judges
are classified according to the courts over which they pre-
side. Building maintenance and building management are
classified differently. However, butter and eggs are still
teamed.

The International's advice to the big city clubs is to
avoid such general classifications as insurance, medicine,
law, etc., and split them up as much as makes sense. On
the other hand, mutually exclusive classifications sometimes
present a problem in small towns. Does the member in
the furniture and undertaking line hold down one classification or two?

Local conditions, i.e., the size of the town and the
type of business it supports, decide policy in these matters
just about automatically. Besides, the clubs have discovered the advantages of what is known in service-club
circles as juggling. Vocational classification, waived in the
small towns, can be tightened up in the big cities if that
is felt to be in the best interests of the club. And some
classification or other can always be provided in which to
tuck a particularly desirable prospect. Fredericksburg,

Texas, in a fever over the success of a local boy in the business at Midway and the Coral Sea, conferred membership on Admiral Chester William Nimitz in 1942, creating a special classification for him.

In 1930, Vincent C. Hascall, later International President, urged on fellow Board members at a meeting in Chicago, a concentrated drive for members in smaller towns.

As set forth in an editorial published in the January, 1931, issue of THE LION:

"Lions Clubs in towns and small cities enjoy one great advantage over those in large population centers: It is easier to interest the very highest class of men and get them to take leadership in the club.

"One circumstance which sometimes handicaps the large city club is that many of the members live in far outlying suburbs, often in another county, or even in another state, and have not the intense personal interest in the physical and cultural development of the business district which they have in their home town.

"On the other hand, in the small town the best and most influential man is vitally interested in everything that affects the prosperity of the community, the churches which his family and friends attend, the schools where his children are educated. . . . He can realize more readily than the city man what a field for service the Lions Club offers, and to his credit he almost invariably takes up the work with enthusiasm and carries it on with vigor."

However in October, 1935, THE LION issued a timely reminder that this Lionizing of the common man, or at any rate the average man, should not be carried so far as to imperil the balance of the organization. "No man," the editorial asserted, "is too big to be a Lion.

"Are you holding your Lions Club in so narrow a channel that it is unable to serve its community to the best advantage? A few club officers do that. A limited membership may, in unusual cases, be advisable; but it can be overdone.

"One club which shall be nameless has been in a rut for years because it fails to avail itself of rich material which could easily be had. Membership is confined to a little circle of little business—the grocer, the laundryman, the manager of the chain store, the plumber, the school-teacher, the preacher, the manager of the motion-picture theater—all fine men, all good material, but not enough of them.

"Outside this narrow limit there are scores of men in that town who are heads of the great businesses in a near-by city, who are high in their professions in the city, who own industrial plants in the city, and most of whom own fine residences and spend much money for taxes and for expenses in the small town. But they are not local businessmen, and they are not taken into the Lions Club in the small town. It is a tragic loss to the club and to that town.

"No man is too good in any way to be a good Lion. As a matter of fact, the 'big' man is often a bit lonely and would appreciate being asked to join with the Lions in his home town. Take him in and put him to work."

The Lions pride themselves on taking in a wider economic angle of membership than some other groups, through the device of the active-and-associate and father-and-son general membership classifications. Students of the service-club movement in general have determined that the average age of Lion members is less than that of the members of the other large similar organizations. However, the number of members in a service club below thirty or over sixty is always limited by the fact that a condition of membership is that the members come from the employing, managerial group.

Because they have a like-minded attitude toward the problems of their group, they are able to submerge other differences. There is no great consciousness of variations of educational, religious, or racial background among Lions Club members. You'll find college professors hobnobbing with men whose formal schooling was less extensive, Protestants with Catholics and Jews, first-generation Americans with F.F.V.'s. "To those who are not Lions, one of the amazing things about Lionism is the harmony that reigns in an organization made up of men of all shades of opinion," THE LION wrote in April, 1931. "That harmony is a matter of pride to Lions. Every club has in its membership men of all political parties, all shades of opinion, all of the important religious beliefs, and they get along with never a clash."

The policy of permitting more than one Lions Club to a city was authorized by the Oakland, California, Convention in July, 1921, in what Melvin Jones calls the most significant of the changes made in the constitution since it was first approved. The portions of the article covering this point have read as follows since the revised constitution was adopted in 1926 by the San Francisco Convention:

"In any municipality in which there is an established Lions Club or Clubs, no additional club shall be chartered in such municipality without the adoption of a resolution by the local board of directors or by the members of the original club or clubs, authorizing the establishing of a new club in such municipality. And such resolution must set forth the boundary lines of the territory within which the new club may meet and obtain members, such lines to be clearly and specifically defined in the resolution giving consent to the organization of the new club. . . .

"Each club shall be known by the name of the municipality in which it is located, as 'The Lions Club of . . . . ,' except in municipalities having more than one club, in which event each club in such municipality shall add a distinguishing designation before the name of the municipality."

So even in the biggest cities the Lions have contrived, by dividing the territory along community lines, to sustain the feeling of neighborliness which it has been shown means so much to the men who gather in service clubs, as well as to extend the scope of the Lions Club in its service to the community and city. In this way all the communities of a large city would be better served.

To this matter Melvin Jones adds what Lions accept as a final word:

"I have often been asked why I refer to the Lions as being the first *service* club. My answer is that we are the first association to insert into our constitution the flat statement 'that no club shall hold out as one of its objects financial benefits to its members.' This was done at the first convention of Lions in Dallas, Texas, October, 1917.

"Up to this time the membership of the associations which were classifying and limiting their membership to a certain number of members in each line of business or profession, practically had an understanding with each other that they would receive financial benefits through business reciprocity. In fact, some of the clubs that were taken into the Lions Association were patterned along those lines.

"When the Lions inserted this clause into their constitution, it virtually revolutionized the classification organizations, for we find that in less than four years some of the other associations had adopted other objects and placed other interpretations on those they had. As, for instance, one association changed its motto from 'We Trade' to 'We Build.' Out of all this came the real service clubs. But the Lions led the way and enjoy the distinction of being the first."

7

ACCORDING TO THE CODE

THERE is probably no truth whatever in the report that Melvin Jones has a framed copy of the Lions Code of Ethics on the wall of his bedroom where he can see it on first rising or that he decks it each evening with votive offerings of beautiful flowers. Jones doesn't need to emblazon the code on the walls because he has it tattooed on his mind, and the copy of it that he carries constantly in his wallet in the space most men reserve for pictures of their grandchildren or their wives or sweethearts is merely for the edification of the less enlightened.

The story is not completely impossible, however. If he *had* a framed copy of the code on his bedroom wall, one can easily imagine him hanging it with garlands. His life and Lionism have been one, and Lionism is *The Code.* He believes, with complete justification, that no organization is better than its basic principles. From the first he has preached the gospel that success is the reward for complete adherence to a set of standards. To reach an objective, in other words, one must first decide what it is.

Unlike many of its rivals in the service-club movement, The International Association of Lions Clubs knew where it was going when it got its original charter—or at any rate Jones did. One of the first jobs of business at the first convention of the new Association was the statement of a code of ethics such as that set forth in a general way by the secretary in his call for the affiliation of the individual clubs.

The organizational meeting in Chicago had adjourned without setting a date for the first convention because some of the delegates had asked for a delay of ninety days in which the clubs they represented could consider the matter of affiliation with The Lions. According to this arrangement the first general convention was held in Dallas, Texas, on October 9, 10, and 11, 1917, to ratify the action of the Chicago meeting. About twenty-five clubs, still patently individual, took part in the proceedings. One gathers that there was a noticeable lack of sweetness and light.

For three months the Chicago organizers, assisted by their local constituents, had had a chance to think over what they had done. The siren voices of such speakers as Jones were not so insistent in the memory and a little more difficult to revive when the home-town boys began to get critical. So the Dallas Convention began with a promise of argument that was not slow of fulfillment. The child had been born, but the birth pains lingered on.

The erstwhile Vortex Club, currently represented as the St. Louis Lions Club, opened the wrangle by demanding that the choice of a name be reconsidered. The object of this, of course, needed hardly any explanation. The St. Louis boys wanted the Association to forget the Old Monarch and adopt the stirring name of Vortex. This was easily understood by at least three other delegates who had come to Texas with similar projects. It was also understood—and resented—by the bulk of the delegates, who were already pretty good Lions, at least to the extent that they didn't want to be called anything else. So some of the groups changed their minds about joining an international organization and went home. Those that remained found new subjects for bickering . . . what sort of outfit was this going to be, anyway? . . . who was going to pay for it, who was going to collect? . . . how was it going to be run, who was going to be in it, whom was it going to profit, what did it stand for?

Out of this melee in a dynamite factory there came presently, and unaccountably, a real basis for permanent unity. Whatever else the loud-voiced delegates ran up their blood pressure about, they were at least in vague agreement on the fundamental reason for their existence as an Association. The whole fundamental law of Lionism could be reconstructed from the one idea they made part of the constitution that the convention finally adopted: *No member would be permitted to make a racket of his club by using it as a means of financial gain.* By indirection at least this was an echo of the old theory—"You don't get anywhere until you do something for somebody else."

Finally there was unanimity, likewise, in the choice of the name. The people who wanted to call the Lions Vortex or Phalanx or Sigmoid or Elmer had already gone away. The delegates voted for gold and purple as the Lions' colors, formally approved the granting of charters, named Melvin Jones Secretary-Treasurer, designated Chicago as the headquarters under Jones's supervision, and adjourned in almost breathless harmony.

As everybody had foreseen, a large number of matters that were later to be of great importance in the development of Lionism had to be left for the action of subsequent conventions. And the chief of these was the preparation and adoption of a formal code. A committee had been appointed to prepare a statement of objects and principles for action by the next convention. But in the end this work was done as a labor of love by the late G. M. Cunningham, then Secretary of the Houston Lions Club, who had not been present at the Dallas Convention.

Jones finds it easy to get sentimental over the devotion of Cunningham. If there were such a thing as a book of Lionism's martyrs, this "typical Texan" would have first place in it, for there is no doubt that his labors in behalf of the organization's philosophy cost him his life. Even though he had been warned by his doctors to stay at home and rest in 1923, he started on a long tour to spread the gospel of Lionism through the West. In Ogden, Utah, while on this tour, he dropped dead.

"He was sorely missed," Jones says of him. "I'll never quit being grateful for the work he did for Lionism when it was really needed. But at least he had the satisfaction of getting recognized for the work he did on the Code."

Cunningham wrote the first draft of this historic document and submitted it to Jones. Jones passed it on to R. E. Kleinschmidt and Walter Lybrand, attorneys, of Oklahoma City, for a legal review, but not before he had given it some careful consideration on his own account. With his customary thoroughness he had made a comparative study of every code known to history from Hammurabi of Babylon (2250 B.C.) to Napoleon, through the Mosaic commandments and the Justinian Codex, and he had been struck by one feature common to all of them.

"Of course," he says, "they were all legal codes and filled with negative command—'Thou shalt not. . .' A code like that was outside our province. What we finally got was what you might call a 'Leadership Code,' and there isn't a 'Thou shalt not' in it. The points the other fellows and I on the committee wanted to emphasize were that you must give the other fellow the benefit of the doubt; that friendship is an end, not a means; that a man must accept nothing that has a string tied to it. 'What we will, we are, and what we love, we yet will be.' "

As early as January, 1918, copies of the Cunningham-Jones-Kleinschmidt-Lybrand code were distributed through the organization in a limited way for practice and discussion. At the convention held in St. Louis the following August, J. Hirsch was appointed chairman of a committee to consider its merits. K. H. Warren, E. F. Hurst, Arlie J. Cripe, and H. F. Endsley served with him. They mulled the Code over at two night sessions, then recommended its adoption. The delegates concurred and the Code has been an inseparable part of Lionism ever since.

"I guess you might say it's permanent," Jones says. "You might as well try to change the Bible as to monkey with that Code. It's been tried, of course. I recall that some delegate wanted a few amendments at the convention at Hot Springs in 1922, and you should have heard the uproar!"

Reading it, one has little difficulty understanding why

the rank and file of the boys are proud of it. It is simple, direct, unequivocal, and you get the idea that a normal man can recite it without feeling like a pharisee or a fool or announcing by his self-conscious manner, 'Look at me, I am about to think some noble thoughts.' It is free from the cornflowers of uplifting literature not entirely confined to service clubs. Here, as it has been handed down from the beginning, is the text of it:

"To show my faith in the worthiness of my vocation by industrious application, to the end that I may merit a reputation for quality of service.

"To seek success and to demand all fair remuneration or profit as my just due, but to accept no profit or success at the price of my own self-respect lost because of unfair advantage taken or because of questionable acts on my part.

"To remember that in building up my business it is not necessary to tear down another's; to be loyal to my clients or customers and true to myself.

"Whenever a doubt arises as to the right or ethics of my position or action towards my fellow men, to resolve such doubt against myself.

"To hold friendship as an end and not a means. To hold that true friendship exists not on account of the service performed by one to another, but that true friendship demands nothing, but accepts service in the spirit in which it is given.

"Always to bear in mind my obligations as a citizen to my nation, my state, and my community and to give to them my unswerving loyalty in word, act, and deed; to give them freely of my time, labor, and means.

"To aid my fellow men by giving my sympathy to

those in distress, my aid to the weak, and my substance to the needy.

"To be careful with my criticisms and liberal with my praise; to build up and not destroy."

Jones, as he frequently mentions in inspirational talks before newly chartered clubs, believes that the greatest beauty of thought in the Code of Ethics is in the fourth clause (or verse, as he prefers to call it), "To hold friendship as an end and not as a means," and in the other lines setting forth the relationship between friendship and service.

"This thought if put into action," he declares, "makes a man a real leader, a big man. For it makes him big enough, in questions of ethics, to resolve all his doubts against himself.

"This verse means to value friends not for what you can get out of them but for what they are—and this Code, which is for the individual Lion, has gone a long way toward making Lions International first among the service organizations of the world.

"Many students of ethics have stated that ours is one of the most thorough and yet most practical codes ever written, and the greatest thing in the Code of Ethics— the really fundamental soul of the Code—is contained in the third paragraph: '. . . to be loyal to my clients or customers and true to myself,' for as Shakespeare puts it in Hamlet:

> *To thine ownself be true,*
> *And it must follow, as the night the day,*
> *Thou canst not then be false to any man."*

8

THE WHY OF IT

IT is significant that the Lions in formulating a Code gave their first consideration to actions of the members and not to ends, to the conduct of individual Lions rather than to any noble goal for a great international organization At a time when everybody in the world seemed bent on putting everybody else's house in order but his own, this seemed to be a refreshing idea.

The Code of Ethics for individual Lions was adopted in 1918 after it had been foreshadowed in the constitution of 1917. But it wasn't until 1919, after the International Association had been in business a full two years, that the declaration of the *Objects* of the Lions was adopted by vote of the annual convention. The Objects, as well as the need for a slogan and club emblem, had been discussed at length at St. Louis, Missouri, in 1918. By 1919 the delegates knew what they wanted and, as the remarkable written record shows, every one of them talked about it.

In those days Lions conventions were small enough—
less than thirty clubs had representatives at Chicago in
1919—to permit the delegates to thresh things out on the
floor. And it was on the floor, with everybody having
his say and causing as much noise and confusion as the
rules of order would permit, that these delegates pounded
out a draft of the Objects of the Association durable
enough to stand unchanged for ten years.

In 1930, the first paragraph of the recital of Objects
was changed as the result of some convention oratory at
Denver, Colorado, by the late Dr. Walter F. Dexter
(International President, 1938-39) and at the insistence of
a fellow Californian, Ray L. Riley, who was International
President at the time. The Dexter address, a scholarly
performance worthy of the distinguished educator who
was superintendent of public instruction in his state, contained the words that since have led all the rest among
the Objects to which all Lions are dedicated.

"We are here to create and foster a spirit of generous
consideration among the peoples of the world through a
study of the problems of international relationships from
the standpoint of business and professional ethics," Lion
Dexter said. "May we all go to our homes, put on a program of international idealism by inviting speakers of
other countries to appear before our Lions Clubs, by passing resolutions of friendship and fellowship, and by dis-
seminating our knowledge and our philosophy to the
uttermost parts of the earth."

Every Lion, whether or not he stumbles over the later
parts of the litany, can roar confidently the text of
Object I:

To create and foster a spirit of "generous consideration" among the peoples of the world through a study of the problems of international relationships.

The words, "from the standpoint of business and professional ethics," originally tacked to the end of this paragraph were deleted by constitutional amendment from the *Objects* a few years ago as expressing too limited a view.

The remainder of the official draft setting forth the Objects of The International Association of Lions Clubs runs:

To promote the theory and practice of the principles of good government and good citizenship.

To take an active interest in the civic, commercial, social, and moral welfare of the community.

To unite the members in the bonds of friendship, goodfellowship, and mutual understanding.

To provide a forum for the full and free discussion of all matters of public interest—partisan politics and sectarian religion alone excepted.

To encourage efficiency and promote high ethical standards in business and professions; provided that no club shall hold out as one of its objects financial benefit to members.

Secretary-General Jones, analyzing these *Objects*, points out:

"Lions are fundamentally engaged in service work, and each of the six paragraphs comprising the formal expression of our Objects develops a separate but integral part of service work.

"The first paragraph refers to welfare at the international level, the second considers the national welfare, and the third the welfare of the community, that great field in which most of the service of the Lions is performed.

"The next object deals with the personal relations of the members, one to another. Here we have the foundations of a Lions Club. There must be mutual understanding among the members and there must be good fellowship in a Lions Club in order that it may function properly.

"Intelligence in action is a prerequisite to community service. Lions should have the advantage of all available information in order to determine the wisest course to follow. Therefore the fifth object. . . . This (keeping informed) keeps the club alive to the needs of the community and the problems of the state and nation. It provides for full discussion, and knowledge on the part of all members, of the problems under consideration by the club. . . .

"Because Lions Clubs take the initiative in community service, membership in a Lions Club marks a man as a leader in his community. To maintain this leadership in a collective capacity, the Lions Club must be made up of men of the highest qualifications. A man must be a credit to his business or profession before he can be an asset to the Lions Club. Therefore a Lions Club is interested in the pre-eminence of its members and so we have the sixth and last object. .

"The second clause of this object," and here Jones draws the distinction between the Lions and some of the *so-called* service clubs, "safeguards the service nature of a Lions Club. It keeps the club and the members from going out to prospective members and saying, 'Join our club and we will give you business.' It puts the restriction in such a way that a man must join the club to serve. He must serve the club and the community, and by serving he naturally develops himself.

"If a Lions Club follows out its Objects, it will have a full program. It will be interested in world affairs, in national problems, in the needs of its own local community, and in the welfare of the individual members."

The *Objects* set forth by Lions International are integrated with those listed in the constitution which is standard for every local Lions Club:

"1. To form a body of men thoroughly representative of the business and professional interests of the City of . . . ., to unite its members in the closest bonds of fellowship, and to promote a closer business and social union among them.

"2. To encourage active participation in all things that have to do with commercial, civic, and industrial betterment.

"3. To uphold the principles of good government.

"4. To assist in every honorable way in furthering the interests of its members and toward bringing about a better understanding among men.

"5. To teach that organization, co-operation, and reciprocity are better than rivalry, strife, and destructive competition.

"6. To encourage the application of the highest ethical standards in business and endeavor, by the exchange of methods and ideas, to increase efficiency in all lines represented."

Being what they were, the Lions naturally had to have a rallying cry, a slogan. But also, because of what they were—men of a thousand varying interests from hundreds of widely scattered and differing places—it was difficult to find one that would arouse them all at once.

Individual clubs had supplied the need by adopting slogans of their own. All of these and a few more were in the hopper when the Chicago Convention (1919) undertook to select a slogan that should be the summation of Lionism. The Lions had only just finished their choice of *Objects* for the official list when they took up the task of putting them into capsule form.

The selectors had their work cut out for them. Slogans have a way of becoming catch phrases that through endless repetition lose their inspiration and rouse in the listener no emotion save a distaste for slogan makers. The Lions committee heard them all from "Twenty-three! Skiddoo!" to "Do it now!"

Some of the contributed war cries had been subjected to less wear and tear than these two samples. "Always faithful!" wasn't so bad, it seemed, if the U.S. marines hadn't already heard about its Latin translation. "At the Nation's right hand," was another that was fairly well received, and there was a pretty good percentage in favor of "We serve best."

"However," says Melvin Jones, "none of these seemed broad enough or deep enough for the purpose. A slogan is an inspiriting message, the clarion call, the rallying cry.

We were groping to find some expression that would have the vitality of a rallying cry but a rallying cry expressive of the purposes of Lionism."

Some consideration was given, he recalls, to the drafting of a creed. But he said no, a slogan was what was needed to bring the boys to their feet.

"A creed," he said, "is something you hang on a wall. Churches have creeds, and more often than not, creeds have the effect of a fence, keeping men apart rather than drawing them together." After that there was a long impasse.

Even in 1919, two years after the name Lions had been adopted and reaffirmed as the best possible choice, clubs that had sacrificed their own identities in the interest of unity would succumb to nostalgic regret. There would be mumbling in the cloak rooms. . . . The world was better when the Lions Club of Whoosisburg had been the Parabola club. . . . You could get a good steak dinner for two bits . . . and you didn't have to worry about the income tax . . . and there wasn't any of this I.W.W. And presently another campaign would be afoot to make the Association of Lions Clubs into the Interplanetary Association of Parabola Clubs.

One of these moves was afoot in the Chicago Convention when Halsted Ritter, an eloquent member of the bar from Denver, Colorado, came onto the floor and made a speech which in the annals of Lionism has a rating something like the one that the history textbooks give Daniel Webster's reply to Hayne.

"What an aggregation we have," exulted the orator from the Rockies as he warmed to his subject. "What a glorious meaning it has. Its name is more significant

than any other. It spells not only the king of beasts,
typifying all the qualities we love to extol; it stands not
only for fraternity, good fellowship, strength of character and purpose; but above all, its combination of letters,
L-I-O-N-S, heralds to the country the true meaning and
basis of American citizenship—*Liberty, Intelligence, Our
Nation's Safety*.

"Analyze carefully and behold the very cornerstone
of our civilization. Liberty and Ignorance bring blood-
shed, chaos, Bolshevism, anarchy, and general ruin. Liberty
and Intelligence signed the Declaration of Independence,
gathered the Minute Men at Concord, and won at York-
town. They have preserved our nation in every crisis.
An intelligent citizenry is the hope of democracy. It is
the ideal of Lionism. In its promotion and protection is
the opportunity we seek.

"The time is ripe for a new baptism of liberty and
intelligence. We must all be immersed in the river of
patriotism, and shout our salvation and preach its reality.
We must have reason for the faith that is within us. The
River Yukon gathers to itself such a volume of pure water
that when it flows into the sea it pushes the salty brine
back from its mouth for ten miles. So should every Lions
Club force a pure, clean stream of intelligent American-
ism into its community life. In a few years, methinks,
with many such streams pouring into the nation's life, the
muddy, murky, and death-spreading waters of ignorance,
disease, and poverty will be cleansed and purified.

"Write it on your banners, Lions; inscribe it in your
hearts; hold it high that everyone may see the magic,
electrified letters — Liberty, Intelligence, Our Nation's
Safety."

And that did it. Lion Ritter, whose talents later were recognized in his elevation to the bench, had every man in the auditorium with him as he concluded. Nothing further was heard from the dissenters. Everybody, it appeared, liked the acrostic idea. Earlier attempts to develop it had been somewhat strained, but Ritter had rung the bell.

"Liberty had been thought of as the first word in connection with the letter 'L' in the Lions emblem," Jones recalls. "It seemed reasonable to everyone that liberty be coupled with education, judgment, consideration of the rights of others—in other words, intelligence. And since our slogan was not intended for the individual but for all, and for every Lion country, it was altogether right to use the plural pronoun 'our' in speaking of the nation's safety. The slogan is so phrased as to be applicable to any nation represented in the International Association.

"So there we had a slogan durable enough to have stood the test of our first thirty years and, I'm ready to predict, to stand the test of our first hundred and thirty."

CITIZENSHIP AND PATRIOTISM

A "Citizenship and Patriotism Code" for Lions International was copyrighted in 1939 to meet a need of which the directorate had been conscious for some time. Things were going wrong in the world and the increasing tension had emphasized the need for such a code for the use of citizenship and patriotism committees in the local clubs.

The Citizenship and Patriotism Code was not developed in convention nor submitted to a convention body for approval. A preliminary draft was worked out in the

International office in Chicago from proposals submitted
by many Lions Clubs and individuals.

The Secretary-General acknowledged his indebtedness
to the Rev. W. Murray Allan, now (1949) filling a pulpit
at Ames, Iowa, for his aid in phrasing the final draft of
the Code. Jones felt that the sentiments of patriotism and
good citizenship that the code was supposed to embody
would be meaningless unless combined with religion or,
as he put it, the soul. He immediately thought of "Bill"
Allan, whose attractive Scottish burr, acquired at the
University of Edinburgh, had made him popular with
Lions audiences. Allan was a member of the International
Board of Directors at the time. At Jones's request, he
took time from his duties as pastor of Plymouth Congre-
gational Church in Grand Forks, North Dakota, to meet
the Secretary-General in Minneapolis. The Lions "Citizenship and Patriotism Code," as subscribed to today, was
completed as a result of this meeting.

A complication in the proper framing of the Code was
that thought had to be taken of institutions and customs
in foreign countries, Lions having been truly international
by this time, with clubs springing up on four continents in
addition to North America. The Code of Citizenship and
Patriotism in its final form is so phrased as to be applicable
to any country professing to uphold democratic principles.

Lions Code of Citizenship and Patriotism

"To create by precept and example a civic and patriotic conscience by fostering an idealistic attitude toward
my country, its historic past, its spiritual heritage, its free
institutions, its boundless natural resources, its great men
and women, its wonderful privileges, and its solemn re-

sponsibilities, that we may give it our full measure of devotion and love.

"To develop a greater knowledge and understanding of the principles of democratic government and the institutions which are the sources of liberty, happiness, and freedom of thought and action; a respect and reverence for the flag; obedience to law and authority; and a sustained and intelligent interest in public affairs.

"To uphold the principles of democratic government by supporting such movements as seek to save a country from its own apathy; by awakening my fellow countrymen to their obligations of citizenship; by stimulating an interest in governmental policies on the part of future voters; by supporting Lions 'Of Age' ceremonies; by encouraging and expediting naturalization of eligible aliens; by furnishing speakers and programs for patriotic events; and by observing patriotic holidays and displaying my country's flag.

"To perpetuate in the public memory historical episodes worthy of emphasis by aiding in the erection and maintenance of memorials, plaques, historical-site markers, and other suitable evidences.

"To obtain suitable recognition for outstanding civic service by the presentation of awards and honors to those whose personal sacrifice and service on the field of battle and in the service of mankind in peace are worthy of the highest tribute.

"To reaffirm my belief in the government of a free people—whose inspiration is wisdom, whose greatest cause is justice, and whose noblest objects are peace and liberty —ever remembering our slogan:

"Liberty, Intelligence, Our Nation's Safety!"

9

GROWING PAINS

ONE of the obvious and
important features of the growth of the Lions has been
its entire freedom from hidebound restraint. Without precedent to guide them, Secretary-General Jones and his aids
had to meet each new situation as it arose . . . and there
were plenty of them. Even without thought of profits,
such a rapidly expanding organization must presently become Big Business with Big Business' numerous problems
and headaches. The leaders of the movement got little
sleep in the early days. So far as Mrs. Jones was concerned, the Lions Clubs as a going concern were little
different than The Business Circle had been when the little
eohippus was deciding to be a horse. There was still work
to be done far into the night, still emergency calls that
took her husband journeying to far places. It was still
impossible for her to make social engagements a week in
advance or plan to have her husband with her for Sunday
dinner.

"Is this ever going to end?" she inquired one day when he came home for a change of shirts after one of his long absences.

"I don't know," he said. "There's never been anything like it before."

Nor had there been. The Lions, having decided what they were going to be and what, eventually, they were going to do, then proceeded to plunge themselves into what to the untutored eye might look like complete confusion. The voice of the Association as expressed in its conventions had been loud and vigorous from the beginning. As more and more Lions crowded into these meetings and thousands of prospective Lions made their voices heard through the district officers, mere turmoil became bedlam and bedlam began to resemble chaos. An outsider might be permitted to wonder why this great movement did not finish like the one it so closely approximated, the battle of the Kilkenny cats.

The end might have been the same except for the flexibility and stubbornness and youthful energy of the skillful opportunists who sat in the front office. Their business operations were largely a matter of cut and try. But in the end they evolved a lot of techniques that are still spectacular in a world of marvels. It is no accident that today the Secretary-General can tell you in a matter of seconds the name of the latest Lion to join up in Belle Fourche, South Dakota, or whether or not some member of a club in South America has paid his dues.

For reasons presently to become apparent, Melvin Jones persuaded the Directors at the St. Louis Convention in 1918 to apply for a charter in Illinois. This charter was granted on August 25, 1919, to The International Association of Lions Clubs, doing business as Lions International. As a matter of convenience, the two names have become interchangeable in common usage. Lions International, except in legal documents, is more often used because of its brevity.

Looking back on the matter, the Lions really got a lot done in those formative years. The Code of Ethics was adopted, and the Objects—prima-facie evidence of a basic coherence and unanimity of purpose that weren't immediately evident in subsequent bickering.

One of the novelties of Lions' progress in those days was the carefree attitude of the members toward their constitution. The average American is accustomed to thinking of a constitution—any constitution—as something contrived by the Medes and the Persians, unchanging and unchangeable, the same today, tomorrow, and forever, *saecula saeculorum*. As proof of this, one has only to cite the attempts of any party or faction or coalition to change the constitution of any state. But nothing was sacred to the Lions—not unless it worked.

So, with virtually no to-do at all, the 1917 constitution was turned in on a new model in 1918. This one lasted until 1919. The 1920 convention in Denver went through the same rigmarole. The constitution committee sweated it out in the accepted tradition in smoke-filled rooms in the Albany Hotel and on the floor of the convention at the Civic Auditorium. Bleary-eyed with panatella fumes and late hours, delegates and committee members—among them Kleinschmidt and Lybrand, the able barristers who had helped formulate the Code of Ethics—continued to battle somewhat inappropriately at the side of Buffalo Bill's grave after a convention side trip had taken them to the top of Lookout Mountain. By the next morning, however, everybody seems to have been tired enough to compromise. There wasn't even an argument when the adoption of the revised and amended constitution was moved.

The weariness of the committee members doesn't seem to have been exceptional. After the vote had been taken and the International President, Dr. C. C. Reid of Denver, was about to move on to the next order of business, a delegate from Peoria, H. R. Armstrong, got to his feet.

"I move," he said feelingly, "that this constitution be made permanent."

He was wildly cheered.

Despite the attitude of the rank and file, however, the perfectionists and parliamentarians continued their tinkering from year to year until, at San Francisco in the summer of 1926, a further revised instrument was adopted that has required only minor alterations during the twenty-odd years that have gone by since. These have involved merely a letting out of seams to ease the strain of the Lions' phenomenal growth.

Reflecting that growth, as well as fostering it, has been the addition from time to time of new general membership classifications. Active and associate members, of course, make up the great body of Lionism. At Philadelphia in 1946, a rephrasing of the article on membership in the constitution defined active members as "proprietors, partners, corporate officers or managers, or those substantially interested in the business or profession which they represent." Associate members were defined as the partners or associates of active members. There is also the *father-*

son membership classification. In it, either may be designated as the active holder of the classification, with the
other having the right of an associate without cutting in
on the rights of a previously existing associate in the classification. Thus, instead of having a single representative
in each line of business, Lions Clubs may have as many
as three. At Miami in 1927, the international convention
created the *member-at-large* classification for the accommodation of members who move from the community
and desire to retain membership in the club.

The *pioneer member* classification was created by the
Toronto Convention in 1942. Members who have been
Lions twenty-five years or more may become *pioneers*
without any other change in status. Or they may become
retired pioneers, in which case they pay only nominal dues
and yield up their right to hold office and the occupational
classification they hold in the club to a newcomer.

In 1922, life membership in the Association was conferred on all retiring International Presidents.

There has been a tendency to clamp down on the lavish
distribution of honorary memberships since one convention
—the session at Cedar Point, Ohio, in 1925—ladled them
out at a single dishing to Helen Keller, James West (Chief
Scout of the Boy Scouts of America), and a lovely young
woman who had sung what must have been a very fine
song at the opening meeting.

"A convention," observes Jones with a grin, "can do
anything."

The convention at Denver in 1930, however, put a
limit on this sort of generosity by approving honorary
membership only for distinguished citizens local clubs
might wish to honor for services to the community and

then only after the International Board had approved.

The International Board of Directors early shaped up to a membership of nine Directors elected for staggered three-year terms, plus the international officers who are elected every year. The Immediate Past President was added to the roster of the Board of Directors by a revision of the Constitution in 1923. The chairman of the Board of Governors was assigned and still holds a place on the International Board as an ex-officio member. The chairman of the International Council (now Board of International Relations) is also an ex-officio board member. The international convention at Louisville in 1929 provided that the Board might appoint other ex-officio members from countries other than the United States if they had no regular representation on the Board.

The Secretary-Treasurer, later Secretary-General — and by either name, Melvin Jones—has been an ex-officio member of the Board, and its Secretary, since the beginning.

Keeping pace with the expanding membership, the number of Directors from the United States elected by the international convention was upped to ten and the term reduced to two years in 1930. Delegates sitting in Toronto the following year authorized election by the convention body of a Director from any country outside the United States having at least forty-five Lions Clubs. In 1946, the number of elective Directors had been increased to sixteen from within the United States plus one from each other country which had at least forty-five clubs. The President, Immediate Past President, and three Vice-Presidents round out the directorate.

The Board of Governors is a court of appeal from any

action the Board of Directors may take as result of a vote
of less than two thirds of the Directors present and voting.
A constitutional revision, passed at Atlantic City back in
1923, requires that the Board of Directors prepare a budget
showing anticipated receipts and expenditures, this budget
to be submitted to and approved by the Board of Governors at their annual meeting, held at the same time as
the international convention.

District conventions at which District Governors are
elected are usually held a month or so before the annual
convention of the Association. Members of the Board of
Governors are those District Governors who have served
during the preceding year and whose successors have been
duly elected.

As Lions Clubs sprang up all across the map, the problem of administering them through the International Association was met by carving up the territory into smaller
and smaller districts, each presided over by a District Governor. At first there were only nine districts, numbered
serially from the West Coast eastward with the states of
California, Oregon, Washington, and Nevada then sharing
the designation of District No. 1. Today the districts on
the North American continent coincide with state, terri-
torial, or provincial boundaries, and even then all but about
a half dozen districts have more than one Governor.

As the mother district, Illinois is now District No. 1
and among its eight subdivisions, the Chicago area is 1-A.
As runner-up for the honor of pioneering in Lionism,
Texas' eight subdivisions are designated as belonging to
District No. 2.

The ratio of one Governor for every fifty clubs was
fixed in 1930. There had been complaining murmurs for

years from Governors conscientiously trying to keep up
with schedules which required them to visit at least once
during their terms of office every club in their districts.
Back in 1920 the Board was instructing the Secretary-
Treasurer, as he was then, to redistrict certain areas "especially adjacent to Chicago . . . into small territories
containing only such number of clubs as can be visited
by the District Governor with reasonable convenience."

In 1936, the Board of Directors approved the Standard
District Organization plan. Under this plan, each District
Governor appoints Deputy District Governors and Zone
Chairmen to assist him in the administration of his terri-
tory.

At last count, Lionism embraced 206 gubernatorial
districts, a jump from 189 during the 1948-49 club year.
Over a good part of the habitable world, the organizational
network of Lionism is spread by these district divisions
as well as by the traveling representatives of the home
office. Melvin Jones's report for 1948–49 showed that
within that fiscal period the 189 District Governors traveled 1,245,231 miles in making 10,129 visits to the clubs
within their jurisdictions. This is not counting Ladies'
Nights, Charter Nights, and other purely social affairs.
Then there are the approximately 650 Deputy District
Governors who swing around the regions allotted to them,
and the more than 1,300 Zone Chairmen who gyrate in a
territory embracing approximately eight clubs. The Zone
Chairmen, Jones estimated, conducted 2,631 advisory committee meetings during the 1948–49 club year.

The International President of the Association, of
course, has to be a sort of one-man combination of Admiral
Byrd, Burton Holmes, and the Ringling Brothers. During

his year in office, he is expected to show himself in every district, stow away at least 600 banquets, accept 1,500 scrolls, souvenirs, and samples of local produce, neglect his wife, children, and business, and love it all.

In the middle thirties, Lions Clubs in all countries were adopting a standard club-organization plan that had been proposed by the International Board of Directors. "Forty per cent of our clubs have seized upon the new plan as something to help them materially in their work," THE LION exulted as early as August, 1935. "Without doubt many other clubs also recognize the merit of the plan but prefer to wait until the new club officers take charge before committing themselves to it officially. Every member of every Lions Club should study that plan. It is the most masterly presentation of the duties of committees, their interrelations, and their possibilities ever worked out by any organization. And since every Lion is, or ought to be, a member of several committees, he should be familiar with the wealth of information the plan offers him. If every club in the Association adopts the standard plan, there should not be an inactive club in any district by the end of this fiscal year."

The year 1936 saw the creation, by the Providence, Rhode Island, Convention, of the International Council, to become known later (1943) as the Board of International Relations. This body is made up of representatives from every country where there are Lions Clubs. Its function is to advise the International Board of Directors on international policy. In setting it up, the Lions forever ranged themselves with the one-worlders against the isolationists at a time when isolationism was prevalent in the United States.

After a dozen years in which international relationships have become virtually the chief concern of everybody in the United States, the Board of International
Relations is still functioning with no apparent need for
change. The International President appoints, with the
approval of the Directors, a representative from the United
States. Selections by the clubs of other countries must
also be submitted to the Board of Directors for approval.

The most recent group to be bound into the organizational structure of The International Association of Lions
Clubs are the International Counsellors. They are the
elder statesmen of Lions International, an honorary body
created not by constitution fiat but by action of the Board
of Directors in 1940.

At a Directors' meeting in Chicago in 1946, Assistant
Secretary-General R. Roy Keaton read a definition of an
International Counsellor:

"He holds a unique position in the International Association. His title is one of merit and honor. It was conferred on him due to special service and loyalty to his
district and to Lions International. All past District Governors are not International Counsellors. However, International Counsellors are all former Lions Governors, for
the title cannot be obtained by a Lion without his first
having served in the capacity of District Governor."

The Counsellors have no independent organization but
function through the Governors' honorary committee, in
company with past International Officers and Directors
in the district.

However, as those who created them point out, the
Counsellors do have a title for life, a broad sphere of in-

fluence, a chance to remain active and useful in Lionism, and a place at the speakers' table wherever Lions meet.

A section of the by-laws dating back to 1926 had sanctioned associations of chartered clubs and associations of officers in the various districts. This provision has now been repealed, but while it was on the books, the club Presidents and Secretaries, District Governors, International Counsellors, International and Past International Officers residing in the district were privileged to meet once a year, adopt a constitution, elect officers, and "consider matters of interest within the district and submit reports thereon to the district convention."

In the beginning, the number of Lions at International conventions was so modest that no convention hall was taxed by the rule authorizing one delegate and one alternate for every ten members. But by 1926 the number of delegates a chartered club might send to the International convention had been reduced to one apiece for every twenty-five members of the club in good standing.

At district conventions, every Lion in good standing from any club in the district may vote on any but two questions. These are the selection of the next District Governor and the next convention city. There the rule of one delegate vote to every ten members of the club applies.

INTERNATIONAL ASSOCIATION OF LIONS CLUBS

CASH RECEIPTS AND DISBURSEMENTS
October 9th, 1917 to August 15th,1918

REPORT OF SECRETARY-TREASURER MELVIN JONES

SECOND ANNUAL CONVENTION

ST. LOUIS, MISSOURI

Balance on hand October 9, 1917	$72.05	
Dues from all Clubs	1346 83	
Entrance fees new members accepted by all Clubs	535.00	
Entrance fees new Clubs organized	479.00	
		$2432.88

DISBURSEMENTS

Miscellaneous	$95 79
Rent	230.00
Telephone	33.00
Telegrams	18.55
Postage	156.27
Stationery	43.50
Printing	344.75
Stenographer & Addressing	633 01
Office File	20.00
Exchange	.55
Railroad fare & Traveling	109.51
Secretary-Treasurer	200.00
Stereotypes	57.75
	$1944.68

Balance in Bank $ 488.20

• • •

Estimated

Number of Clubs in good standing October 9,1917	28
Clubs organized and chartered by the Association	18
Organized Clubs chartered (formerly operating under another name)	3
Total -	49
Clubs dropped	1
Total number of Clubs in good standing Aug.15,1918	48

Secretary-Treasurer's Report to the Second Annual Convention, St Louis, Mo., August 19–21, 1918

INTERNATIONAL ASSOCIATION OF LIONS CLUBS

CASH RECEIPTS AND DISBURSEMENTS
August 19, 1918 to July 10, 1919.

REPORT OF SECRETARY-TREASURER MELVIN JONES

THIRD ANNUAL CONVENTION

CHICAGO, ILLINOIS

Balance on hand August 19, 1918		$488.20
Received		
Dues from all Clubs		2625.61
Entrance fees for new members accepted by all Club . . .	1375.50	
Charter fees	230.00	
Miscellaneous	89.65	
Magazine for advertising	1205.00	
" Miscellaneous	12.00	
Total		$6116.16

DISBURSEMENTS

Office furniture		$40.00	
Exchange		5.71	
Rent & Telephone		358.04	
Stenographer		781.10	
Miscellaneous		81.10	
Telegrams		54.85	
Traveling expenses		190.07	
Postage		128.12	
Stationery & Supplies		45.60	
Printing		199.00	
Melvin Jones,Salary,bal.1917-1918 $300			
1918-1919 750			
		1050.00	
		$2924.59	
Magazine			$2087.89

Balance on hand $5912.48

$ 203.68

Secretary-Treasurer's Report to the Third Annual Convention, Chicago, Ill., July 9–11, 1919

Mr. and Mrs. Melvin Jones at a banquet in Odessa, Texas, in 1949, celebrating her birthday and their fortieth wedding anniversary—June 29

10

HOME OFFICE

SOMEWHAT anomalously, the Lions, who publicly frown on business efficiency as an end in itself, have no hesitancy about practicing it in their own affairs. Anyone who has followed the history of the organization thus far will not need much of a refresher course on how the routine endeavors of the organization, the book-and-paper work, the pencil-and-pen work, were carried out. In the early days the Board of Directors delegated much of the administrative work of the International to committees and then there were sub-committees reporting to committees and so on ad infinitum. And committees, it seems, are committees—even Lions committees. So the shift from the committee form of management to something tidier was accomplished as soon as Melvin Jones, the Secretary-General, had the International Office sufficiently organized to take over.

Cramped quarters was one of the first plagues that beset Jones as he struggled (once more with the experienced assistance of Mrs. Jones) to set up, for the mush-rooming organization, procedures that wouldn't be out-grown before he could put them to use. He moved the International Office four times, after relinquishing his Insurance Exchange suite and brokerage business, before coming to rest in the McCormick Building on Chicago's Michigan Avenue at Van Buren Street. Lions International has been in that sturdy old block ever since April 15, 1921, spreading out from time to time until floor space rented in the building in 1949 totaled more than 24,000 square feet. The headquarters staff has grown with the years from the husband-and-wife team of Jones and Jones to a present complement of more than two hundred secretaries, clerks, auditors, and executives.

From the time the first Board of Directors elected him, until 1946, Melvin Jones was the only salaried officer in the Lions organization. Recognizing that under his management Lions International had grown in size and complexity to a point where he could use a few noncoms to keep things going, the convention that year authorized the appointment at headquarters of a paid Assistant Secre-tary-General, Secretary, Treasurer, "and such other sec-retaries as may be designated by the Board of Directors."

The departmentalization of International business be-gan early. Jones organized sundry divisions of his office to act as information centers for the guidance of commit-tees in the individual clubs. This relieved committees set up by the International conventions or Boards, of administra-tive detail they were poorly equipped to handle.

Visitors to the International Office—and better than a thousand visiting Lions drop in on the Secretary-General each year when passing through Chicago—are invariably amazed at the speed and efficiency with which the great mass of detailed work is handled. The office occupies the major portion of the third floor of the McCormick Building. Stepping from the elevator, the visitor immediately notes the large Lions emblem welcoming him to headquarters. At once he is reminded of the international aspect of the organization as he passes along the corridor, which is flanked by the national flags of all the Lions countries. In the reception hall he is greeted with a smile and a sincere word of welcome by the receptionist, who serves also as one of the operators of the busy telephone switchboard. By the time he has signed his name in the visitors' register, the office manager is waiting to conduct him personally on a tour of the office. In the meantime, the receptionist is dispatching the news of his visit to the secretary of his home Lions Club so that he may be credited with an attendance make-up.

Just about the first thing every visiting Lion wants to do is to shake hands with Melvin Jones, and he is greatly pleased to find the jovial Secretary-General awaiting him at his office door, his hand extended. An air of unpretentious informality pervades Jones's book-lined office, and the visitor feels very much at ease chatting with this greatest Lion of them all. However, if you are the average visitor you may blush with embarrassment at not being able to recall some obscure event which occurred in your home club, perhaps years ago, as Jones's remarkable memory unfolds for you the minute details of that event.

Besides supervising the International Office, convention matters, and matters of policy, the Secretary-General has established some twenty-eight departments at Chicago headquarters to handle all phases of Lions work. Among those which the visitor usually finds most interesting are:

Club Activities Department: This department is organized to aid clubs in selecting activities and to furnish them with information and suggestions so that their projects will be successful. The department files have been built up to a point where they cover virtually every aspect of Lions activity "from an Easter egg hunt to building an airport." Most of this information has been compiled from actual experiences of Lions Clubs.

Club Service Department: Club difficulties, as differentiated from community difficulties, are diagnosed by this department, to the end that the proper remedy may be applied. Like the service department of an automobile agency, the department's business is to keep every Lions Club in good running condition.

Extension Department: This is the department that can take much of the credit for the rapid multiplication of officially chartered Lions Clubs. When a new one is formed, its officers and directors are instructed in their duties and the committee chairmen are given suggestions. The extension service seeks to supply every help to a new club to develop into a strong, active club.

Membership Department: Plans and suggestions for building and holding a representative membership; key, club, and special awards to stimulate interest in membership development; and informative literature of interest to prospective members, are the province of this department.

Department of Accounts: This department keeps a record of receipts and disbursements, names and addresses of members, statistical information on the Association, the districts, and the clubs, and a continuous record of membership reports.

District Administration Department: The primary concern of this department is the co-ordination of activities of the District Governors, Deputy District Governors, Zone Chairmen, Cabinet Secretary-Treasurers, State Secretaries, and other district officers. The closely knit, smoothly running district organizations are evidence of the effectiveness of its work.

Magazine Department: The Association's official publication — THE LION — is issued monthly and mailed to 355,000 leading business and professional men throughout the English-speaking countries in Lionism. The Spanish edition — EL LEON — goes to 20,000 members of Lions Clubs in Spanish-speaking countries.

To the visitor, the headquarters filing system seems uncanny. Name any town where there is a Lions Club— And where isn't there one?—and a card will be whipped out of the files bringing you completely up to date on the status and activities of that club since its organization down to the last dollar and the newest member and the latest clambake. You have a good deal the same feeling, when the little cards turn up, as if you were watching one of those think-of-a-card tricks. Monthly reports relayed from club secretary to International, with copies to the District Governors, Deputy District Governors, and Zone Chairmen, are the obvious explanation of this phenomenon, and the less obvious one is the field representative from headquarters, who, unhalted by rain, snow, sleet, high wind, or dark of night, makes his appointed rounds among the clubs. It is his job to get new clubs started and to help the old ones to stay in business.

One fantastic result of the efficiency of the headquarters records is that clubs sometimes find it easier to get an over-all picture of their condition by consulting the compact International file than by plowing through their own.

Since the war, the Lions have entertained intermittent hopes of putting up a building of their own. But in this they have been repeatedly blocked by the postwar construction deadlock.

In the meantime, spare corridors and vaults of the McCormick Building are bursting with "supplies"—literally tons of charts and folders and booklets which the International distributes to its 7,500 member-clubs. More than a million pieces of mail were handled by the mailing division during the club year 1948–49. Thousands of packages of various supplies, as well as awards, were shipped to the clubs. Merchandise ordered by clubs is handled on a nonprofit basis as a special service. Mailing plates are kept for more than 90,000 officers and committee chairmen so that a complete mailing can be made, if necessary, in one day.

And it is not only the "plant" from which the International directs the individual clubs that needs more and more space as time goes on. Individual clubs are finding it advantageous to acquire quarters of their own rather than be pushed around by harried maîtres d'hôtel with overcrowded schedules. In towns where the Lions have achieved this independence, their rooms or buildings are invariably in demand as community centers, and that is what they turn out to be.

11

PENNY WATCHING

THAT the Lions contrived to stay solvent during their first five or six years is not the least remarkable thing about them. They had no endowments, no visible means of support except the money that came in for dues. Organization expenses ran above estimates, as they always do, and the no-assessment rule prevented them from sharing the burden among themselves.

Jones recalls the story of one of the men who developed hybrid corn and came to the climax of his long work in the middle of the worst drought on record in the United States. All of the field he had planted shriveled up except for two stalks. If those two stalks went with the rest he would have no seed with which to go on with another year of experiment, and one of his assistants suggested that he give the parched plants a little water.

"No," he said, "if this corn can't take it, it's no good to anybody. Let it shrivel." Out of the few ears he salvaged when the stalks survived has grown a tremendous industry in a corn variety that doesn't have to be coddled.

The Secretary-General reads into this a significant allegory.

In forming the Association there was no income. There had been considerable outlay for traveling, stenographic expense, and the entertaining of individuals and groups. The clubs that accepted the invitation into the affiliation began to pay dues after a constitution was adopted in which the amount that they should pay was stated— which was then only $1.00 per year. All this was worked out at the Dallas meeting on October 9, 10, and 11, 1917, at which time it was definitely decided that Melvin Jones would be the Secretary-Treasurer of the Association and that the office of the Association would be in the city in which the Secretary-Treasurer was located.

So the Secretary-Treasurer returned to Chicago, opened an office in the Insurance Exchange Building, and proceeded without funds and without compensation. He made a report to the St. Louis Convention on August 15, 1918, of a total income from October 9 to August 15 of $2,432.88. It had always been a contention that the St. Louis meeting, instead of being called the Second Annual Convention, should be called the First as, after all, the meeting in Dallas on October 9, 1917, was not actually a convention but was the completion of an organization. Nevertheless, the meeting in Chicago in 1919 got to be known as the Third Annual Convention, and all conventions have been numbered from the Dallas meeting in 1917. In examining these two reports,* it is well to note that at the conclusion of the 1918 Convention, after

* See illustration facing page 86.

Melvin Jones's report at the end of the year, he had $488.20 to the good. Also, at the end of the convention in July, 1919, he had a balance on hand of $205.68. That year the total expense was $5,912.48. Of this, Melvin Jones received compensation to the extent of $1,050, which he laughingly remarked probably reimbursed him for a quarter of his expenses that he did not feel should go into the expense accounts.

The question of a salary for him had always been of more interest to others than to himself, and in the early days he remarked, "As long as the insurance business is good, I would be glad to work for nothing and board myself." But in the early twenties the Board of Directors felt that he should be reimbursed for more of his time and voted him an annual salary of $4,000.

At that particular time there was considerable agitation about moving the office to Minneapolis or to Toronto, but Jones proceeded to lay out plans for an office in the McCormick Building, where the Association has made its headquarters ever since.

There was also a movement on foot to reimburse Melvin Jones on the basis of a dollar per year per member and $1.00 for every new member that was brought in. In fact, the Board of Directors voted to pay him on this basis, but Jones thought the matter over and refused to accept any such compensation, nor was he going to allow the Association to be put in a position of paying an executive on this basis. So the records show that the Oakland Convention (1921) created the position of Secretary-General for Jones, making it a full-time position and resolving that Melvin Jones be engaged for a period of five and one half years at a salary of $7,200 per year, with the provision

that the Board of Directors could increase such salary from
time to time as conditions warranted.

At the Atlantic City Convention of 1923 the Board
increased his salary to $10,000.

In 1931 the Board of Directors felt that the Association
and the expenses warranted the raising of Melvin Jones's
salary to $1,000 a month, or $12,000 a year. But, in
December, 1932, the headquarters staff gulped and manfully accepted a 10 per cent salary cut with the Secretary-
General setting the example by voluntarily taking a 25 per
cent cut in salary.

After the depression the Board felt that Melvin Jones's
salary should be restored to $12,000 a year, and as time
went along they raised it to $15,000 a year. Most of these
raises were given despite his opposition to them; and in
discussing his salary with some he openly stated that he did
not want to be rated as a cheap man because his salary
was not in proportion to what some people thought it
should be and was possibly more than others thought it
ought to be. He made a statement to the Board to the
effect that he never had run a foot race in his life with
anyone to see who was the cheapest man. On the other
hand, he did not get into the Association to make money
out of it. If he wanted to make money he would have
stayed where he was—in the commercial field.

On one occasion he stated to a group that every Lion
who joined the Association had to give some of his time
voluntarily; that there was a time when the Association
did not want to reimburse any of the Lions even for their
expenses, but he was always back of the movement to
reimburse the Board of Directors and District Governors
for their actual expenses. The Constitution provided that

no officer except the Secretary-General should receive a salary. He felt that since the Directors and other officers were giving portions of their time and were being reimbursed only for their expenses, he also should make some contribution to the Association. However, he had to live and had home expenses to meet. Since some people seemed to rate a person as a cheap man if he did not get a salary, he felt that it was necessary for him to have some salary.

Furthermore, as his co-workers in the office were not being paid in proportion to what others received in commercial lines, he felt that they, too, were giving to the Association because they believed in the development and growth and the things that the Association was doing. Therefore, he never placed anyone in a position of authority unless he felt that the individual had the welfare of the Association at heart.

But, after all, some consideration must be given to those men who are devoting their entire time to the development of this Association. In answer to inquiries raised by an interviewer relative to his salary and salaries of others, Jones replied by asking these questions: What is the value of a man? What is his worth? What would it be worth to you in your business to have a man or a group of men develop your business in such a way as the Association has been developed or built? What do you think he or they would be worth to you?

"In a sense," Jones continued, "the Lions are the owners of the Association. How much do you think they should pay a man or a group of men who have built it, and what do you think they should pay to a man or group of men to run it? What do you think a man or a group of men are worth if they are able to build an

Association of over 7,400 clubs with more than 380,000 members in 26 countries, to put a million dollars in the treasury, and throughout the years of depression, war, and inflation to keep—without any increase—the dues as low or lower than any other similar organization?

THE ART OF FINANCE

Most of us remember only too well the general financial conditions immediately following the crash of '29. We know it affected every business and organization, most of which were fighting to survive. It is only necessary to refer to the reports on financial operations and other records to see that Jones was not only an expert organizer but also a genius on finance. In fact, the present treasurer, Wilburn L. Wilson, who has worked closely with Jones for almost two decades, points to the wisdom of Jones's management as basic to the continued success of the Association.

The glum year of 1930 brought with it a double challenge in the fact that it affected both membership and finances. This meant proving to each man that he could not afford to relinquish his Lions Club membership. New methods of helping the clubs, and also the individual members who were paying dues to the clubs, had to be devised. The detailed "Jones's operations" involved in this would supply sufficient material for the preparation of a separate book on that subject. However, the effectiveness of his getting organized for the conditions that prevailed is reflected in the fact that there was only one year in which a net loss in membership is recorded. After that year, the growth steadily continued. The certified public accountants' financial statement for the year ending June 30, 1930, showed a net loss of $10,392.55, accounts payable with trade creditors in the amount of $35,455.53, approximately that amount of assets on paper, and only $1,417.89 in the bank. The accounts payable figure is proof enough that Jones had friends who believed in him and the organization. There were times when Jones would cash the employees' pay-roll checks out of his personal funds, holding them until there was sufficient money in the Association's coffers from which they could be cashed.

But Jones never became discouraged, and by 1931 his "depression program" was grinding along in good style. The long hard hours beyond the usual work day contributed by him and by his reduced but loyal staff could spell nothing less than success. The fiscal year 1931 closed with a net excess of income over expenses of $2,442.15. The following few years were rough, but this young, aggressive organization surged forward. The income of the year ending June 30, 1940, exceeded expenses by $13,494.56 and gave the Association a net worth of $4,358.34. After going through the financial difficulties of the thirties, Jones resolved that this should not happen again. His solution involved not only the International Association's funds, but also those of the individual clubs. The clubs have been furnished all the know-how of a good financial program and, while carrying on more and more worth-while activities, have at the same time built up healthy reserves both in their administrative fund and in their activities fund.

The year 1941 called for a new type of planning involving the uncertainty of wartime conditions, the inevitable inflation, and the effect on individual clubs. It was definite that the war effort would need the help of strong

Lions Clubs, and Jones reasoned that building membership in existing clubs, increasing the organization of new clubs, and continuing to suggest new ideas with respect to Association economy would more than offset the financial rigors of war and inflation. He had never been so right, because this three-way program gave splendid support to the war effort, made Lions International the largest and most active service-club organization in the world, made it possible to retain dues (including the magazine subscription) at $4.50 per year, and brought the total net worth and reserves for contingencies up to more than one half million dollars as of June 30, 1949. Jones is indeed a wizard on finance and management and seemed to thrive on the challenge of depression, war, and inflation.

12

LIONS IN PRINT

As we have mentioned somewhere before, the second convention of the Lions (St. Louis, 1918) in a moment of great expansiveness voted to establish an official monthly magazine. And as has also been mentioned, Melvin Jones found himself designated Editor and Publisher. There was nothing surprising about it. The delegates naturally assumed that the myriad-minded Secretary-General would be able to get out a magazine, as he had learned to do so many other things, in his spare time. Whatever Jones may have thought about it, he lived up to expectations. Two months after the convention, the first copy of THE LIONS CLUB MAGAZINE went into the mails from his insurance office, 231 Insurance Exchange Building, Chicago. The only change he had found necessary in his already jammed headquarters was a new sign on the door.

Jones had never been an editor. His experience as a publisher had been confined to the production of insurance biochures. On the other hand, as he has frequently observed, experience is the cheapest thing a man can buy and the quickest delivered. Anyway, the first issue of the magazine made it apparent that Jones, and whoever it was that he got to help him whitewash his fence, had ingenuity and resourcefulness. The 28-page issue that Lions began to receive the next day in the mails had a gratifying collection of advertisements, mostly from Chicago firms. The pure reading matter consisted of timely discussion of the war and war problems, war gardens, Spanish influenza, and Lionism.

A two-page spread of a picture taken at the St. Louis Convention carried the legend: "Those who have been in touch with Lions Club activities will recognize many familiar faces in this group picture, although it shows only a portion of those who attended the convention at St. Louis. The photograph was taken on the occasion of a delightful automobile sight-seeing trip tendered to Lions and their ladies on the afternoon of August 20, just preceding the formal banquet." That will give you a general idea of the tone of the magazine at its inception. It was plain, unassuming, folksy, somewhat haphazard in make-up. Certainly it looked little like the important national slick-paper publication that it was presently to become. But the Lions loved it, and with considerable reason they looked upon Jones as a sort of magician for having produced it without any funds for that purpose.

The next year the Lions, convening in Chicago, authorized the Board of Directors to name a committee on publications. The committee's chief function was to look about for a new editor for the magazine. Through succeeding editorial regimes, however, the name of Jones has remained on the masthead as editor and business manager. In what was undeniably a promotion in pay, the Board confirmed his appointment to the editorial post in 1920 at a salary of a dollar a year.

The magazine acquired its present format—eight and one half by eleven inches—with the issue of January, 1922. That same year the number of pages was increased to 48. As Lions multiplied, more space was needed to keep the individual clubs abreast of what the òther clubs were doing. Art covers in two or three colors began to appear and the size of the magazine increased until it reached the present standard size of 64 pages.

But policy as to editorial content and advertising jelled slowly. In spite of the quantity of advertising in the first issues, the trend from the start was toward a magazine that would be strictly a house organ.

THE LIONS CLUB MAGAZINE—not until later was it to be titled THE LION: A MAGAZINE FOR LIONS—at one period of its development competed with great national publications for big names. Writers of the status of Peter B. Kyne, Mary Roberts Rinehart, Ellis Parker Butler, James Oliver Curwood, and Irvin S. Cobb were among the contributors in the 1920's. But by degrees it came to be understood that the principal function of the magazine was to print news items relative to the activities of the various clubs, and articles of "such character as may be of interest and benefit primarily to members of the clubs."

The general directory of the clubs, with names of presidents and secretaries, time and place of meeting, etc., now a separate publication, at first was included in the body of THE LIONS CLUB MAGAZINE.

As early as 1922, Jones discouraged the idea of relying

on advertising in a publication of THE LIONS CLUB MAGA-
ZINE type.

"In checking on other club magazines," he said, "we
have found that it costs them nearly as much to increase
the size of their publications in order to carry advertising
as the advertising brought in."

President Cameron agreed.

"I haven't been able to see we were justified in having
a lot of advertising we didn't get a good price for,"
Cameron said. "I think we should keep a high standard
of cost and, if an advertiser wants the back page, let him
pay accordingly. Let the advertisers pay so the magazine
is not chock-full of advertising. We'll get along just as
well."

He explained this idea—which most publishers would
have considered sheer heresy—quite simply:

"The membership is paying for the magazine now—
paying for the cost of it and it is financing itself, which
practically no other magazine in the country is doing on
subscriptions alone."

And Lion John S. Noel made a similar comment:

"In one way," he said, "we are *giving* our membership
that magazine. Don't send them a big magazine full of
advertising. We want to give them the essence of Lionism."

In 1925, the Board decided that the magazine would
accept no advertising in which the name of any individual Lion was mentioned and would print no professional
cards as advertising.

During the ensuing years, paid contributions all but
disappeared from the pages of THE LION. The magazine
had run over its budget in 1939, a year when Association

finances generally were at a low ebb, and in 1941 the
Board considered means for stepping up the official publication's revenues. The question of payment for editorial
material was discussed and Jones demurred.

To buy articles for publication, he declared, with the
subscription rate being what it was—a dollar a year—
would only insure an annual deficit. Oscar C. Kurtz, the
advertising manager and now managing editor, explained
the peculiar position of THE LION as an advertising medium. Agencies felt that if they used one publication of
this type they would have to use others in the same category, and they figured they could reach all THE LION
readers more economically in the long run through general
national magazines.

All of this discussion at one point prompted Ray L.
Riley, Past International President, to burst out:

"Well, THE LION 's a dollar's worth, isn't it? If we
go beyond the limitations of a club organ, we'll get in too
deep."

However, one day in the late summer of 1932 Melvin
Jones stormed into the Magazine Department and issued
the ultimatum that the magazine had to be made more
readable, that the contents be made livelier—"even if you
have to run crossword puzzles"—something to make the
members drop what they are doing when the magazine
is delivered each month, and read it. During the weeks
that followed, many ideas were suggested and tested, and
some of the best were developed and used.

"Hm-m-m. 'Even if you have to run crossword puzzles.' I wonder," mused Oscar C. Kurtz one day when
inspecting books of crossword puzzles in a store. "I wonder if I can make up a crossword puzzle."

Well, he did. It was run in the November, 1932, issue of the magazine. In the meantime he prepared another which became a part of the December issue. "Since then," says Kurtz, "I have not had to make up another puzzle except to introduce a new type. The puzzle fans have kept us well supplied with excellent contributions."

That was a modest statement, because so many contributions rained on the Magazine Department from interested fans that after a few years mimeographed supplements were issued "to use up the surplus puzzles" and the supplements mailed to the Lion members who had gotten on the puzzle-fan mailing list. This move, however, served only to increase the flow of contributions, and the supplements are now issued monthly. Up to the early part of 1949, a total of 1,484 puzzles had been printed on the last page of the magazine, while 1,826 had appeared in the 68 supplements issued to the same date. Believe it or not, some of the puzzle fans have solved correctly nearly all of those 3,310 puzzles.

Pamphlets are issued describing the various types and forms of puzzles used, and a special lapel button is awarded to those who solve correctly at least ten puzzles. The puzzle editor is O'Casey, a *nom de puzzle* used so the fans could bawl out the editor without seeming to be personal.

Charles J. Stevenson, editor and broadcaster, then a member of the Board of Directors from Cambridge, New York, voiced the following sentiment in an editorial which was classified as definitive when it ran in the February, 1943, issue of THE LION:

"We've been in the publishing business a good many years," Stevenson wrote, "and we think THE LION is a splendid job in every way. Of course it isn't a second

Saturday Evening Post and the only fiction it carries are some reports from clubs in our neck of the woods.

"In short, some misguided individuals have somehow got the foolish idea that THE LION is a publication of general circulation instead of a fine specialty magazine which carries only materials pertinent to the Lion world. There probably are a few members of this great and growing organization who think the magazine should carry a 'How to Keep Well' column, a few choice recipes for making blackberry pie (or brandy), and a Dorothy Dix corner.

"Just how do they get that way? Aren't there enough magazines of general publication in the market to meet this demand? If you are looking for fiction, boys, we can recommend a number of bang-up publications, but don't expect any 'true confessions' to be printed in these pages.

"Then we have a few bluebloods who whine because *The Readers' Digest* doesn't reprint articles from THE LION. You don't happen to have seen any articles reprinted from any one of the hundred or more leading specialty magazines either, have you? . . . Our magazine is just for Lions. . . ."

Lion Stevenson appears to have had the last word. The International President, Edward H. Paine, Michigan City, Indiana, told the Directors when he next called them together that he had heard no further criticism of THE LION.

The extension of Lionism beyond the boundaries of the United States has necessitated publication in several languages. A separate section of the regular magazine was brought out in 1937 for Lions in Spanish-speaking countries. This has now grown into a special Spanish-language edition, EL LEON, which has won a wide and loyal readership among the many leading men of Latin America who, because of their high ideals, public-spiritedness and ambition to serve, have adopted Lionism as their cause. EL LEON has exerted strong influence in stimulating the expansion and growth of Lionism throughout the Latin-American countries, thus linking them ever closer in friendship and mutual understanding, not only to each other, but also to their Lion neighbors to the north and across the seas. EL LEON, furthermore, through its word-and-picture reporting of the virile Lionism practiced by the Latin-American clubs, has focused world attention on them and their activities, as object lessons of the constructive power of the Lions in behalf of their respective communities and nations.

Ernst A. Stewart is the Managing Editor of EL LEON, and Fidel Torres V. is the Editor.

Getting out the magazine is only a fraction of the work of the editorial talent at headquarters. In addition they keep district and club officers briefed with periodic reprints of the Secretary-General's monthly letters. They furnish basic material on Lionism to all new officers, directors, committee chairmen, and members. They prepare a new edition of the directory annually and—periodically —special programs, activities suggestions, etc. The directory for confidential use of Lions Clubs officers and traveling Lions has gone through 33 editions. It has grown to 208 pages in a six-by-nine-inch format. The pages list names and addresses of international, district, and club officers, as well as information about club meetings. The list of the editorial department's standard pamphlets, available to clubs or members on request, runs to over 100 items in English and almost as many in Spanish, with several also published in French and the Scandinavian languages.

Familiar purple-and-gold highway signs and hotel-lobby banners, wherever you go, show the way to the nearest Lions Club and are the organization's most familiar means of telling the world.

The clubs rely on their local papers to print advance notices of their meetings, cover newsworthy programs, and give an occasional friendly plug to their drives. Otherwise the Lions ask few publicity favors. In fact, on the contrary, the International has a policy, unique among service organizations, of buying newspaper space to thank cities for hospitality extended at convention time. Individual clubs are urged to follow a similar policy, buying a page of advertising space on which to render an account of the year's activities to the community.

Life Magazine once devoted its "Life Goes to a Party" pages to the annual Halloween Barn Dance of the Binghamton, New York, Lions Club. Publications devoted to recreation, library work, and other phases of welfare work in which the clubs are interested periodically give the clubs their due. But by no possible stretch of the imagination could the Lions be called publicity grabbers. And you are more likely to find the Lions promoting their community than their club to the general public. You'll find them represented with a float in every parade, if indeed they aren't in charge of the show. But in their boosting efforts you'll find little of the shallow exhibitionism that so bores the outsider.

California has let itself go to the extent of an annual district-wide essay contest on the subject, "What the Lions Club Can Do for Our Community." Composer of the best 500 words discussing this topic gets $500 and a trip to the next convention city.

That business of Admiral Halsey's saddle, a Lions promotion, wasn't kept a secret, exactly. But the credit and the national publicity went to Montrose, Colorado, rather than to the Lions Club which developed the stunt. Bruce Torgney, a Montrose Lion, suggested it after reading the Admiral's assertion that he would ride Hirohito's white horse down Tokyo's main drag. Lion Walter Allison, purveyor of saddles to all the cow country round, set to work on the finest saddle his skill could turn out. Sixty-three local cattle men were delighted to chip in $10 apiece to have their brands stamped into the leather work. Lion Allison also made the bridle and breast strap and adorned them with cattle brands. The blanket, white with a red center field, was woven for the Lions by an old Indian who lived at near-by Towaoc. Woven into one side, in blue, are the words, "Admiral Halsey." "Montrose, Colorado" is woven on the other side and the word "Lions" is at one end. Admiral Halsey, who never did get around to riding that horse, has sent the gear to the United States Naval Museum at Annapolis, Maryland.

The Lions were adequately represented in the prewar series of World's Fairs. The extent of their participation in each succeeding one has a certain significance beyond its mere promotional value. It offers also an interesting gauge of Lionism's growth.

In 1932, "in view of present economic conditions," the Board of Directors recoiled in shock from the proposal of a representative of Chicago's A Century of Progress committee that they spend $10,000 on participation in the Fair during the five months of 1933 that it was to be open. The suggested $10,000 was pared down to $1,000 for an allotted plot in the Social Science Building on Northerly

Island during that first year. But the Directors were quite willing to raise the ante for the 1934 season. They furthermore decided that registration at the Lions exhibit at A Century of Progress might be considered a make-up for club attendance.

In 1939, the Lions had their special "days" at both the San Francisco and New York fairs. In the Court of Peace, Mayor Fiorello La Guardia and Grover Whelan, Fair president, welcomed 1,000 Lions who came on to New York from their convention in Pittsburgh. On Treasure Island, 4,000 visiting Lions were honored with a special program.

13

ROAR! YOU LIONS!

MELVIN JONES, who is still remembered in Chicago as a soloist whose strong, resonant tenor for many years was a part of the offerings of the Apollo Club, the city's principal choral society, soon had the Lions singing like birds. Nobody was surprised.

"I introduced songs the first thing," he recalls. "It seemed to me that the meetings were pretty dead until we limbered them up with community song. Everybody talked business with his neighbor at the luncheon table; and when that subject was exhausted, he shut up and kept his eyes on his plate. A few rounds of 'Tipperary' and 'I Want a Girl Just Like the Girl' ended all that. There's always some fellow in a club who can perform at the piano and someone to lead the singing."

Jones's sensing of the need to limber up with song was reflected in THE LIONS MAGAZINE in 1919. Under the heading "Not Roars but Music," the March issue carried this editorial:

"He to whom the term 'lion' suggests roaring must be a nonmember of our leonine fellowship, for where is the club that is not using the charm and power of music to enhance the pleasure and effectiveness of its gatherings?

" 'Such as the music is, such is the music of the commonwealth,' says an old Turkish proverb, as if anticipating the interest which was to be shown many centuries later by the commonwealth-uplifting groups that comprise our fellowship. As might be expected, patriotic music was much in evidence during the war, but the termination of the great conflict has by no means brought a cessation of the singing. Worthy talent is always available among the club members, and for the occasional ladies' nights the wives and daughters may also be among the enjoyable contributors to such variety-lending parts of the program.

"Some clubs have quartets or double quartets of their own, and one recent announcement referred to the next meeting as a 'Sing Song,' evidently implying one of those community singing festivals which are deservedly growing in popularity. At Chicago, the last annual meeting was enlivened partly by a series of short parodies of popular songs, written at the expense of the newly elected officers and appropriately following the brief speech of acceptance made by each of the 'surprised' men whose names had been on the successful ticket. Indeed, the general absence of paid entertainers speaks well for our clubs, and while enthusiasm may occasionally be vented in something akin to a yell or a roar, it looks as if our organization might acquire a quite enviable reputation as providers of good music."

From the singing of songs familiar to everyone to the composing of tunes and lyrics exclusively for Lions was a logical progression. Sometimes the Tin-Pan Alley talent that supplied these compositions provided both the words and the music—sometimes only the words. Sixty-three of the 175 songs accepted for the 96-page official songbook are either adaptations or originals especially dedicated to Lionism. The copyrights for some of these are held in the name of The International Association of Lions Clubs, and others are used by permission of the copyright holders. In tone they range all the way from "Munchin' at the luncheon . . . eatin' at the meetin' " to the stately Lions Hymn.

First place in any Lion's book, and heart obviously, is held by "Don't You Hear Those Lions Roar?" for which Lion Joseph W. Thurston of Hartford, Connecticut, contributed the words and Lion Robert Kellogg of the same club the music.

This song, with its accompanying roar, is the one by which Lions make their presence known in convention cities and hotel dining rooms the world over. It goes:

1.

He makes his home in a jungle den,
He feeds on meat and also men;
King of beasts, he kills and preys,
He's the lord of the forest,
'Til he ends his days.
Roaring, he bites 'em!
Snarling, he fights 'em!
Monarch of all he surveys.

CHORUS

Don't you hear those Lions roar?
Don't you hear those Lions roar?

You can hear them roaring ev'ry week,
As they feed and growl for more. (Rah! Rah! Rah!)
You should hear those Lions roar
Their snarling, rumbling roar—
So, roar, Lions! Bite 'em! Bite 'em! Bite 'em!
Don't you hear those Lions, hear those Lions,
Hear those Lions roar!

2.

A jungle queen is now his bride,
A tawny mate lies by his side.
Cubs they raise fifteen or more,
Whom he fills a-plenty with the jungle lore.
Growling, he rambles! Midst bloody shambles,
Ready now for peace or war! (CHORUS)

Anthony Menke, originally a member of the Detroit Lions
Club and later secretary of the Newark, New Jersey,
Club, is credited with inventing the Lions' roar, that splendid paradoxical performance, a good-humored and even
hilarious growl. Thanks to Menke's origination of this
unique sound, the Lions have been roaring, with fine rah-
rah spirit, since they were the merest cubs. The roar goes
like this:

Roar Lions! Roar Lions! Roar Lions!
Bite 'em! Bite 'em! Bite 'em!

At other times they bend down as one man and come
up with a rumbling "R-r-r-o-o-o-ar-r-r," like a lower-
octave skyrocket.

Without taking any polls—as indeed who would want
to—it is apparent that "God Bless America" ranks first

among the non-Lion songs to be heard everywhere Lions
gather in the United States. On occasions, patriotic and
otherwise, when Lions meet, "God Bless America" has
become as indispensable as the chairman's gavel.

The evolution of the official *Songs for Lions* was slow
and sometimes painful. The International Board had begun
prospecting for publication of a songbook as early as 1921
during the administration of President Ewen W. Cameron
of Minneapolis. However, some thought it should be one
kind of book and others thought it should be another
kind, and each new Board of Directors would wrestle with
the problem awhile and then pass it along to its successor.
Finally, in 1925, the late Benjamin F. Jones, then the International President, informed the Board of Directors that
"a questionnaire has been sent to all Lions Clubs for the
purpose of ascertaining the most popular songs, and arrangements are being made to obtain permission from publishers of popular music to use the words and music of
certain songs."

And so it was that in 1926, after much procrastination,
Lions International had finally achieved an official songbook. Apparently the results have not been too bad because the book, with its purple-and-gold cover, is now in
its fifth printing and is still going strong.

Almost as long as most Lions can remember, Tom
Warrilow, head of a Gary, Indiana, sign business, has been
official song leader at Lions International conventions,
with Al Green, a Gary C.P.A., at the piano. Warrilow
doesn't turn as many actual handsprings as he once did in
directing some of the more spirited choruses. But he still
must—and can—do a few mental ones on occasions such
as the 1948 convention in New York.

A choral group from Amarillo, Texas, was down on the program for a rendition of "The Lord's Prayer." But, at the time for their scheduled performance, Jones, looking frantically into the wings from his position on the rostrum, saw no signs of them. The stage wait that followed was no longer than it took Jones to assure himself that Lions Warrilow and Green were in their accustomed place, with all avenues of escape shut off.

"And now," Chairman Fred W. Smith said airily, "we are privileged to hear 'The Lord's Prayer' "—and he nodded to the startled pair at the piano.

It was what might have been a bad moment for some people. But a man doesn't spend the time Tom Warrilow has spent in getting Lions gatherings into full voice without acquiring a certain aplomb. Warrilow's baritone rolled out a sort of Gregorian chant to a hastily improvised accompaniment by Green, with enough assurance to satisfy the audience that he had put in long hours practicing for this impressive moment. As the "Amen" died away, the chorus from Amarillo drifted back. It seems there had been some bad judgment on just how urgently the Lions were standing in the need of prayer, and how long it would take to slip out for a cup of coffee.

14

INCREASE AND MULTIPLY

IF you have needed any proof that unselfish service brings its rewards, you need only look at the statistics. It is significant that of the million or so men who have contracted the lunch-club habit in the United States and other countries where the American organizations have offshoots, more than one third are Lions. There are more Lions in the U.S.A. alone than the next largest luncheon-classification club can muster in the entire world. As of June 30, 1949, Lions International had 381,426 members in 7,427 clubs in twenty-six countries on five continents.

The Lions International membership, estimated at 800 in 1917, had reached eight times 800 and extended to Canada by 1920. During the administration of Dr. C. C. Reid of Denver, International President in the year 1921–22, the directors recognized that the growth of the organization was going to be something beyond all precedent and set their goal at "a new club every day." The goal

Lion dignitaries and guests meeting at a banquet at the Waldorf-Astoria Hotel, in celebration of the Thirtieth Anniversary of the founding of Lions International, in New York in October, 1947

First Annual Convention of The International Association of Lions Clubs, Dallas, Texas, October 8–10, 1917

More than 25,000 Lions fill Madison Square Garden to overflowing at the Association's Thirty-first Annual Convention in New York City, July 26–29, 1948

was attained a few years later and passed in the forties. The rate of growth of considerably better than "a club a day" has been steadily maintained and improved. During the three-year period from 1946 to 1949, there was an average of more than 825 new clubs organized each year, or two and three fourths a day, exclusive of Sundays and holidays. The average net membership increase for that same period exceeded 35,000 per year.

A big factor in the vitality of the Lions membership structure is the seeming nonchalance with which the International will cancel out substandard clubs. Charters are summarily annulled at the discretion of the Directors for failure to meet financial and other obligations. The constitution further provides that clubs paid up in full to the International may resign at will.

"If a club is persistently inactive, we'd better get rid of it and work with a new one, perhaps in the same community, frequently with some of the same membership," Melvin Jones explains.

However, this isn't saying that the International doesn't at all times stand ready to administer first aid to ailing clubs. That is what the headquarters service department is there for . . . counselling, devising programs for any weak clubs, reorganizing inactive ones. The Lions insist that their clubs be active.

Clubs that got into difficulties during the depression were given tender nursing. There were about 350 clubs which the International wasn't even going to bother to bill, Jones reported to the Directors in the spring of 1931. A year later, average membership had dropped to 32, collections were a headache, and the International was in the red. But as the depression lifted, the Lions showed the flash of speed that put them permanently ahead of competitors for top rating in membership.

By 1923, the policy of establishing minimum charter membership requirements on the basis of population was pretty well formulated. The Directors that year decided that representatives must secure at least 20 paid, active members before a charter would be granted to clubs in the smaller communities. This scale was graduated upward in the larger communities. Representatives were required to bring new clubs up to a further minimum membership by the end of six months.

Asked what is the ideal size for a service club, Jones will tell you there isn't any such. It varies with the community. A maximum membership is attained only when all civic-minded men eligible to membership have become members of the Lions Club, he says. Or, putting it another way, when every business and professional classification in the community has been filled. Membership in Lions Clubs runs all the way from 20 to 900. Some 25-member clubs have more of an impact than others ten times their size. There was the case of Cut Bank, Montana (pop. 1,500), where the Lions, stalking new members, brought in 45 in a single week in 1936 and claimed "the biggest percentage of increase ever made by a single club."

Calipatria, California, Lions, failing to meet a quota of one new member a month (suggested to the clubs back in 1930 by Secretary-General Jones), pointed instead to what they claimed was a record in the cub department: "August 27—a boy to Lion George Gullett; October 2— a boy to Lion Phil Benson; December 2—a boy to Lion C. R. Prince; December 26—a girl to Lion Harold Brandt." The International conceded that this might be a record for a 25-member club, all right, but not along the lines the International had in mind.

The statistical table of Lionism's growth, measured in the number of members and clubs and reckoned as of June 30 of each year, runs as follows:

1917 (approx.) 25 clubs	800 members
1918........ 28 "	1,526 "
1919........ 42 "	2,364 "
1920........ 113 "	6,451 "
1921........ 245 "	13,739 "
1922........ 495 "	25,429 "
1923........ 640 "	32,477 "
1924........ 761 "	36,943 "
1925........ 939 "	43,647 "
1926........1,086 "	49,230 "
1927........1,183 "	52,965 "
1928........1,458 "	60,859 "
1929........2,044 "	74,238 "
1930........2,339 "	79,863 "
1931........2,491 "	80,456 "
1932........2,660 "	79,203 "
1933........2,670 "	75,725 "
1934........2,692 "	77,470 "
1935........2,709 "	78,240 "
1936........2,725 "	85,539 "
1937........2,789 "	91,948 "
1938........3,042 "	104,818 "
1939........3,432 "	120,251 "
1940........3,817 "	137,727 "
1941........4,082 "	147,407 "
1942........4,171 "	147,909 "

1943	4,326 clubs	150,024 members
1944	4,477 "	177,579 "
1945	4,856 "	218,184 "
1946	5,400 "	279,116 "
1947	6,117 "	326,448 "
1948	6,808 "	358,144 "
1949	7,427 "	381,426 "

GEOGRAPHY LESSON

Lionism and other businessmen's clubs may have had their original impetus from the population drift from country to city with additional stimulus after the boys of World War I had seen Paree. But a reversal is indicated in the directions in which Lionism has spread. The big cities probably always will boast the biggest, richest clubs. But it is the small towns that set great store by the community leadership that Lionism can provide.

The small, independent businessman, backbone of the service-club movement, has been absorbed in the personality of the big corporations in the cities. In the rural and semirural areas, small business still rates, and it's a brash lot of city fathers who will lay down a piece of paving or set up a bandstand without first sounding out Lion sentiment—unless indeed, as frequently happens, the Lions Club and the city fathers are interchangeable.

So it has come about that the density of Lions Clubs, geographically speaking, often has been in inverse ratio to the density of population. A recent survey, taking in the entire service-club field, showed that 72 per cent of such clubs were in towns of under 25,000, 38 per cent in towns of less than 10,000, and 20 per cent in towns of less than 3,000.

At the time of the first International convention in Dallas in October of 1917, four months after the decision to found the Association had been made, Lions Clubs were in business in 32 cities in ten States. The cities were: Waco, Austin, Beaumont, Fort Worth, Dallas, Houston, Wichita Falls, Texarkana, Paris, Abilene, Orange, Port Arthur, San Angelo, Temple, and Greenville, Texas; Oklahoma City, Muskogee, Tulsa, Chickasha, El Reno, Okmulgee, and Ardmore, Oklahoma; Pueblo, Denver, and Colorado Springs, Colorado; Little Rock, Arkansas; Shreveport, Louisiana; Memphis, Tennessee; St. Louis, Missouri; Oakland, California; Chicago, Illinois; and St. Paul, Minnesota.

Some of these original clubs have remained continually active. Denver arrived at first place among Lionism's 2,670 clubs in 1933. Next year Oakland had moved up from second to first place, pushing Denver back a notch. Oakland stayed there until 1935 when Mexico City took the lead and Denver dropped into third place. Central Club of Chicago was out in front in the late thirties. But by 1941, Havana, Cuba, with more than 900 members had become the largest Lions Club and hence the largest service club in the world, and no challenger since has succeeded in taking away that title.

Columbus, Ohio, has been in an "often-a-bridesmaid-but-never-a-bride" predicament for years, never rising above third place nor sinking below fifth among the "Big Ten" of Lionism. Grand Rapids, Oklahoma City, Houston, Baltimore, North Little Rock, Austin, Raleigh, San Antonio, New York City, Metairie, Lubbock, Stockton, Lake Charles, Pittsburgh (East Liberty); San Salvador, El Salvador; Caracas, Venezuela; Lima, Peru; and Rio Piedras and San Juan, Puerto Rico, are among the cities that vie monthly for positions on the "Big Ten" list. Texas was the first state to organize more than 500 Lions Clubs. The next most Lionized states are Pennsylvania and California.

For the second year in succession, District C–2 (Cuba) led all the rest in rate of membership increase during the 1949 Founders' Month Program by averaging sixteen new members per club. Second, third, and fourth places in the District standings also fell to Cuba, with Districts C–6, C–5, and C–3 running up totals of 8.33, 7.67, and 7.13 new members per club, respectively. The Lions Club of Guines, Cuba, had the greatest individual club increase with 80 new members. Odessa, Texas, was second with 74; Havana, Cuba, third with 73. The over-all average increase was slightly over four members for each club in the Association.

Of the 757 new Lions Clubs admitted into the Association during the year ending June 30, 1949, 638 were in the United States; 31 in Canada; 21 in Mexico; 17 in Colombia; 11 in Chile; five in Hawaii; five in Sweden; five in Venezuela; four in the Philippines; four in Bolivia; four in Cuba; three in Peru; three in Puerto Rico; one in Alaska; one in Australia; one in Ecuador; one in France; one in Norway; and one in Switzerland.

The Lions crashed across the border to found a club in Windsor, Ontario, in 1920. From this beginning, more than 325 clubs have been established in the Dominion.

The organization owed its first venture over international boundaries to the Downtown Lions Club of Detroit under the inspiration of Anthony Menke. The Detroiters sponsored the Windsor Lions, who elected

John Hewer as their first president. The Windsor Lions Club claims the distinction of having been the first to introduce the white cane into the Dominion as a safety identification for blind persons.

In 1927, the International Board learned, from correspondence having to do with prospective clubs in 225 cities, that one Theodore E. Simmang of Tientsin, China, had established a club at Tsingtao.

But the main drift of extension at the time was toward Mexico. The first club south of the United States border was established at Nuevo Laredo in March, 1925. Much of the credit for the success of expansion throughout Mexico must be given to the late Colonel Bill Higgins, first and perennial president of the Lions Club of San Antonio, Texas.

In the southwest the Colonel was known both as a colorful figure and as a civic asset. Among other projects, he brought the Chicago Civic Opera Company to San Antonio every season in the days of Garden, Muratore, and Galli-Curci. Founder of a trade bureau for Mexico in the San Antonio Chamber of Commerce, he became an emissary of Lionism on countless trips across the border. He was named District Governor of Mexico after the first clubs were founded there.

For a group as sensitive to the "one-big-mutually-helpful-world" concept as the Lions have shown themselves to be, they've been noticeably "cagey" about spreading themselves to other continents. There was no basic difficulty about establishing clubs in either Canada or Mexico. They entered Cuba and Puerto Rico without much apprehension. Havana furnished them with an International President in the person of Dr. Ramiro Collazo in 1945. But throughout much of the troubled thirties, they obviously shared the prevailing feeling that there was safety in aloofness. They were in no hurry to expand to other continents. In the days when the organization was young, such expansion was held to be too costly. There were also international copyright complications involving protection of the Lions name and emblem.

The war, of course, put an end temporarily to any plans that might have been shaping up as a result of "where-do-we-go-from-here" discussions whenever the Board met. A year before V-E Day, however, faint stirrings, suggestive of action, began to be heard. Dr. Collazo, then First Vice-President, proposed another mission to South America, where some clubs had already been established. Secretary-General Jones went over again in detail the hazards of foreign extension. Obviously he was for taking it easy and making certain that the development of Lionism in other countries when it came should be stable rather than spectacular.

In the meantime the enemy blackout still enshrouded the Lions Club that had carried on so bravely in Tientsin. After December 7, 1941, mail addressed to the Lions Clubs of Tsingtao and Tientsin was returned to the International Office stamped "Service Suspended." When service was resumed in 1945, Lion Denis Conings, president of the Tientsin Club, filed his report:

"After the eighth of December," he wrote, "our club had to go into hiding. Some members were thrown in jail, some were repatriated, some—of whom I was one— were sent to prison camps for years. Others, being neutrals, had to be very careful. Our secretary, E. 'Bis' de Laderbis, however, kept our records in his house, which was twice searched by the Japanese during the war and our funds confiscated, and all by himself he carried on our pet activity, the financing of a brilliant but poor Chinese boy at a French college. The war was hardly over and some of us were still in prison camps when Lion 'Bis' was already on the job, re-forming our Club."

THE LION, in March of 1948, carried an item to the effect that the Tientsin Club's protégé had been graduated with honors and taken into the office of the club treasurer as junior assistant. To raise money to continue their scholarship fund, the Tientsin clubmen gave a dinner dance, de Laderbis mentioned, which netted $35,000,000 in local currency.

Another report from the Pacific carrying about the same date tells of the chartering of a club in the famous leper settlement at Kalaupapa, Molokai, Territory of Hawaii. Delegations from eight other clubs on near-by islands attended. More than half the 31 members of the Kalaupapa club are lepers.

Whatever difficulties it may create, extension into new lands has also swept away some old prejudices. In 1926, the International approved admission of members representing all Pacific races into the Pan-Pacific club in Honolulu, "making possible, perhaps the first . . . *international* club of any of the great American weekly luncheon organizations taking the name 'international' after their titles. . . . The Pan-Pacific Club begins service with its own clubhouse and spacious grounds in the center of the city. . . . On each Tuesday at lunch, fifty to a hundred leaders among the Anglo-Saxons, Latin Americans, Chinese, Japanese, Koreans, Russians, Filipinos, and Hawaiians [attend]."

Lionism, as Jean-Paul Galland has pointed out, is "a

window opening on the world." When he made this statement, the president of the Lions Club of Geneva, Switzerland, was citing the predicament of his own country, "superorganized . . . with 1,800 to 2,000 associations . . . but still with a place for Lionism [which] presents a vehicle for larger participation in the affairs of the world." Through Lionism, Galland said, he hoped that his countrymen might overcome the national claustrophobia from which they had suffered as a result of being ringed in by Axis-occupied countries.

15

HAPPY BIRTHDAY

THERE is a wide choice of days in the calendar which might reasonably be celebrated as the birth date of Lionism. There is June 7, 1917, when the clubs later welded into the International Association first came together to talk it over. There is October 9 of that same year when the first Lions convention was held in Dallas. There is August 25, 1919, when the Illinois charter was granted. No wonder the perfectionists were thrown by this wealth of possibilities and only official convention action could end the confusion. ("Conventions," as Melvin Jones says, "can do anything," and apparently this includes calendar tinkering.)

What was done in the summer of 1931, fifteenth jubilee year of Lionism, was to decide that:

"Whereas, no birth date or Founders' Day has ever been designated or set aside for the proper observance by the members of this organization, on which might be held suitable celebrations and annual meetings, now therefore be it

"Resolved, by the fifteenth annual convention of Lions International now assembled at Toronto, Canada, that January 13 be designated hereafter as Founders' Day and so established by the organization, and that each club within the Association be requested to observe the same with suitable recognition and ceremony."

There was nothing arbitrary about the convention choice. It was Melvin Jones's birthday. Jones and Lionism being interchangeable in the minds of the delegates, what more natural than for them to fix the founding of the one on the same day as the founding of the other?

Jones wasn't as used to demonstrations in his honor then as he has had to become since his birthday was made a sort of semipublic holiday. In 1946, the flag that flew over the Capitol of the United States on his sixty-sixth birthday was presented to him by the Southwest Harbor Lions Club of Washington, D.C. Jones had gone to Washington at the time for the charter ceremony of the Southwest Harbor Club, the 5,000th to be inducted into Lionism. But fifteen years earlier he had made only a modest beginning toward accumulation of the honors that have piled up on him in later life. So he had been singularly moved when, several months before the Toronto Convention, the Lions Clubs of Cook County (Illinois) had surprised him with a lot of rhetoric and a gold watch as he sat with other survivors of the old Business Circle at a banquet in their honor.

"I used to think," the usually serene, white-maned Secretary-General responded shakily on that occasion, "that there couldn't be anything closer to a man's heart than Lionism. I find there is something that gets closer still—the friendship that Lionism brings us. It is when I stand here and look into the faces of the fellows who stood by me in 1916 and 1917 that I realize what friends there are among the Lions. . . . No one man can build an organization. The whole gang stood by. One after another I've had to call on every one of these fellows at the table in times past when we got into a hole. . . . I know you boys love me. I love you all. There is among us a friendship beyond understanding. . . ." Friendship of others for Jones is well exemplified in the many foreign decorations which have been showered upon him and the scores of honors from national organizations.

At the same time a move had been started to honor all old-timers of the Association by designating them "Old Monarchs" and dedicating to them the second week in October, anniversary of the Dallas Convention. The idea was to bring members who had strayed from the clubs back into them at that time. "These men may well be typified by Rosa Bonheur's great painting, 'The Monarch,' which decorates the front cover of this issue," THE LION wrote in October, 1931. "He is typical of the quiet strength, the supreme self-confidence, the serene tranquillity, the hidden power which lies in every member of a Lions Club."

Old Monarchs—Lions of at least ten years' duration—wear chevrons on their special lapel pins signifying the number of years during which they have been members—ten, twenty, twenty-five, thirty, as the case may be. Charter Monarchs, Old Monarchs who, moreover, were in at the chartering of a club, are similarly decorated.

The distribution of chevrons by the club president calls for special arrangements by the program committee. Most clubs prefer an evening dinner meeting for this little ceremony, with the ladies present. There is likely to be a birthday cake symbolic of the passing years and a few solemn words about the meaning of Lionism before the chevrons are passed out to the candidates lined up before the speaker's rostrum.

By the end of April, 1949, 21,295 charter chevrons had been presented to men who had been Lions for ten years and also had been charter members of their clubs. Old Monarch chevrons to the number of 32,113 had been distributed to Lions who, while not charter members, had been in the organization for ten years. There had been 5,547 twenty-year charter chevrons distributed and 3,663 twenty-year Old Monarch chevrons; 2,400 twenty-five year charter chevrons and 736 twenty-five year Old Monarch chevrons; 119 thirty-year charter chevrons and 22 thirty-year Old Monarch chevrons.

The grand total of chevron awards up to April 30, 1949, was 65,895. Since the Association only just celebrated its thirtieth birthday in 1947, the first thirty-year awards were made in 1948.

Old Monarchs always will be honored in the insignia they wear and in the prestige they enjoy. But with the celebration of the first official Founders' Day in 1932, Melvin Jones's birthday became Lionism's chief rallying time. At first only the day was observed, then the observance stretched out into the week in which the birthday occurred, with the clubs honoring their charter members and bestowing earned chevrons during that period. Initiation of the Melvin Jones birthday program in 1936 has diverted this into a month-long birthday celebration.

The International Office in the McCormick Building was a bower of bloom on that first Founders' Day. Tele-

graph messengers wore a path in the marble corridor leading to it. But the note of congratulation that meant most
to Jones was the one he couldn't read because it was written in Braille by the children of a sight-saving class sponsored by the Lions Club of Youngstown, Ohio. Central
Club of Chicago held its 1932 Founders' Day meeting in
the Hotel LaSalle where the International was organized
in 1917. A good many of the old Business Circle crowd
were still about—Maury Blink, Milton Page, Lewis Nutter,
Frank Fry, "Bill" Livingston, Joe Trienens, George Smalley, S. J. Reynolds, F. W. Fullmer, George Aigner, Andy
Comstock, Maurice Wallbrun, Gus Meyer, E. J. Raber,
and Dennis Sattler. On behalf of the Club, International
Director Joseph R. Adams presented the Secretary-General with a book with space for the autograph of every
member of the Club.

Founders' Day continued to be considered a purely
sentimental occasion until 1936, when Bob J. Lyles, then
a member of the International Board, worked out a
membership development activity for his home club in
Austin, Texas. It caught on so well that the Board of
Directors approved it as an International annual event.

January used to be the month when Lions Club membership figures showed a seasonal drop, so in getting born
in that month Melvin Jones showed the co-operative spirit
that has come to be expected of him. However, he can
claim no further credit for initiating the Melvin Jones
Birthday and Founders' Program than having got himself
born at a convenient time. He was not present when
Lyles described to fellow Directors in 1936 the plan that
had worked so well in Austin and recommended that it
be adopted on an International scale. Jones's objection to

use of his name in the program led to a compromise—an expansion of the original plan, really—by which each club was to honor not only the founder of the Association during the month of his birth, but also the founders of their own club.

"Any business would remain at a standstill or be retarded if continual and special efforts were not made to perpetuate itself," Lion Melvin B. Wright wrote, in his capacity as Chairman of the Board of Governors, in a letter to all District Governors in 1948. The International Directors have designated the Chairman of the Board of Governors as official chairman of the birthday program. "Modern society places great emphasis on perpetuating itself by bringing into the world a stronger, healthier, and more vigorous new generation. By the same token, the Officers and Directors of Lions International have, through the years, put emphasis on building, strengthening, and enlarging the membership of individual clubs so that the clubs and the Association will perpetuate themselves. Through the Birthday and Founders' Program, Lions International has not only perpetuated itself but has taken its rightful place as the largest, most active, and most useful service-club organization in the world. Lions International would not be where it is today had it not been for proper emphasis and attention to a well-organized plan for growth and self-perpetuation.

"I have come in contact with many clubs who do not wish to continually discuss membership at every meeting or every month during the year. They inform me they prefer to concentrate on membership development by a well-organized plan once a year whereby they can carefully choose their prospective members, concentrate on getting them into the club, and properly induct them.

"It is true that every man who joins a Lions Club may not stay, regardless of when he joined. . . . We must keep in mind that Lions Clubs are made up of men—human beings—human beings who possess all the virtues and weaknesses inherited by the human race. Men drop out of the club because of many things—the rise and fall of their successes, their health, their ages, their temperaments, and all other things pertaining to human life."

January, 1937, saw 3,054 new Lions brought in as a result of the Birthday and Founders' Program. Successive annual observances, up to and including 1949, have added over 150,000 members to the Association's roster. At a birthday dinner-dance honoring the founder and Mrs. Jones on January 13, 1938, he was presented with a grand master key for having brought 50 members into Chicago's Central Club and was promised two new members from every club as a birthday present. A total of 5,518 members had been added by the end of the month. The birthday score was 8,712 in 1939. Under the definitely unfavorable conditions of January, 1942, when the United States was reeling from the blow at Pearl Harbor, the Lions' membership gain was 7,513. Since then the increases during January have run: 9,249 in 1943; 14,376 in 1944; 19,855 in 1945; 28,538 in 1946, the year the greatest number of servicemen were reconverted into civilians; 27,850 in 1947; 25,551 in 1948; and 27,213 in 1949.

The Lions have been particularly fortunate in experiencing inflation in the number of their members rather than in the amount an individual member must pay to maintain himself and his club in good standing. The constitution requires that members of each chartered club pay dues of not less than $12 a year. A special committee appointed by the Directors has recommended that this minimum apply only to clubs of 25 members or less, that clubs of from 25 to 75 members pay annual dues of at least $25, and clubs with more than 75 members pay annual dues of not less than $40 a year. The per capita remitted to the International Office by the club for its members in semiannual installments of $2.25 is covered by the membership dues. The per capita, in turn, includes the member's $1 annual subscription to THE LION and his 50¢ annual convention fund tax.

WHEN THE ROLL IS CALLED ON TUESDAY

Service clubs are unique among voluntarily organized secular institutions in the obligation of attendance they impose on their members. Once a man becomes a lodge brother in the Elks, Moose, or Eagles, say, he's in good standing as long as he pays his dues. But when he becomes a Lion he finds himself hooked for committee work, assorted community boosting, and the regular eatin' meetin', come every Tuesday. "The name of any member who shall absent himself from four consecutive meetings of the club without acceptable cause being given to the attendance committee or the secretary shall be submitted to the board of directors," states a "forfeiture of membership" clause in the standard form constitution and by-laws. It is then up to the board to decide within 30 days whether to retain the member on the rolls or give him the old heave-ho.

"We've passed the 'eat it and beat it' stage in club work," Lion Russell B. Brown, Ardmore, Oklahoma, a member of the Board, said in delivering a typical charge to fellow Directors in 1930. "We can't come and eat, sing, and beat it out as soon as we finish. We have to render actual service. That is what I had in mind when I spoke of putting more stress on the character of a club than on the number of men in it, though I appreciate that we must have numbers also." Lion Brown then proposed a "School of Lionism" to be conducted by two or three members for the briefing of the about-to-be-inducted.

"If each new member can be sold on the value of attendance, you never have to worry about the old members," an executive secretary out in Oakland, California, once said.

As a matter of fact, the care and feeding of new members has become the special responsibility of two standing committees in every local club, the committees on Lions information and on membership. Among its other chores, the membership committee is supposed to make the new member feel so completely at home that he will have no thought but to bat 100 per cent in attendance. The new member has come into the club under what is known as "the buddy system," with a sponsoring member. He is seated at a table with the club's more accomplished greeters. He is put on a committee right off and the president mentions his name from the rostrum. "At the second or third meeting," the International suggests, "have the new member tell about himself—when and where he was born, the various kinds of work he has done, how many in his family, how he happened to choose the city as his place of residence, etc." Of such stuff is the impulse to attain perfect attendance records made.

With the average member, obligation to his service club comes somewhere after obligation to his church and ahead of devotion to the general run of other organizations founded on such interests as golf or veteran activities. How seriously Lions themselves feel about being AWOL was indicated in 1934 when an earnest member from Waycross, Georgia, queried the International Office as to whether he could get attendance credit when traveling by going to luncheons of clubs other than Lions. The rules permit granting of credit to "visiting firemen" from other Lions Clubs, but the Directors advised the Lion from Waycross that approving his proposition would be carrying the thing a little too far.

Because of the arrangement for "making up" absences by attending meetings in other cities, as well as because of a natural interest in what neighboring or distant clubs are up to, there is a good deal of interclub visiting back and forth by Lions members who happen to be making a swing around the circuit. A desirable result of this exchange has been the growing tendency to discredit local and regional views and prejudices.

Lost attendance through absence from a regular meeting of the member's particular club may be made up within six days before and six days after the date of the missed meeting by appearing at some other Lions gathering, such as (a) a meeting of any other Lions Club, (b) a meeting of the home club board of directors, (c) a home club committee meeting, (d) a special meeting or function of the home club, (e) a regional meeting, (f) a zone meeting, (g) the International Office, (h) a district convention, (i) an International convention. An excuse signed by the attending physician is acceptable in case of illness. But THE LION regularly reports instances where some Lion, hospitalized or immobilized by a broken leg, is spared from having his attendance record jeopardized by sympathetic fellow members who gather at his bed of pain and hold their meeting there.

Club secretaries send out routine reminder cards to members suspected of an inclination to play hookey. The Lions Club of Port Arthur, Texas, has organized the staff of the hotel where the club regularly meets to jog members' memories by giving them a jingle on meeting day. Some clubs use a "dawn patrol," routing out any member who has missed three consecutive meetings by telephone at 5:00 A.M. on the day of the fourth meeting, as an ungentle reminder. Other Lions Clubs post the names of absentees as some social clubs post the financially delinquent.

All these mechanical pressures probably wouldn't be worth much in maintaining high report-card attendance averages, however, without three added inducements. These are the International and local attendance contests and awards, the stunts and penalties that are the life of every luncheon, and programs that include a minimum of duds.

The International holds attendance contests for clubs during two ten-week periods each year, one in the fall and one in the spring. The International's contest for individual Lions extends over a period of 32 meetings, from mid-September to the latter part of April.

Eight major attendance awards are given each year. Railroad and Pullman fare for one member to the International convention, plus a suitably inscribed banner, are offered the largest club having 100 per cent attendance during both the fall and spring contests. The same prizes are assured the club with the greatest number of points attained by multiplying average attendance during the two contest periods by the number of members in the club. Second place in each of these two classes carries the same awards as first place. For third place in either class, the award is $60, no banner; for fourth place, $50.

Top attendance contest winners for 1948-49 were: First place, Guines, Habana, Cuba, and Denver, Colorado; second place, Pomona, California, and Beaumont, Texas.

There were also prizes that year of $25 for the top club in each of eleven divisions into which the clubs are grouped according to the size of the membership. Group A is for clubs of 20 or under, Group K for clubs of 176 or over. The winning club in each divisional contest is the one with the largest membership with perfect or most nearly perfect attendance during both the spring and fall campaigns.

The International authorized members with 100 per cent attendance records during the 32-week club year to wear special lapel insignia indicating their achievement. In addition, the International makes special awards to club members who have maintained continuous perfect attendance records for periods of five, ten, fifteen, twenty, twenty-five, and thirty years.

During the twelve months ended April 30, 1949, these perfect attendance awards were issued: One year, 85,523; five years, 1,923; ten years, 478; fifteen years, 109; twenty years, 41; twenty-five years, 14.

At the local level, the strategy of stimulating attendance is less formalized and more fun. The clubs have tried everything, from a point system with prizes for the winners and penalties for the losers, to conniving with the cop on the beat to bring in the truants in irons. Members of one club chose up sides, with the avoirdupois as equally distributed as possible. The side with the most "weight" at the meetings over the period of the contest took the prize. "Pot of gold" drawings, with the pot accumulating from meeting to meeting and members who played hookey out of luck if their names are drawn, have produced gratifying results. At Nyack, New York, the club secretary sent notices of the next meeting to the members' wives, along with word that the weekly attendance prize would be sent directly to the wife of the winner. And were the boys in their seats at roll call!

The Lions Club of Tygart Valley, West Virginia, found a sure cure for tardiness in "Little Beaver." "Little Beaver" was a detestable rag doll which became the special charge of the last man to arrive. This unfortunate had to give "Little Beaver" a mother's tender care and was fined if, in the judgment of the safety committee, he got too flip with safety pins or otherwise failed in his maternal duty. The club in Auburn Park, a Chicago community, found a more solemn device effective. Members there hate not to be prompt since meetings have opened with the display of a fluttering flag in a darkened room while the club sings the national anthem and repeats the pledge of allegiance.

Three general membership classifications enjoy exemption from the obligations entailed in roll call. The honorary members, retired pioneer members, and members at large don't have to worry about the attendance mark on their report cards.

16

EATIN' MEETIN'

TUESDAY is traditionally
the preferred day, when the Lion Tamer has presumably
polished off the identification badges and the members
pick them off the rack as they file in for the weekly hour
and a quarter of chicken croquettes, fun, frolic, and up-
lift. "A man has burrowed out from under the Monday
mail by Tuesday and has a bit of a breather before things
begin piling up on him toward the end of the week," says
Melvin Jones in explaining the popularity of the second
day of the business week.

However much the unbeliever may smile at the big
badges blazoned with the member's nickname and business
connection, their influence on American social custom
can't be ignored. A quarter of a century ago, people were
on stiffish "Mr." and "Mrs." terms for years before ven-
turing to first-name each other. In by-passing the etiquette
books and dropping formal titles outside the personal circle as well as in it, the service clubs of America started a

practice so pleasant that it has been universally adopted.

The Lions Clubs have grown up in depression and have been tempered in the fires of war. Much of the exuberance of early meetings has been toned down. But so long as the Tail Twister flourishes and the chairman's equipment includes a gavel and gong with which to choke off the long-winded, no Lions meeting can be completely dull.

Something of the spirit that animated those early meetings is reflected in a document that has become a classic of Lionism: C. C. Lasher's letter to fellow members when he was secretary of the Ardmore, Oklahoma, Club, on the subject, "I Lost My Hat."

"I lost my hat," Lasher wrote. "I got it back again with several others that I do not care to own. Without making exact count, I think every member present at the last luncheon, and one outsider, returned a hat to me. This indicates to me that every one there exchanged hats with someone in an effort to get a better hat. The extra hat probably was sent by some guest who became conscience-stricken after seeing my appeal in the paper.

"The following letter came with one of the hats:

" 'Deer Mr. Lasher: I noticed in the last nite's paper that someone had exchanged hats with you without your knowledge or concent at the Lyons club luncheon. One would think from the roar you made you had sustained a very great loss. Now I have been keeping up with the doeings of the lions club with much interest and have developed a very great regard for its aimes and purposes and have hitherto observed that when a lion makes a roar either collectively or individually it means something, that there is something worth while behind it. I have also understood that before a man is eligible to membership in your club, symbolizing all the fine atributs of the king of beasts, he must prove that what is good for one is good enough for the others. No doubt the hat you lost was not altogether as good as the one you got back but for the sake of charity and kindness toward some brother, could you not have worn and endured, perhaps to the pleasure and enjoyment of some Bro Lion, that old straw ford a few weeks longer that he has worn for two long summers? Think this over and if my idea of a real Lions meets with your approval I shall be glad if you should see in me some of the atributs of a real Lion and invite me to join you. Yours very respectfully, A Friend.

"'P.S. If you still want your old hat here's hoping you will get it.'

"From the above I have made the following findings of fact: (1) That the man who wrote the above letter is a member of the Lions Club of Ardmore. (2) That he is president of the club. (3) That he deals in shoes, including gumshoes. (4) That his name is J. Ed Hamilton. (5) That he took my hat. (6) That he could have taken any hat in the bunch and made a good trade. (7) That there was nothing personal about the whole affair—just an honest effort to get a good hat. (8) That he will not try the same stunt again.

"But you should have seen the hats I got. Black, blue, gray, spotted, brown, striped, and some of no color except that of the ground. Hats with high crowns and some with no crowns at all. Old hats, new hats, dirty hats, clean hats, felt hats, panama, straw, and hay. Hard hats, soft hats, summer hats, and one for a winter day. But I can't tell you all the different kinds of hats. Yours for a new hat,   (Signed) O. C. LASHER."

Aside from such interludes as the tail twister and personalities like Mr. Lasher may provide, the members are in the hands of the program committee and at the mercy of speakers who sometimes seem to have come out of a grab bag. Mediocrity of the average lunch-club speaker is not entirely the fault of the program committee which must take what it can get, a condition depending more on the geographic location of the club and the time of year than on the judgment of the committee.

Severe critic of the service clubs though he is, Mr. Bruce Bliven found it in his heart to sympathize with them in their postluncheon sufferings.

"First," he wrote,* "there is the product of the rank novice, the prominent business man of your own or some near-by city who takes a long time (and it seems longer) to deliver a ten-minute speech on 'Main Developments in the Cold Storage Industry, 1920–1927,' or 'The Trust Company: Your Friend, Your Counsellor, Your Guide.' This gentleman is usually suffering from an acute case of exhibitionism, with nothing to justify it. He dearly loves to read in public the papers written for him by his advertising man, who has been careful to work in generous reference to his own company, its resources and facilities.

"The other standard type, just as bad, is the 'inspirational' address. Even today, after all the ridicule that has been rained on this weird product, it is still being uttered, day in and day out, North, East, South, and West— especially West. Every member of every club ought to know it by heart—but seemingly he doesn't, for he tolerates its endless reiteration. . . .

"It is no answer to my criticism to say that most of

*Forum, December, 1928.

this inspirational stuff is true. What if it is? It is also true that the world is round."

It is noticeable, however, that there is a tendency to secure more liberal speakers in times of national trouble, either because the speakers themselves take a liberal turn at such times or because people are willing to listen at such times to discussions they generally would prefer not to hear.

One thing the program committee can—and does—do that contributes to the success of the meeting and that is, to see that it opens at 12:15 sharp and ends promptly at 1:30. The order of business in between is pretty well pre-scribed: National song, flag salute, luncheon, introductions, announcements and committee reports, entertainment and speaker, final business, closing song—with the tail twister in operation throughout the session.

The by-law outlining the duties of the program com-mittee also suggests types of programs: Discussional, Out-of-Town Day, Inter-City Meeting, Ladies' Night Meet-ing, Charter Anniversary Meeting, District Governor's Meeting, International Convention Meeting, Installation of Officers Meeting, Stunt Meetings, Lions Informational Meetings, Classification Meetings, as well as programs in charge of the various activities committees.

The stunts that can be interspersed between the more serious program features are limited only by time and the ingenuity of the committee. Quizzes, games of "penny poison" and "string pass," "human lotto," "driving the pig to market" pleasantly fill odd chinks of an evening program, when time is not of the essence. Even in the noontide rush, one of those vest-buttoning relays can be run off or the calisthenic gag in which the chairman in-

vites everyone to stand up and stretch, just after the committee reports and before the main event. He puts the
crowd through some informal upsetting exercises, then
commands sharply, "Shake hands with the fellow behind
you." Everyone turns, only to find the other fellow's back
turned to him. The Cumberland, Maryland, Club, with a
number of newly acquired members, recently held a get-
acquainted contest in the form of an apron derby. Every
member collected as many signatures as he could on the
white butcher's apron provided him for that purpose.
Top collector was prize winner.

Lions Clubs will go to any length to make periodic
Ladies' Nights memorable occasions. But that, one sus-
pects, is to enable the clubs to continue on a firmly non-
coeducational basis with reasonably clear consciences. Some
of these Ladies' Nights are very white-tie while others
are as packed with horseplay as any regular Tuesday noon
meeting. In Springfield, Colorado, some of the wives participated in a hoax that completely fooled their husbands.
They rose in meeting to protest against the recently elected
council, which included some Lion husbands, and shrilly
demanded control of the city. Whenever a councilman
rose to defend himself he was told he was out of order.
When International Counsellor Bob Burrows walked out
of the meeting in disgust, his wife refused to accompany
him.

Just as the meeting got completely out of control, the
law arrived, followed by newsboys with bogus extras
screaming "Riot at Lions Meet."

Other clubs have contrived a sprightly evening with a
"fashion show." The show proceeds with three dummy,
preferably headless, models borrowed from a department

store. Three Lions are asked by the master of ceremonies to come to the platform. Three ladies are asked to act as judges. The models are trotted out and presented, one to each of the men, who then are asked to dress them from boxes of clothing provided for the purpose. The man who turns out the best-dressed model gets a prize. All he would need do to qualify would be to put the dress on neatly, but contestants invariably struggle with foundation garments and other odds and ends, adding considerably to the interest. A fashion magazine makes a nice prize.

Another Ladies' Night stunt requires participation by three known dog lovers among the club membership. The wife of one must be taken into the confidence of the entertainment committee and agree to smuggle his dog into the meeting. The master of ceremonies asks the other two, in turn, to come forward. The M.C. inquires of each whether they own dogs, what the dogs look like, etc., and concludes by having them show the audience how they call their dogs. Each is given a can of dog food as a reward for a good job of dog calling. Then the third man, whose dog is in an anteroom, is called up and asked to call his dog, with results that are a surprise to nearly everyone except, probably, the dog.

At the risk of upsetting the popular notion of the service club as one that foregathers at the noon hour, it must be set down that the majority of Lions Clubs, though not the majority of Lions, do their getting together of an evening. Because of hotel-reservation complications and one thing and another, a late check showed approximately 75 per cent of the clubs were meeting at the dinner hour or later. Of the remaining one fourth, most were convening at the traditional luncheon time. However, five

desperate groups reported that the only time they could
find a meeting place was in the morning. But it is the
big city groups that cling pretty steadfastly to the midday
custom. In the agricultural belt, evening meetings seem
more expedient.

To pour on further statistics from the same report,
1,556 clubs said they met on Monday, 2,162 on Tuesday,
1,315 on Wednesday, 1,730 on Thursday, 440 on Friday,
46 on Saturday. There are even some 30 clubs, mainly
in Latin America, which hold their meetings on Sunday.
While some clubs can't seem to come together oftener
than on alternate weeks, the International snubs mention
of this fact. The theory is that meetings are held weekly
and lapses in practice do not pass unnoticed by the International Office.

17

FUN WITH FINES

AND so we come to that once controversial figure in Lionism, the tail twister. The clowning of this character, circulating among the luncheon tables banging a gong which signifies that bald-headed Lion Joe Doakes has been fined a dime for not combing his hair, strikes the uninitiated as somewhat on the juvenile side.

But no Lions Club would dream of dispensing with its tail twister. Without the fines he industriously collects, the club's welfare activities might be in a bad way. Without his merry what-next quips, many a meeting would bog down into dreary celery-chomping and fork-shoveling. The tail twister has proved his value to an extent where he has been given an honored place on the roster of club officers along with the lion tamer, or sergeant-at-arms.

As a matter of fact, the origin of his office is older than Lionism. Records of the clubs that flourished in the

London of Addison and Steele and Dr. Johnson contain such house committee rules as:

"Every member shall fill his pipe out of his own box; if any member absents himself he shall forfeit a penny for the use of the club, unless in case of sickness or imprisonment; if any member tells stories in the club that are not true, he shall forfeit for every third lie a halfpenny; if any member's wife comes to fetch him home, she shall speak to him without the door."

The Lions have broken away from this precedent to the extent of holding an occasional Ladies' Night. Going to jail no longer is considered good enough form to serve as an acceptable excuse for absenteeism. But in the tail twister, tradition survives.

The tail twister has made good as an accepted institution, however, in the face of skepticism and snide cracks and an abortive attempt at one time to foist on him the name of "spizzerinkter."

No lexicographer has successfully challenged the Lions' claim to having thought up, or dreamed up, this term all by themselves. Thus the best authority on its origin would seem to be the Lions' official magazine. In July, 1936, this erudite source said:

"Some readers may be wondering about the word 'spizzerinkter' used in conjunction with 'tail twister.' Spizzerinkters began to pop up in clubs throughout the Association some months ago. They are close relatives of tail twisters—blood brothers, in fact, and there is a definition—not by Webster—of their name. Here it is:

"Spizzerinkter, *n*. 1. A fire-eater; a live wire; a gouger; a snapper; a cutter; a pusher; a trail blazer; a wisecracker. 2. A Lion with the qualities of dynamite, pepper, ginger, great heat, T.N.T. 3. An official in a Lions Club who is redheaded, sharp, witty, alive, awake, quick, sizzling, speedy, high-stepping, gate-crashing. Implies reckless partiality. 4. One who is in a state of perpetual eruption, as a volcano. One who has great zip.

"The spizzerinkter has also been variously described as worse than a revolution, more 'touching' than your most shiftless relative, and about as subtle as an avalanche, and as a new name for an old-fashioned affliction — tail twister."

But some way, the plain term of tail twister has outlasted its more hifalutin' synonym, and you hear more today of tail twisters than of spizzerinkters.

The first effort at innocent merriment in meeting took the form of pep committees supposed to prod members into the spirit of the occasion. A. D. Shaw, a field representative of the day, initiated this practice at the chartering of the downtown Detroit club in 1920. The pep committees seem to have sifted down, as committees will, to a single energetic personality on each one, and presently these stalwarts came to be known—only Melvin Jones recalls exactly how—as tail twisters.

"Back in the early twenties we were trying to find some way to liven up Lion meetings," Jones says. "For instance, after everyone was seated, with maybe five members of the pep committee at different parts of the table, one would say 'hummh!' Another committee member across the table would say 'hummh!' Then the third, fourth, fifth, members would repeat this grunting monosyllable. If no one noticed, they'd repeat. As a matter of fact, they'd repeat so often there'd be howls to take them out and choke them. Then the idea of fining them was proposed. About this time, membership on the pep committees had begun to dwindle and the survivors got the idea that they should be the ones to do the fining.

"One Sunday afternoon three or four of us were discussing this matter of putting pep into the meetings. One fellow who had been born on a farm said that what we needed was to do what used to be done on the farm. When a cow refused to go through the gate, someone would grab her by the tail and twist. We all laughed but one of the boys said, 'Why isn't that a good name— tail twister?' We already had decided on the name 'lion tamer' for the sergeant-at-arms, so it seemed logical to confer the title of 'tail twister' on the chairman of the pep committee."

But the International Board, in a huff of offended dignity, issued an edict to the clubs against use of the low-comedy term.

"I remember," Melvin Jones says, "how the issue came to a head late in 1920 in Columbus. The Board was there for ceremonies at which fourteen clubs were being chartered. Word came out from the room where the Board was in session before luncheon that the term 'tail twister' was prohibited. The rank-and-file membership took matters into their own hands during luncheon by passing a motion in favor of tail twisting. The Board agreed to reconsider and the question was batted about at Board meetings for years after that. Other names, to represent the same office, were suggested. Like spizzerinkter. However, the consensus of the Board remained pretty much the same—that the terms 'tail twister,' 'cub,' 'lion tamer,' and 'den' should be dropped from Lionism—until Ray Riley (International President, 1929–30) got up at a session in Washington one day and told them they were taking themselves too seriously. Besides, Riley added, he suspected the clubs were going to go right on having tail twisters whether the Board liked it or not."

So the official magazine of the International Association of Lions Clubs could write in 1941:

"Of all the novel and rich experiences which await the new Lion, none strikes him so forcibly as his introduction to that 'Demon of the Dime,' that 'Debunker of Dignity,' known as 'The Spizzerinkter,' or 'Tail Twister.'

"The tail twister, as we prefer to call him, is about the only absolute dictator we know who enjoys the affection of those whom he oppresses. The tolls he exacts profit him not, but find their way into his little bank, from which they eventually emerge to do some altruistic service.

"The novitiate oftens stands in red-necked and crestfallen embarrassment when ordered by the tail twister to give explanation for his tardiness, his use of a formal address to a fellow Lion, or just for living. Or, for that matter, for anything which the fertile brain of the efficient tail twister can concoct that will serve as a 'crime' and bring on the penalty. . . .

"Of all the officers in the club, he alone has no rigid code, no well-defined plan of action. He must be a Lion of originality; a merciless prosecutor of friend and foe; one who stands not in awe of the most unbending Lion or highest visiting dignitary."

A Lion from Weatherford, Texas, named Larry Taylor, put it more succinctly:

"It is natural for men to have fun together but not so natural to start this fun on their own initiative for fear of seeming out of place."

So the game of forfeits goes on, providing not merely revenue but the spark that keeps the members interested.

A tail twister with his heart in his work can be an indispensable officer of his club, the International now concedes. He can find enough reasons for assessing fines without resorting to fining for imaginary offenses, the International goes on, and suggests a few: Tardiness, failure to wear name badge or Lions button, failure properly to register guests, improper address to officers, plugging business, becoming a bridegroom or a papa, having a birthday, winning a golf prize, breaking into print, being promoted in business or elected to office, referring to another member as "Mister" or "gentleman," singing too noisily or not noisily enough.

From the tail twister's fine there is no appeal, and the tail twister may not be fined himself except by unanimous vote of all present, including himself. Members are protected against triple jeopardy, i.e., being fined more than twice at the same meeting, and, as a rule, only the most hardened offenders are nicked for more than a dime. Some fine boxes play tunes when the lids are lifted. Others make less musical noises. Tail Twister Walter Hundt, Morris, Illinois, has been using, along with his fine box, a wheel which sets the amount of the fine from one to twenty-five cents. John C. Douglas, tail twister of McCook, Nebraska, had made a good thing out of renting advertising space on his receptacle for fines, setting up a sort of chain reaction, since advertising within the club is a fineable offense in itself.

Tail twisters find it profitable to toy with the no-advertising ban, giving a member's business a forbidden plug and then fining him for it. Tail Twister C. W.

Carlson of Arcadia, California, got hold of members' business cards and placed them at each place at the luncheon tables with profitable results.

At Wood River, Illinois, the fine box jingled as members were haled into a "Soakum and Sockum" traffic court set up to make the club traffic-conscious. Warrants were issued for real traffic violations or, lacking those, for imaginary ones. Court sessions were held and fines assessed at regular meetings.

Tail twisters know how to deal effectively with the absentees. In Hugo, Oklahoma, members who had offended by being absent were hauled to the club meeting in an ambulance. In Lakeview, Illinois, they were carried in on stretchers. In Tyler, Texas, they were brought in irons and had to manage the creamed chicken and apple pie with the bracelets still circling their wrists. Absenteeism was unknown in Owensville, Missouri, after the tail twister there acquired a goat and sent the animal to board with any member who had played hookey.

In many clubs, failure to show up with a Lions lapel button is corrected by compelling the culprit to invest in another, or to buy an automobile decal, at a profit to the club.

A typical tail twister trick is a roll call in which middle names are read off. Fines are dished out to members failing to recognize their middle names when called. A lot of members in a Washington club preferred to forfeit a dime rather than get up and make a speech proving to the club that they were no fools.

A tail twister, smarting under criticism of his methods, appointed his critic as his assistant. The assistant went into action by auctioning the clothes right off the tail twister's back, rolling up the sum of $60.81 for the activities fund.

Some tail twisters have tapped still another source of revenue. They conduct impromptu quizzes concerning items which have appeared in the very latest issue of the official Lions magazine. Those members who have read the magazine from cover to cover, stand a little better than even chance of not being nicked for a dime, that is unless the tail twister pops up with a question he "just happened to dream up."

From which it may be judged that the tail twister is here not only to stay but to get away with murder. In Fort Worth, Texas, he has won recognition for the club poet laureate:

> *Tail Twister! Tail Twister! I've known you of*
> *   old;*
> *You've robbed my poor pockets of silver and gold;*
> *You've kicked me and cuffed me, you've been my*
> *   downfall;*
> *You've cheated and crooked me; but I love you*
> *   for all.*

18

THE WORLD'S BIGGEST DOERS

Who gives himself with his alms feeds three—
Himself, his hungering neighbor, and Me.
  —Lowell, *Vision of Sir Launfal*

This eagerness to serve, to be useful, to give of
yourself—that is where Lionism gets its strength. For
nothing unites men more closely than the sameness of
purpose insofar as that purpose is inspired by high
ideals and aims.
  —Mariano Roca Gutierrez, in an address
    before the Lions Club of Santiago, Cuba

DOERS AND PROUD OF IT

THE man who joins a
Lions Club in good faith presently is up to his belt in
activities which, he may find, overlap at some points welfare work of his church and the community boosting that
is the *raison d'être* of the local Chamber of Commerce.

Not that there isn't enough of either to go around
among them all. Moreover, church and social agency

workers have confessed to a frank envy of the efficiency
of the Lions Clubs, which can commandeer the best business brains of the community when they want to get
something done.

Lions Club presidents appoint committees to plan activities. But the carrying out of the plans is likely to be
a whole-club activity. In one of his homely heart-to-
heart talks with his assistants, Melvin Jones once cited the
example of an outstanding Lions Club "whose name appears on the banner in the first, second, or third position
year after year."

"The board of directors of this club," Jones cited,
"first went into a huddle, then they invited into the huddle at a later meeting a third of the membership, later
invited another third, and still later the remaining third
of the membership, until all of the members were in the
huddle. Out of such conferences comes combined or
organized leadership."

One of the strongest appeals of the service club to the
busy executive, it has been said, is that the club furnishes
him a convenient channel through which to carry out
better his obligations as a citizen. On the other hand, the
man who hasn't been overly conscious of such obligations
is exposed to some concentrated education about them
as soon as he bumps up against the club activities program. THE LION recently carried an item about a member
in Chattanooga who was delegated to investigate an appeal
that had been made to the club to aid a young Negro girl
who had lost her sight. The upshot of the member's formal
investigation was that he assumed full charge of the case,
guaranteeing the girl—on behalf of the club—whatever
care and means were needed to give her as normal a life

as possible. That one instance is representative of a common pattern.

"A Lion's participation in welfare activities through his club fulfills a two-sided purpose," a Lions International Counsellor said recently. "This participation brings a program of service to those who need it and at the same time it brings to the Lion a sense of well-being for having given of his substance or time. . . ."

"I'm part of an organization that is doing a world of good," a new Lion exulted. "Every pair of glasses we buy for an underprivileged child, every time we feed the St. John's orphans, every time we give a white cane to some blind person, I get a feeling of joy out of it. When I walk into the post office and see old blind Charley behind his cigar counter, it makes me feel good because our club made it possible for this poor fellow to live again—he is actually happy now. I have more respect for myself since I joined the Lions Club because our club is always doing something that gives a fellow a feeling that he is of some benefit to the world."

"The activities program embraces every opportunity for community service," the International sums up. "The Lions Club, therefore, presents an unrivaled medium through which every civic-minded, public-spirited individual may serve in the particular field in which he is most interested."

A study of the Secretary-General's annual report shows literally thousands of activities in the three major divisions of social welfare, community improvement, and aid to business. But emphasis is easily on the second. Of 101,736 separate activities undertaken during the twelve months ending June 30, 1949, 44,696 came under the heading of "community betterment." Describing what Lionism seeks to do in the fewest possible words, it might be said that its fundamental purpose is to make the club's home town, or community, a better place in which to live. This objective automatically puts the Lions into everything that goes on around town. It also points up a distinguishing characteristic of Lions. No job is too small for them, which may explain why they have accomplished so many big ones.

Professionals in the welfare field have raised the point that Lions activity in this field is unplanned, that it meets only the immediate emergency. The Lions' own record in doing just that, without smothering everyone concerned in red tape, is of course the best retort to this criticism.

Since the day they were founded, the Lions have been paying burial expenses for lonely old ladies, sending coal to the shivering and doctors to the sick—while other agencies were preparing case histories in triplicate. Lions are not above painting a fence, repairing a pavement, or sitting with a baby if the circumstances are urgent. Somebody has to do these things and Lions never have found a job too small for them if it is something that really needs doing.

Back in 1918, one of the clubs got a request that, it was felt at the time, was unduly flattering. "The reputation of some of the prominent Lions as connoisseurs of food and drink evidently has been well established," THE LION commented. "Otherwise why should the conservation bureau of the American Red Cross write to one of our clubs urging its members to save the lead tops of champagne bottles?" But in the thirty years since then,

Lions have become used to appeals more strange than that
—and to responding to them.

Here again the International's card index system pays
out. A club embarking on a new phase of activity can
almost certainly profit from the experience of some other
club, and the International, through its activities file, most
certainly can refer the one club to the other.

International Office records show that club expenditures for activities ran to more than $10,000,000 during
the fiscal year 1948–49, or approximately $1,500 per club.
Top divisions, as Lions divide up the work, were: Community betterment, $2,400,000; civic improvements, more
than $2,000,000; boys' and girls' activities, $2,000,000;
health and welfare, $1,500,000. These figures are exclusive
of Lions' participation in projects in co-operation with
other agencies such as the Red Cross, March of Dimes,
Community Chest, Boy Scouts, Friendship Train, etc.

The Secretary-General's report places particular emphasis on juvenile delinquency prevention, programs leading to improvement of the lot of the schoolteachers, community surveys of health and education facilities, war
memorials, and veterans' housing, as representative of the
present activities trend among the clubs.

LET THE LIONS DO IT

Service in any one of the ten committee divisions under which Lions Club activities function is a far from
confining experience. As the activities have been divided,
each committee must be concerned at times in welfare
work, community service, and—to a lesser extent—business promotion.

In one year alone, 1948–49, the clubs turned in reports

of activities which the Secretary-General consolidated as follows:

Boys' and girls' activities. Sponsored baseball, basketball, and hockey teams, games, and leagues; provided equipment and raised funds. Staged model airplane, pet, soapbox, marble, and kite contests and gave prizes. Organized, chaperoned, entertained, and donated to youth clubs and teen-age canteens. Sponsored, maintained, and donated to youth camps. Held field days and provided transportation. Co-operated with officials to curb juvenile delinquency and held dances and lectures for youth. Sponsored Christmas parties, Easter-egg hunts and Halloween parades. Held father-son-daughter nights. Sponsored Boy, Girl, Cub, Sea, and Air Scouts, and Camp Fire Girls; provided equipment, meeting places, buildings, camps, and transportation, held courts of honor, took care of week-end outings, and entertained them and also their executives. Sent youths to Boys State and Girls State and to camp. Observed Youth Week and Boy Scout Week.

Citizenship and patriotism activities. Held special observances of Armistice Day, Army Day, Columbus Day, Washington's and Lincoln's Birthdays, Independence Day, Dominion Day, Memorial Day, Navy Day, Remembrance Day, and V-E and V-J Days. Co-operated with American Legion and Canadian Legion and Veterans of Foreign Wars. Arranged classes for new citizens and entertained them. Bought and sold government bonds, stamps, and flags. Sponsored and donated to overseas relief drives. Entertained hospitalized veterans. Assisted in securing state and national guard units for locality. Urged citizens to vote and provided transportation to polls. Sponsored war memorials and service boards. Assisted and entertained service men. Promoted showing of flags on patriotic holidays. Presented citizenship awards. Observed Physically Handicapped Week.

Civic-improvement activities. Promoted and helped to obtain airports and the installation of air markers. Sponsored street signs and house-numbering projects. Cleaned and beautified cemeteries. Secured road and bridge construction and improvement. Sponsored city cleanups, placement of trash receptacles, and designated dump sites. Established libraries, gave financial aid, and provided books. Secured home mail-delivery service. Sponsored fish- and game-conservation movements. Prepared parking lots to improve parking situations. Established, equipped, lighted, and improved athletic fields, swimming pools, tennis courts, playgrounds, and skating rinks; provided supervisors and swimming lessons. Secured improved electric, telephone, bus, and train service. Installed street lights. Helped to secure water- and sewerage-system improvements.

Community-betterment activities. Sponsored baseball, bowling, donkey ball, basketball, curling, and softball teams, games, and leagues. Sponsored special newspaper editions. Took census of towns. Held banquets, dances, stag parties, barbecues, picnics, and steak fries. Staged auctions, bingo and card parties, carnivals, circuses, rodeos and horse shows, turtle derbies, fairs, home-comings, parades, jamborees, turkey shoots, clambakes, and fish fries. Sponsored air, amateur, magician, boxing, and minstrel shows, movies, plays, and concerts. Operated concessions and booths. Held public meetings. Conducted labor surveys and secured industries, toured plants and factories, and printed brochures to advertise locality. Sponsored beauty and float contests and entrants. Co-operated with Y.M.C.A., Chambers of Commerce and other service organizations. Sponsored Christmas, Easter, Halloween, New Year's Eve, and Thanksgiving activities. Entertained government officials. Assisted bands and sponsored quartets. Conducted scrap drives.

Educational activities. Entertained students, athletes, faculty, school officials, and musical groups. Sponsored contests, gave prizes, and entertained contestants. Gave awards and entertained honor students. Made donations, purchased uniforms and equipment for bands, orchestras, and choral groups. Held meetings and financially assisted P.T.A. Presented scholarships and provided student aid. Secured, equipped, and financially assisted vocational schools. Sponsored, equipped, and provided transportation for teams, backed games and sold tickets, presented awards, and held athletic banquets. Sponsored drives, provided equipment, and cleaned school buildings and grounds. Sponsored and donated to athletic training camps. Financed physical examinations and paid insurance for athletes. Secured athletic instructors. Sponsored track, swimming, and field meets. Backed the Indian Educational Plan. Observed National Education Week. Sent children to view Freedom Train. Provided transportation for children to school. Presented "Moral Code for Youth" to schools. Published school papers and donated to yearbooks. Donated to schools. Promoted school appropriations and increased teachers' salaries.

Health and welfare activities. Sponsored drives and donated to cancer control, Community Chest, infantile paralysis, Red Cross, Salvation Army, blood banks, welfare funds, and heart associations. Financed, equipped, and sent persons to fresh-air camps. Provided blood-type tests and transfusions. Financed and sponsored clinics. Observed Child Health Week. Provided braces, entertainment, and transportation for crippled children. Secured doctors for towns. Purchased ambulances, crutches, hospital beds, iron lungs, wheel chairs, and ceiling projectors for community use. Provided clothing, food, and funds for disaster areas. Sprayed town with DDT and conducted rodent and insect campaigns. Purchased and sold TB bonds and Easter seals. Sponsored TB X-ray survey. Sent gifts and flowers to shut-ins and entertained them. Provided milk for undernourished school pupils, families, and babies. Sponsored school-lunch programs. Secured and financially aided visiting nurse. Financed tonsillectomy and "blue baby" operations. Supplied medicines and vaccinations for needy. Financially assisted and held parties, picnics, dinners, and Christmas and Easter parties for orphanages. Backed Blue Cross Plan. Equipped, improved, and financially assisted hospitals. Provided hearing aids and artificial limbs for needy. Entertained and presented gifts to inmates of homes for aged. Supplied clothing, shoes, food, fuel, and funds for needy. Adopted resolution favoring establishment of polio center at Ontario Hot Springs, California.

Safety activities. Entertained firemen, police, and school safety patrols. Distributed safety book covers to schools. Sponsored safety campaigns and contests. Donated, organized, and provided equipment for fire departments and school safety patrols. Conducted safety meetings. Sponsored and equipped driving schools. Provided inhalators and resuscitators to communities for first aid. Erected traffic signs, improved traffic regulations, and eliminated hazards. Observed Fire Prevention Week.

WATCH OUT for KIDS

NORTH HOLLYWOOD LIONS CLUB

and Kleiser

SAFETY

EDUCATION

Lions Clubs are interested in every opportunity for unselfish service to the community, and to this end their activities are grouped under ten major headings: Agriculture—Boys and Girls—Citizenship and Patriotism—Civic Improvements—Community Betterment—Education—Health and Welfare—Safety—Sight Conservation and Blind—and United Nations. On this and the following three pages are illustrated Lions Clubs' projects typical of each of these ten major categories.

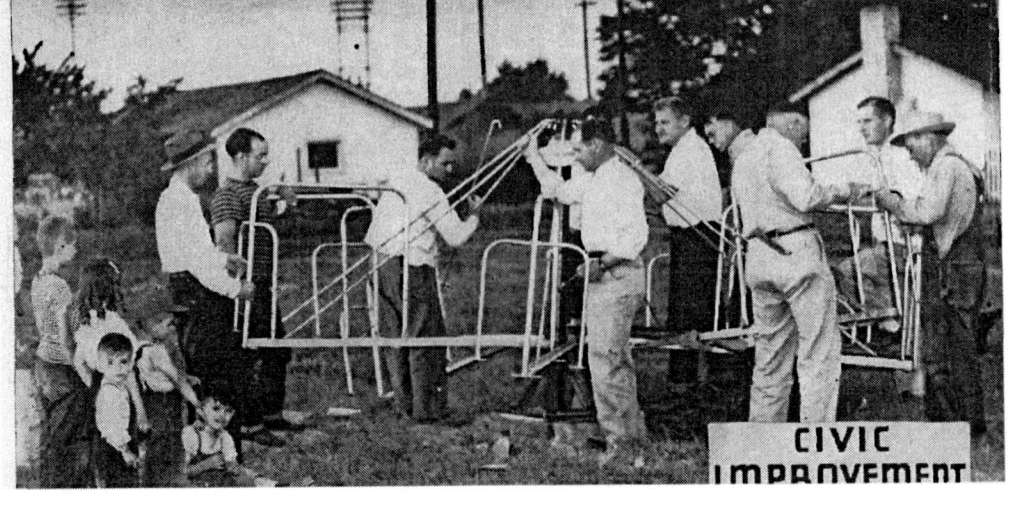

AGRICULTURE

BROWN COUNTY CRAFTS

COMMUNITY
BETTERMENT

CIVIC
IMPROVEMENT

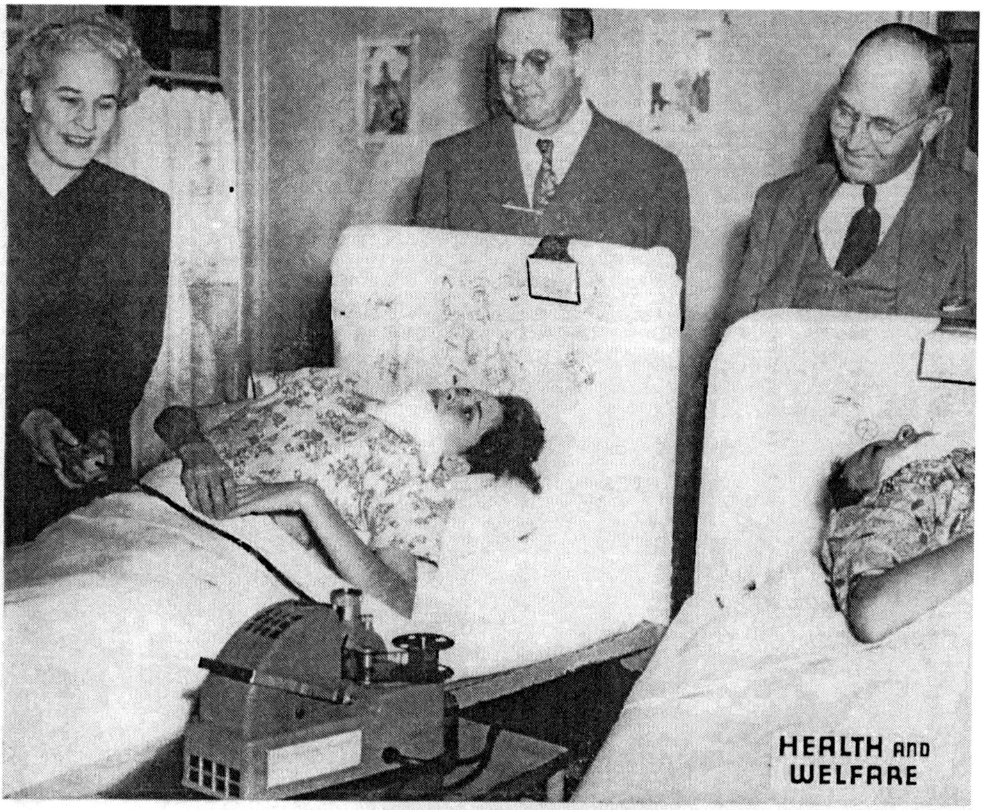

HEALTH and WELFARE

BOYS AND GIRLS

UNITED NATIONS
FOR PEACE

UNITED NATIONS

SIGHT CONSERVATION
AND BLIND

CITIZENSHIP AND
PATRIOTISM

Sight conservation and activities for the blind. Provided clothing, food, household goods, and funds for the blind. Sponsored, maintained, and raised funds for and contributed to sight clinics. Conducted sight surveys, bought sight-testing equipment, and improved school lighting. Held Christmas parties and provided gifts and baskets. Supplied Braille books, Braille writers, typewriters, talking books, and radios. Sponsored Braille instruction and readers. Sponsored sight-saving classes and assisted students financially. Sponsored bowling teams and parties, and provided transportation. Financed purchase of glasses, artificial eyes, and white canes, examinations, medical supplies, hospital bills, treatments, and operations. Provided employment and equipment and assisted with sales of merchandise made by the blind. Sponsored workshops for the blind. Paid salaries of case workers with the blind. Joined state associations for the blind. Repaired talking books, radios, and white canes. Entertained blind at picnics and concerts. Provided guide dogs. Sponsored White Cane Week sales and other financial drives.

Agricultural activities. Donated to agricultural associations. Promoted milk ordinances and dairy programs, staged dairymen's meetings, and observed Dairy Week. Held Farmers' Days and field days. Presented awards to outstanding farmers. Assisted farmers with harvests and in securing laborers. Promoted soil-conservation programs and meetings. Sponsored livestock and crop fairs. Promoted pasture, corn, "Enrich Our Soil," and cattle-growing contests. Observed Cotton Week and promoted cultivation of cotton. Bought cattle at fairs to promote participation in later years. Opposed reduced agricultural appropriations. Staged farm safety campaigns. Sponsored

Bangs testing for cattle and research in hoof-and-mouth disease. Entertained Farm Bureau, agricultural association representatives, and County Agents.

United Nations activities. Sent telegrams of support to United Nations on arrival in New York. Observed United Nations Week. Participated in United Nations parade. Entertained representatives of United Nations Assembly. Favored elimination of veto power. Held model United Nations meetings.

The Secretary-General tabulated the number of projects accomplished by the clubs in each division as follows: Boys and girls, 13,677; citizenship and patriotism, 3,006; civic improvement, 5,789, community betterment, 44,696; education, 8,255; health and welfare, 12,892; safety, 2,673; sight conservation and blind, 7,905; agriculture, 1,681; United Nations, 1,162.

All this division of club activities into committees looks very pigeonholed and trim. But attaining the present tidy organization took more doing than appears on the surface. There were times, in the early days of The International Association of Lions Clubs, when the organization was pestered to the point of distraction by do-gooder pressure groups within the membership, each with its own world-saving panacea which it wished the Association to espouse to the exclusion of all others.

So it came about that in 1923 Judge Hubert Utterbach of Des Moines was asked by International President Edgar S. Vaught of Oklahoma City, now a U.S. district judge, to head up, not so much an International activities committee, as a committee to sort out and evaluate the activities for which professional sociologists, medical men, jurists, and other worthies among the membership were agitating. The judge himself was interested in juvenile delinquency problems and so was Halsted Ritter of Denver. Then there was Charles H. Hatton, later International President, who thought distribution of the "Moral Code for Youth" with an accompanying series of textbooks called "Studies in Conduct" should be the Lions' chosen work. Dr. M. F. McCarthy, chairman of the Ohio state welfare committee, was lobbying for a Braille magazine he was anxious to circulate among blind children under Lions auspices.

Melvin Jones dropped a quiet unobtrusive word to President Vaught as the annual convention converged on Atlantic City that summer. "Put all these fellows with an ax to grind on Utterbach's committee and let them fight it out," he suggested.

"Well, sir," Jones chuckles today in recollection, "Utterbach and Ritter had a bedroom in the hotel next to the suite where I was working. Every time a fellow came in with some new activity proposal, I'd send him down to that bedroom. The parade began on the pre-convention Saturday. Utterbach and Ritter got no sleep from then on. Finally, the first of the next week, Utterbach came to me. He looked pretty worn down. 'We're never going to narrow it down to one major activity,' he acknowledged. 'Looks like we'd have to have fourteen.'

"His report to the convention recommended fourteen different activities. The convention accepted the report, but in 1925 I got hold of Alex Wells, who had succeeded Utterbach, and said the activities committees should be scaled down to ten. He agreed and the thing was worked out that way."

19

KIND HEARTS

Leaf through any monthly issue of The Lion. You'll find it packed with the sort of modest and moving little stories newspapers used to print in quantity until the brutal blow-by-blow report of a world trying to destroy itself pushed "human interest" out of the paper.

Well, here are the Canadian Clubs, by international courtesy given precedence over the "A's" among the states. Let's see what they did in, say, Ontario:

"Toronto (Danforth) . . . provided needy family with groceries and paid part of a medical bill . . . gave $1,000 to General Hospital toward furnishing Orthopedic Ward with new wing, and pledged additional $9,000 . . . furnished clothing and furniture for family . . . fitted two needy persons with glasses . . . furnished coal for family and installed plumbing . . .

"Ancaster . . . provided food and toys for ten families at Christmas . . . sponsored blood-donor service for hospitalized citizens . . . bought $100 of equipment for Junior Hockey League . . . bought artificial limb for man . . .

"Howick . . . paid expenses of crippled girl's stay in camp . . . donated $200 toward development of community park . . . held Halloween party for children . . . donated to British flood relief . . . financed hospitalization for child . . .

"Leaside . . . donated $7,500 to community-center project . . . established $600 yearly scholarship at university . . . five-day carnival, including parade, huge success, carnival equipment being property of the club; nearly 13,000 paid admissions at ten cents a head, children free . . . installed drinking fountain in public park . . .

"Ottawa . . . provided orthopedic boot for crippled woman . . . gave Braille typewriters to blind veterans . . . purchased invalid chair for woman . . . distributed food and clothing to two families . . . provided clothing for needy children . . .

"Parry Sound . . . sponsored mobile X-ray chest unit . . . arranged for medical checkup and treatment for youngster . . . provided hearing aid for girl . . . fitted four persons with glasses . . . paid for cross-eye correction for boy . . ."

And so on throughout the Dominion. While in outposts of Lionism more distant from the home port the routine ran:

"Lismore, Australia . . . helped the Red Cross ladies unpack clothing parcels for flood relief, even though nearly every Lion was personally affected by the flood . . . raised twenty pounds sterling toward hundred-pound contribution to children's home . . .

"Hamilton, Bermuda . . . twenty-one underprivileged boys entertained at regular club meeting . . . proceeds of moonlight cruise for Lions and ladies donated to home for underprivileged children . . .

"Stockholm, Sweden . . . sent through Lions International Office message of need for special chemicals and other research material by Stockholm printing house . . . son of Stockholm Lion, visiting the United States and planning to fly back to Sweden, received message and took material back with him so that it was received within a day's time . . .

"Geneva, Switzerland . . . established 500-Swiss franc scholarship award for needy student at university . . . "

And within the boundaries of the United States:

"Bessemer, Alabama . . . held ball game for benefit of Alabama sight work . . . contributed $400 for tennis courts in connection with recreation program for Negroes . . .

"Montgomery, Alabama . . . purchased machine for testing eyes of school children and furnished eyeglasses and examinations for all pupils recommended by school authorities . . . sent 77 working boys to summer camp . . . bought Braille writer for blind family . . .

"Tuskegee, Alabama . . . collected $1,000 for junior baseball teams . . . sent a boy to Boys' State . . .

"Phoenix, Arizona . . . purchased 26 scales at cost of $3,750, to be placed in favorable locations and revenue to be used for sight-conservation work, to which Phoenix Club contributed $5,133 in previous fiscal year . . . furnished school room for near-blind children . . . repaired radio for blind persons . . . staged Christmas party for children and furnished clothing and toys . . .

"Batesville, Arkansas . . . raised money to mark streets with permanent metal markers . . . bought an artificial eye for an indigent person . . .

"Manila, Arkansas . . . raised $2,500 for purchase of city fire truck . . . sponsored basketball game to finance purchase of Christmas baskets for needy . . . gave $60 to aged man for hospital bill . . . rebuilt home and provided furniture, food, and fuel for disaster-stricken family . . . raised $1,000 to provide free tuition for members of 50-piece school band . . .

"Monticello, Arkansas . . . netted over $400 for sight-conservation program from minstrel show attended by over 1,000 . . . with local doctors contributing services, 192 children examined in club-sponsored sight-conservation clinic . . . glasses purchased for those needing them."

And so on through the alphabet and across other borders. These aren't special cases, just run of the mill. The notable thing about them is the number that, in an age when "charity" has been streamlined and specialized, still display the personal touch.

Going back into the files of Lions Club activities, however, it is easy to trace the origin of an attitude that Lions have no intention of giving up, for all the production-line philanthropy in the world.

"I saw Lions standing about with tears in their eyes," the secretary of the Shelbyville, Indiana, club reported in describing an early Christmas party. "Imagine a boy nine years old in a prosperous city of the United States' Middle West, who had never seen fried chicken, mashed potatoes, and creamed peas and was afraid to eat them, but thought it a great treat when a Lion ran out and fetched him a hot dog. Imagine many of the 114 children at that table, wrapping their pieces of chicken in paper napkins to take home to a small brother or sister or a mother who wasn't invited to the party. Many of our members had their eyes opened. . . ."

In 1923, the Norfolk, Virginia, Lions Club became interested in a ten-year-old named Russell who "caused quite a stir every time he came into juvenile court, and that was on more than three occasions." The Norfolk Lions looked into Russell's case. They found he was unusually bright and didn't himself think he was in the wrong. After some loosening of red tape, the court approved a sort of informal adoption of Russell by the club, and he was scrubbed up and sent to a military school in a different part of the state. When he came home, he asked to attend a club meeting and thank the members in person for the chance they had given him.

The Norfolk Lions were spurred to further adoptions. The committee flushed up another boy, William, whose worst offense was playing hookey. At eleven, William was on his own, looking out for a younger brother and cooking meals while his mother was employed. William, too, was sent to school, at the Lions' expense.

The "adoption" device spread to other clubs. Lions in Aberdeen, South Dakota, adopted two young paralytics. "As these young men have every comfort," the report stated, "the plan is not so much to provide material things as to have these boys know the sympathetic interest of the Lions Club members."

Scottsbluff, Nebraska, Lions "practically adopted" Lorrie, whose widowed mother worked in a laundry and had no money, after feeding her large family, to pay for doctors for Lorrie. "Then the Lions came in," THE LION reported. "They furnished the mother groceries and got her a widow's pension. They set dentists and doctors to work on Lorrie. When she was taken to a club meeting she so won the Lions that they voted her the 'club sweetheart.' Now the club is interesting itself in other children, reported by the school nurse as in need of care."

In La Porte, Indiana, only the other day, Lions stepped in when no other organization was willing to take charge of two children of a very poor family, who had been desperately burned. The Lions collected $8,000 and had more pledged in short order. After being treated at a local hospital, the children were removed to one in Indianapolis where they underwent skin grafting and other expensive care.

But perhaps the most characteristic thing about the Lions in the performance of club activities is that they never let lack of specialized or outside help stop them, but pitch in and, if the job is one calling mainly for time, patience, or even muscle, do it themselves.

A member of Price Hill Lions Club in Cincinnati and his wife died within a short time of each other, leaving two small orphans and a drugstore. "So the Price Hill Lions Club did a thing not provided for in either its constitution or its by-laws but has only the sanction of the kindly, lamblike hearts of the Lions—it became a druggist," a Cincinnati paper wrote.

"For the livelihood and proper upbringing of the two children the club took over the operation of the drug store, installing a manager who every month renders an accounting to the Lions Club of Price Hill. The two children continue to live in the home their parents had made for them, and an approved housekeeper looks after them. The drugstore prospers. The Lions function in the father's stead.

" 'To do such things is merely the Lions creed,' is the only comment of Otto Streutker, president of the Price Hill Lions Club."

Lions of Fredonia, Pennsylvania, learned that lightning had destroyed the barn of a newcomer to the neighborhood and with it most of his hay crop. A neighboring farmer had offered the young man use of his barn and two thirds of the hay on his land if the young man could make the hay. The hay was ready to cut. The Lions got busy. With equipment supplied by neighboring farmers they cut, raked, and baled the hay, nearly 55 tons of it. Contributions from Lions and a $25 donation from the farmer with the baler covered expenses and left a surplus for the young farmer who had been burned out.

Springfield, Colorado, Lions helped harvest 7,000,000 bushels of wheat during a shortage of harvest labor and difficulties in obtaining combines in 1947, piling the grain in rows pending arrangements for truck hire and granary space. Then the Lions got up early one Sunday and pruned trees and hoed down weeds in the city park and pledged $300 for further upkeep.

In Monroe, Utah, 200 Lions harvested eight acres of potatoes in six hours' time for a rancher who had been injured in a hunting accident.

In Tularosa, New Mexico, John King, 16, got appendicitis. But his mother seems to have known how to look out for his business interests, which centered in a newspaper route. She called a member of the Lions Club. The Lions took over the route, assuring uninterrupted service to 169 subscribers of the *El Paso Times*.

All the Lions of Emmitsburg, Maryland, turned up with scythes and rakes and tidied up a newly designated playground area of several acres. "Nothing the club has done in years marked so well the contribution a Lions Club makes to a community," Secretary John J. Dillon commented. "For, while club money could not find workers, Lions spirit had all the prominent men of the area doing for the community what members of the community could not be hired to do."

A more ambitious recreation project, including baseball diamond, clay tennis courts, Scout house, picnic ground, speaker's stand, and "the biggest swimming pool in northeast Georgia" was dedicated on time at Lawrenceville because the Lions applied their own muscles to it. "A week before the opening," the report to the International ran, "all members were working diligently during the day and part of the night, building forms, pouring cement, grading ball fields, ditching, laying pipes, building bathhouses, wiring for electricity . . . " This same club has other interests. One is a little girl for whom a fund has been set aside to cover monthly eye examinations for a seven-year period. The other is a 4-H Club pig-chain started by the club's purchase of registered Tamsworth pigs.

Being human, Lions are more likely to glow over helping their neighbors than contributing to some remote cause. In Cordova, Alabama, the club got considerable gratification over installing broom-making machinery in the basement of a blind man, making him partially self-supporting. The Sacramento Lions provided a motor-powered sewing machine for a blind leather worker. Lions of the Elmhurst Club of Oakland, California, heard of a young woman, crippled from birth, who needed a typewriter. Members went to great lengths to break rules and incur the wrath of the tail twister until fines totaling $110, purchase price of the typewriter, had been collected.

Sweetwater, Texas, Lions burst their buttons when a young girl who has been their charge almost since she was blinded with a pair of scissors at the age of three, graduated from her home-town high school with a straight A record. Now they have undertaken to pay part of her expenses at Texas State College for Women.

At Powers, Oregon, the Lions wanted to do something for another sightless sweet girl graduate. They decided on a benefit dance, receipts from which would provide her with eastern schooling and a seeing-eye dog. The plan almost bogged down when it developed that Florence's grandparents, with whom she lived, belonged to a religious sect opposed to dancing and weren't going to let her go to her own party. But they relented in the end and the crowd rained silver dollars on the platform as Florence sang "April Showers."

In Victoria, Texas, the Lions Club saw a sightless young girl through a business course, bought her a dictaphone, and got her a job with the Chamber of Commerce.

Sometimes, of course, as happens to all doers, Lions find themselves in embarrassing predicaments. The club of Soquel-Capitola, California, became a foster papa to two brand-new fawns which had been picked up on the highway by a tourist and were turned over to the club by the State Fish and Game Commission. A home ultimately was provided for the fawns in Big Trees Park in Santa Cruz County.

20

INTO EVERYTHING

IN the darkest depths of the depression, with other clubs folding right and left, the member clubs of The International Association of Lions Clubs managed somehow to keep welfare programs moving. Undoubtedly, hard times were a prod. The greater the occasion, the easier it is to rise to it. So we find among the records of 1932–33, when the Association was only about one fifth its present size, these statistics—to cite just a few examples—statistics dull in themselves but exciting in what they stand for:

> 3,987 children furnished with eyeglasses by 394 clubs;
> 1,198 white canes presented to blind adults;
> $16,697.27 expended by 35 clubs in supplying milk to undernourished school children;
> 475,318 free meals furnished unemployed persons by eighty clubs;
> 12,617 Christmas dinner baskets distributed by 187 clubs;
> 14,660 copies of the Moral Code for Youth presented to schools;

79,843 donated to other welfare and civic organizations;
4,533 underprivileged children given medical attention;
operations performed on 527 children;
2,034 underprivileged and undernourished children provided
   with summer camp vacations;
479 children hospitalized for medical care;
44,117 trees planted throughout the country;
net profits of $118,427.80 reported from various community
   entertainments and events;
1,960,000 baby fish placed in lakes and streams by five
   clubs.

Through the predepression years, the welfare program
had been gradually taking the shape that Lions nowadays
like to think of as peculiarly Lionistic. At first, the clubs
functioned more or less independently in choosing—with
some assistance from their standing committees on health
and welfare and on sight conservation and work with the
blind, etc.—the good deeds they wished to do. Even
today, each club's program is determined by community
needs rather than by mandate from on high. But there
is a certain amount of friendly swapping of advice between the clubs, as well as reliance on the wealth of
data on past experiences in the files at headquarters.

So we see, in 1923, the Bridgeport, Connecticut, Lions
undertaking to put up a $10,000 convalescent children's
home through sale of $100 founder's certificates, and
Los Angeles Lions pledging $50,000 for a new home for
boys. Here a club was hiring a band to gladden Boy
Scouts who had none of their own, and there a club was
putting up a war memorial. Another was sending baskets
of candy, fruit, and flowers to crippled youngsters. Others
battled the spread of tuberculosis, started milk funds, promoted poultry shows and high-school athletics, equipped
hospital wings, and staged Easter-egg hunts. Lions have

been especially identified with Easter-egg hunts for nearly thirty years.

In Mason City, Iowa, in the 1920's, Lions did some pioneering in child placement. In other parts of the country, they were setting up circulating libraries in public schools, sponsoring community Christmas trees and hot school lunches, pressuring town fire departments into rehabilitating toys for children who otherwise might lose their faith in Santa Claus. St. Louis inaugurated a better-babies campaign and Pittsburgh (East Liberty) made possible a hospital ward for premature babies. With the changing times, the clubs bought ceiling projectors and iron lungs and supported blood banks and cancer control. A club in Redland City, California, lately undertook to send letters to shut-in children who have no one but the state or county to love them. One in Kirkland Lake, Ontario, started a school for mentally retarded youngsters.

Vinita, Oklahoma, Lions described in 1934 as "an active organization boasting 28 wide-awake members," went behind the locked doors of an institution for the insane to carry out their welfare program. Through their president, Dr. Powell L. Hays, the Lions got to know Marle Woodson, writer, lecturer, World War I veteran, and discharged dipsomaniac. Dr. Hays used to bring Woodson with him to meetings. Moved by Woodson's description of the lives of men and women with nothing to guide their obsessed minds into rational channels, the Lions established a 3,000-volume library in the hospital where Woodson had been a patient. Woodson died shortly after publication of his book, *Behind the Door of Delusion*, written while in the asylum.

Clearwater, Florida, Lions tackled a somewhat differ-

ent problem and one that, before it was solved, put the
Lions themselves in closer proximity to padded cells than
the people they were trying to help. It seems that in the
spring of 1940, just as the hotel shortage was beginning
to be felt, the well-meaning owner of an island off Clearwater broadcast an invitation to honeymooners to come
one, come all, come on over. The Lions Club co-operated
by furnishing one cottage on the island. They and the
others who had joined in the project got 1,200 requests
for reservations, all for June. The Lions manfully undertook to handle the situation as equitably as possible.
Throughout the summer the club's "honeymoon convention committee" played host to 500 couples, at the rate of
50 a week. To avoid congestion on the island, some had
to be put up in town, with compensating features of free
boat rides, free beach barbecues, bicycling, and deep-sea
fishing. In contrast to this moonlight and honeysuckle
project, Tarentum, Pennsylvania, Lions became involved
in lavender and old lace. They played host to 83 old
ladies of the community at an "Over 80" dinner, gallantly
presenting each with a corsage and a pearl necklace.

Out of this hodgepodge of activities, certain ones
have emerged to occur and recur as an enduring part of
the Lions program. Lions have reason to be proud of
the reception educators have given their textbook project,
designed to provide "A Moral Code For Youth." Free
from sectarian doctrines, it has been accepted as part of
the curriculum of many school systems.

By 1928, sight conservation and aid to the blind had
so captured the imaginations of the Lions that all the
clubs interested themselves in a radio broadcast over forty
stations of the NBC network especially for the entertain-

ment of blind persons. "This will be the first time in history that every Lion will be able to listen to the same message at the same time," THE LION said, in announcing that the International President, the late Irving L. Camp of Johnstown, Pennsylvania, would make some opening remarks. "The realization of the magnitude of this undertaking, the good that can be accomplished, is nothing short of inspirational."

THE LION turned out to be so right. It was long before the days when listeners-in were called away from their radios to be presented with brass bands, refrigerators, airplane tickets, and Hollywood boudoirs. But the chairman of the broadcast committee, had a foretaste of that experience when his phone rang as the broadcast ended and a Philadelphia woman wanted to know to whom to make out a $100,000 check for the aid of the blind. "Don't do anything till I get there—I'll be right over," he managed to gasp.

Among the many contributions that resulted from the broadcast was a dollar bill from a widow in a Wilkinsburg, Pennsylvania, home for the aged. The Pittsburgh Lions were so touched that they ordered a basket of flowers for the donor. Lions have looked out for a lot of old ladies in their time, and they were pretty tickled to come across an old lady who was looking out for them.

Lions have operated clinics for the prevention of blindness, bought eyeglasses by the bale, found jobs for the blind and set them up in business, sold their products, paid their tuition in special schools, lobbied for them, and provided them with white canes and Braille books and writers.

Concern with the special equipment of the blind has

led the Lions into bypaths of research that have contributed to the comfort and happiness of blind persons everywhere. Pressure from Lions Clubs was largely responsible for municipal ordinances penalizing motorists who ignored the stop-traffic signaling of a white cane.

According to reports received by Lions International, credit for invention of the white-cane device belongs to a Lion in Peoria, Illinois. Credit for building up the white cane to the point where its purpose is universally recognized belongs to the Peoria Lions Club.

The 1931 convention of Lions International at Toronto took cognizance of Peoria's contribution. The convention proceedings record:

"This activity, originated, we understand, by the Lions Club of Peoria, Illinois, endorsed by the recent convention of the first district, Illinois, and recommended by it to this International Convention, has for its purpose the presentation to the blind of white canes with the lower six inches thereof painted red, to be used by blind pedestrians in assisting them in safely crossing streets. The cane is held in a horizontal position, pointed in the direction in which it is desired to walk. Observance of this signal by the drivers of vehicles is made mandatory by local ordinances. The adoption of this plan is recommended to our clubs as part of our major activity, Blind Work. Full information as to this plan, including copies of the ordinances which have been adopted, may be obtained through our activities department."

In 1940, the *Peoria Star* told the story this way:

"A blind man crossing a Peoria street one day nearly ten years ago started a movement that has carried to all parts of the country.

"The man, virtually helpless in the swirl of traffic, his cane tapping futilely upon the pavement, was noticed by George A. Bonham, then president of Peoria Lions Club. Thoughts of the man kept coming back and he began to search for some means of helping him and scores of other Peorians in his predicament. There should be some way of warning drivers before it was too late that the man was blind and his fate entirely in their hands.

"The cane—that's it! Paint the cane white and put a wide band of red around it. Then let the blind man hold it extended as he crosses the street. Mr. Bonham presented the idea at the next meeting of the Peoria Lions Club. It gained unanimous approval. The canes were painted and distributed; the city council co-operated by adopting an ordinance giving the right of way to its bearer.

"Furnishing the canes without expense to the blind became an international activity of the Lions organization. Ninety per cent of approximately 135,000 sightless in the country now have them, and once a year they are privileged to renew them. Many states have adopted laws similar to the Peoria ordinance, and even in some other countries the white cane with the red band has become a symbol of the blind to be watched for and heeded."

In 1924, a New York Lions Club underwrote publication of a large-type book for use of the partially blind. The year before, the Cincinnati club began experimental publication of a children's magazine in Braille, using a printing plant operated by the blind at the Clovernook Home on the outskirts of the city. "The magazine is being distributed without charge to all blind children in Ohio between the ages of seven and fifteen," Dr. M. F. McCarthy, chairman of the Ohio state welfare committee, reported at the time. "Our 50-page Christmas number contained three juvenile stories. Cost of production was 50 cents per copy. All our plates are being preserved. There is no reason why this magazine should not become a national or, for that matter, an international one."

Dr. McCarthy spoke prophetically. The next International convention recommended that the International assume responsibility for publication and distribution of the magazine, a departure from the fixed policy of local autonomy in club activities. The Secretary-General's report for the twelve months ending June 30, 1949, contains the information that juvenile Braille magazines were furnished children between eight and fifteen years old in countries as distant as Colombia, Egypt, and the Belgian Congo, as well as in England, Canada, and the United States.

Not to be outdone by Peoria, the Long Beach, California, club promoted a writing board for the blind. This is a contraption which enables a blind person to write on ordinary paper with a pencil and keep the lines regular and parallel. The price was rather steep at first, but in 1932 the club brought out a model which retailed for a dollar. Milwaukee Lions became interested in Braille city maps when Esther Fellows, the St. Paul woman who originated them, explained their practical value to the club. Mrs. Fellows was commissioned to provide enough Braille maps of Milwaukee to go around among all the city's sightless. The Fellows maps employ yarn to mark waterways. Round and long beads strung on thread are car lines. Street names are marked in Morse code. Bridges are indicated by two parallel staples and railroad crossings at street level by a single staple. Important landmarks are listed just as on maps for the sighted, and there is a 'finder' in Braille on the margin.

In 1946, the Lions Club of San Diego gleefully seized on the Banks pocket-Braille writer, a vest-pocket-size machine which enables a blind person to write Braille at shorthand speed. They got in touch with Thomas J. Watson, president of the International Business Machines Corporation, to interest him in the manufacture of the machine. When Watson saw its possibilities, he voluntarily offered to manufacture the first one thousand machines free of charge to be distributed by the Lions to blinded veterans of World War II. Since that time, this activity has spread rapidly throughout the entire Association. Only recently, the Lions Club of Tientsin, China, purchased six of the little Braille writers.

The writer is described as a foolproof device with a keyboard containing the six keys and a space bar. The cover lifts to disclose a roll of narrow paper tape on which Braille characters are embossed by hitting the keys. Dr. Banks invented the writer when he came out of World War I with an eye ailment. A specialist advised him to learn Braille while he still had his sight. His experience with the 150-year-old code for the blind man's written alphabet exasperated him and started him on a 12-year quest for a better method.

Another "first" in service to the blind which may be chalked up to the credit of the Lions is the first Boy Scout troop composed entirely of blind boys. It was organized in 1929 by the Lions Club of Berkeley, California.

Lions have been closely identified with the establishment of blind men and women as newsstand operators on street corners and in public buildings. Camden, New Jersey, Lions, for instance, reported in 1929 that their committee on work for the blind had erected four booths at busy corners, stocked them with newspapers and magazines, and installed in them four blind men who previously had been almost helpless. The Camden project has been repeated many times over in cities in all parts of the country.

A few years ago, when the Tulsa, Oklahoma, Lions started a project to provide steady employment for two blind broommakers, they probably had no idea of the proportions to which this activity would grow. During the first two weeks of operation the two blind men turned out 600 brooms, and three blind helpers sold them. As more and more blind workers and helpers became interested and more and more brooms were produced, the little factory had to be expanded. Today, this thriving industry, known as Broomtown, furnishes employment for many blind persons, and its products have a nationwide distribution.

Detroit (East Side), Michigan, Lions preened themselves a little when, in 1935, Ned H. Smith, a blind man to whom they had made friendly gifts of "Talking Books," attributed his appointment as judge of the Common Pleas Court in large part to the help given him by the club.

In 1933, Dr. J. E. Glaydes told the Lions something about work their support had made possible in the West Virginia School for the Blind:

"In the latter part of 1930, the 114 students enrolled in the school at Romney were examined, and it was found that by surgery probably 27 of them could be helped. It was agreed that the surgical work would be done without compensation of any kind, but about $3,000 was needed for transportation and hospitalization. Not until the Lions Clubs of the state came to the financial assistance of these children were we able to proceed with our plan.

"The operative work was begun in the summer of 1931. Each child underwent from two to seven operations. Of the 27 who received surgical treatment, nine have entered public school with normal sight, two were not benefited, and 16 received vision in degree varying from 20/200 to 20/50, or enough sight to permit them to go about and earn an independent living like normal persons. In addition, three other students were found to have blood conditions which soon would have caused total blindness, but treatment has enabled them to retain sufficient vision to go about by themselves.

". . . It was the behavior of the children after the operations which more than repaid me for what I have been able to contribute to this work. A girl whose sight had been given her, wrote me after she had returned home —a typewritten letter. She told me that for the first time in her life she had seen her mother and father, 'And now I'm able to help them, too,' she said.

". . . Another boy came to my office full of excitement. 'I never dreamed the world was so wonderful,' he exclaimed. 'I've seen the Kanawha Falls and the sky and the clouds and an airplane—oh, I guess I've seen about everything.'

"One little girl came to my office after her operation, and was fitted with glasses. When she found how well she could see, she fell on her knees and, with tears of joy trickling down her face, made a little prayer. As I recall it, her prayer was like this:

" 'Dear God, I want to live a long time. Please, God,

don't ever let anything happen to me; please don't ever take my sight away. I love you, dear God, and I want you to love me. . . .' "

In Lumpkin, Georgia, the other day, a little girl named Mary Corley wrote the Lions Club a letter of thanks for an operation which had corrected a progressive myopic squint. "I am back in school," Mary wrote, "My eyes are well and—oh, goody—they are straight. They look like other little girls' eyes now."

A mother in Andalusia, Alabama, poured out her gratitude last year to the Lions Club, which had arranged for operations by a Lion surgeon which gave sight to her blind son. "When you all helped me to get my son Carl to Mobile for treatment, I doubt that he ever had seen his parents or brother to know us from anybody else," the mother wrote. "Cataracts on his eyes had smothered the sight. You all sent me to Dr. Maury and after the first two orapations he learn colors and by the time he had completed the fourth orapation and fitted him with glasses he was able to place his little finger on the numbers on a ruler. It have been a sad home for us to have to wonder for three long years could there be anything done for Carl. He never eat a meal before by himself or done anything without help. Now he even pick up his toys when he dropped them and to see him get his chair, go to the table, name the food and ask for what he wants, gather his play toys for himself, get him a book and ask me about the pictures in the book—you know there is no words I could tell you that would let you know how much I have to thank you for. . . ."

Sight conservation may no longer overshadow other welfare activities on the programs of the Lions Clubs.

Other newer causes claim a fair share of attention. But no phase of Lionism has been emotionally more satisfying to the Lions themselves.

Dr. McCarthy summed up the way Lions feel about this sight-saving business when he said, in pleading for support for the Braille magazine:

"We have all learned not to waste our time in the sentimental display of pity for blind children. The blind child of today, with our modern methods of training, does not need pity unless it leads to something constructive in the way of a chance to get on. . . . Experience has shown that well-trained blind children can take their places in the modern social order and be creative and self-sustaining individuals.

". . . We have found great unfilled gaps in the lives of the younger blind, unfulfilled wants which approach mental starvation, terrible deserts of monotony which you and I have never known because we have our sight. . . . The great need of the blind is suitable reading material. . . . If a blind child is brought up to be merely a machine with no mental background, you get machinelike results. . . ."

In addition to distributing the Braille magazine through the years, Lions International has taken over another distribution designed to reach the juvenile audience. This is the "Moral Code for Youth," with its supplementary publication, the six-volume "Studies in Conduct" series. Promotion of this project is a major responsibility of the education committees in the individual clubs.

It was the late Charles H. Hatton, Wichita, Kansas, banker and International President, 1932–33, who first brought the "Moral Code" to the attention of the International Board. This was at a time when the Association, in an effort to set the activities program on a straight and consistent course, was eliminating proposals about as fast as they came in. But Hatton's idea of providing framed copies of the code in each schoolroom in the communities in which clubs were located found favor. The code had first been issued by *Collier's* magazine. *Collier's* still holds the copyright, although copies now are available only through Lions International, which furnishes them gratis to the individual clubs.

The code reads:

IN GOD WE TRUST

If I Want To Be a Happy, Useful Citizen I Must Have

COURAGE and HOPE—*I must be brave*—This means I must be brave enough and strong enough to control what I think, and what I say, and what I do, and I must always be hopeful because hope is power for improvement.

WISDOM—*I must act wisely*—In school, at home, playing, working, reading, or talking, I must learn how to choose the good, and how to avoid the bad.

INDUSTRY and GOOD HABITS—*I must make my character strong*—My character is what I am, if not in the eyes of others, then in the eyes of my own conscience. Good thoughts in my mind will keep out bad thoughts. When I am busy doing good I shall have no time to do evil. I can build my character by training myself in good habits.

KNOWLEDGE and USEFULNESS—*I must make my mind strong*—The better I know myself, my fellows, and the world about me, the happier and more useful I shall be. I must always welcome useful knowledge in school, at home, everywhere.

TRUTH and HONESTY—*I must be truthful and honest*—I must know what is true in order to do what is right. I must tell the truth without fear. I must be honest in all my dealings and in all my thoughts. Unless I am honest I cannot have self-respect.

HEALTHFULNESS and CLEANLINESS—*I must make my body strong*—My eyes, my teeth, my heart, my whole body must be healthful so that my mind can work properly. I must keep physically and morally clean.

HELPFULNESS and UNSELFISHNESS—*I must use my strength to help others who need help*—If I am strong I can help others, I can be kind, I can forgive those who hurt me, and I can help and protect the weak, the suffering, the young, and the old, and dumb animals.

CHARITY—*I must love*—I must love God, who created not only this earth but also all men of all races, nations, and creeds, who are my brothers. I must love my parents, my home, my neighbors, my country, and be loyal to all these.

HUMILITY and REVERENCE—*I must know that there are always more things to learn*—What I may know is small compared to what can be known. I must respect all who have more wisdom than I, and have reverence for all that is good. And I must know how and whom to obey.

FAITH and RESPONSIBILITY—I must do all these things because I am accountable to God and humanity for how I live and how I can help my fellows and for the extent to which my fellows may trust and depend upon me.

As new clubs are organized, they are urged to become the agency for the placing of framed copies of the code not only in schools but also in the local Y.M.C.A., Scout cabins, Sunday-school rooms, and other places where youths congregate. In translation, copies of the code travel to the Spanish-speaking countries where Lionism flourishes. Milwaukee, Wisconsin, has been especially enthusiastic in supporting this activity by sponsoring a school-children's essay contest based on the subjects covered in the code.

After the code had been widely circulated, Lion Hatton pointed to the need of some sort of follow-up—something which would make the principles laid down in the code come alive in the minds of boys and girls. The

"Studies in Conduct" series was the result. Three New York schoolteachers, supported by 731 assisting teachers, collaborated in producing texts based on actual experiences of children in choosing between right and wrong.

The State of Florida was the first to adopt these character-story readers as supplementary readers throughout the state. That was in 1929, and since then other state school systems have done likewise.

21

"WHAT'S GOOD FOR BUSINESS—"

OUTSIDE the strictly phil-
anthropic field, two key committees in every club reach
out toward all the other activities demanded of the well-
brought-up Lion. These are the committees dedicated to
civic improvement and community betterment, or boosting. Their duties inevitably interlock. What's good for
one is grist for the other. If the civic-improvement boys
are on their toes in city planning, clean-up campaigns, and
such, the way of the community-betterment committee in
attracting new business and tourist traffic is exceedingly
pleasant. And vice versa.

Sustaining the efforts of the community-betterment
and civic-improvement committees, and even at times over-
lapping with them in a friendly way, is the work of the
committees on boys' and girls' activities, education, safety,
and agriculture. Topping the activities of the first-named
committee is the sponsoring of athletic, camp, contest, and
hobby projects for "Y" and Scout groups of both sexes

and similar juvenile and teen-age enterprises. The committee does its share of worrying over delinquency and is at the elbow of the courts and juvenile-protective agencies in a big-brotherly way. The education committee co-operates with schools, libraries, churches, and the P.T.A., runs book drives, sponsors public lectures, and undertakes vocational guidance and hundreds of other activities of an educational nature. Also in the province of the education committee is the distribution of the "Moral Code For Youth." The safety committee busies itself organizing and equipping junior safety patrols, operating safety lanes and driving schools, removing traffic and fire hazards, engaging pool and beach life guards, conducting classes in first aid and lifesaving, and running safety campaigns and contests in schools, factories, and offices, etc. The agriculture committee maintains liaison between city and country. It makes soil-conservation studies and sends mobile libraries into the kerosene circuits. It checks health and fire hazards of rural man and beast and holds "Farmers Day" and "Home Products Day" meetings and fiestas.

Apart from, yet co-ordinated with all these community-service committees, is the work in citizenship and patriotism which is allocated to a standing committee in every Lions Club. Citizenship and patriotism is the only one of the ten standard activities committees which has been dignified with a copyrighted code. The citizenship and patriotism code was given a place among the fundamental documents of Lionism because of a feeling, particularly as the world prepared for the last war, that Lions as a group should make public profession of their love of country, over and above the sentiments contained in the organization's Objects and Code of Ethics.* Among its myriad duties, the committee especially entrusted with converting patriotic sentiment into action provides street decorations on suitable occasions, instructs in display of the flag, promotes memorials, and aids aliens and new citizens.

Peculiar to Lionism is the "Of-Age" ceremony with which clubs welcome to citizenship young men and women of the community attaining voting age within the year. The preferred time for this occasion, which occurs annually, is the Sunday preceding a national patriotic holiday, such as Washington's Birthday or the Fourth of July.

The International has worked out a ritual of patriotic music and reading calling for participation by such related community groups as the American Legion and Auxiliary, the Scouts, women's clubs, etc. "However," the International cautions, "don't permit the Lions Club to be submerged. This is an exclusive, distinctive Lions Club activity. Keep it that way." An "Of-Age" certificate is presented to each of the young people being honored.

Watch the abstract duties of these assorted activities committees unfold into concrete projects, and you have not only a creditable showing of accomplishment but also a rich chronicle of American folkways. Certainly some of the things Lions have thought to do could have been done nowhere but in the particular regions where they have been done. It took the Lions of Newcastle, on the Wyoming–South Dakota border, for instance, to explore and develop a cave to a point where the federal government was willing, in 1934, to include it among the national

* For text of Code of Citizenship and Patriotism see pages 72–73.

beauty spots as Jewel Cave National Monument. In 1944, Lions of Lake Zurich, a tiny resort area northwest of Chicago, bought the lake for $10,000 and arranged to give it back to the town, putting an end to years of squabbling between owners of riparian frontage and boat concessionaires over pollution. Sentimentally inclined Lions of Southport, North Carolina, recently restored the town "whittler's bench," which, as far back as the memory of the oldest Lion goes, has encircled three trees near the water front. Lions in Burlingame, California, spent $116.33 and several patient evenings one summer attaching strips of luminous tape to the bikes of 600 juvenile menaces to traffic.

Hickory Ridge, Arkansas, has twenty-three street lights, thanks to Lion enterprise and willingness to dig down into the jeans. Citizens of suburban Downer's Grove, Illinois, periodically are presented with an issue of a village directory compiled by the Lions. The directory is free of all advertising, including advertising by Lions Jacksonville, Illinois, Lions laid a concrete walk in a parking-meter area in the city square. "Took us several evenings," the club secretary's economically worded report ran. The Lions of Lark, Utah, were less fortunate. A missing part for what the club took to be a playground jungle gym frustrated the club for weeks. The thing eventually arrived and the Lions successfully assembled their contraption "without anyone getting trapped inside" and learned that, appropriately enough, what they had acquired wasn't a jungle gym at all but something called a run-around.

Lions of another city and another day must have felt they were victims of a run-around when they went through an experience that has become a classic in the annals of Lionism. It seems that this club suddenly blacked out in 1926 and the International despatched the usual trouble shooter down to find out "how come." The man from headquarters found that the club not only had overtaxed itself but had roused local jealousies by assuming responsibilities that would properly belong in the province of a Chamber of Commerce. But the city had no Chamber of Commerce. Learning the diagnosis, the indefatigable Lions promptly set about organizing a Chamber of Commerce, and sweetness and light once more streamed down on the city.

THE LION told the story this way in the March, 1926, issue:

"Here was a body of men, leaders from every walk of life, so sincere, so earnest, and so constructive that they got 'in bad' because of the very nature and extent of their activities.

"Their achievements were remarkable. . . . They have been entirely responsible for the development of the now thriving little town. They drove the pigs from the back gardens and the cows off the streets. They brought about street paving and good sidewalks and safe traffic conditions. They have made possible safe railway crossings and succeeded in stirring up sufficient interest and influence to compel the railroad to run an evening train, part freight, and part passenger. This one feature alone took months of work. . . . The train is running today and is generally known as the Lions Special. . . .

"Further, the club was entirely responsible for the raising of $120,000 necessary to induce the only sizable factory to locate there. This is a shoe factory, employing over 600 hands every day . . . and considered the 'backbone' of the town.

"The Lions have brought about better conditions in the Old People's Home, and individually helped in its more comfortable furnishing. They brought about an anti-tuberculosis campaign among the milk sources. They promoted Boy Scout troops and camps and they have developed a business college and a better school system. As individuals they have been actively . . . behind city bond issues and have helped largely in agricultural matters.

" . . . Obviously such a program could not be carried on without making enemies and receiving hostile criticism from the standpatters whose pockets occasionally were touched by taxation to pay for city improvements that the Lions Club was 'guilty' of promoting.

"By and by it became generally accepted that the Lions Club was 'running the town.' There was some intimation of a boycott and the merchants and the banker, fearing they would lose some trade, dropped away from the club but continued to applaud its work and say, 'Go to it, boys! We're for you but we can't be with you.'

"Later it was known that the Lions Club members— not as a club but as individual citizens—were behind the 'slate' of city officials elected. The talk went around that the Lions Club could not run the political affairs of the city. So the politicians dropped away from the club. Finally there were left only eight faithful souls who didn't give a 'hoot' about hostile criticism or boycotts or political favors or prestige. They knew they had brought about good only . . . and so they continued to meet every week. They collected no dues, enforced no laws, elected no officers. They functioned only as a local club body—a group of real, earnest, and useful men who wanted to stay together for the good of each other and for the town as a whole. Fortunately these men were among the most forceful and representative in the community.

"That club is now back on its feet. It is working in harmony with International, it has the backing of more than 1,000 other Lions Clubs, and it will continue to carry on the civic work for which it was intended and to second all efforts of the Chamber of Commerce. The best men of the city are joining the faithful eight, and the whole domain of Lionism has an object lesson of courage and nerve in the face of opposition."

The Lions evolved their present highly intricate activities program through a willingness to try anything once, maybe twice, in the early days. They swatted houseflies, the billboard nuisance,—and the narcotic traffic. They beautified Port Arthur, Texas, by planting three carloads of palms and selling rosebushes to the populace at one third of cost price. They put up a shelter house for tourists visiting in Boulder, Colorado, and a $150,000 golf course for the "underprivileged golfers" of Denver, where golf greens were a rarity thirty years ago.

Jonesville, Arkansas, Lions were responsible for the installation of a juvenile court in Craighead County in 1920. Lions of Oakland, California, joined with other civic organizations in underwriting a $5,000,000 athletic club. Down in Long Beach, the Lions played newsie to raise money for a newsboys' clubroom. In Atchison, Kansas, the 50-member club took over one day's editions of the *Daily Globe*, changing the name of the 20-page issue they produced to *The Growl*. The Lions solicited the ads and wrote the copy, got over 500 local news items,

edited telegraph news, wrote editorials and features, super-
intended make-up and put in two hours in the mailing
room—with results no more pied than show up from time
to time in struck or semi-struck dailies. *The Growl* netted
the Atchison Lions $900 toward construction of a public
swimming pool.

The year the depression hit, Lions International, in
furtherance of the aid-to-business partition of their activities program, were furnishing 534 newspapers with a series
of 52 articles called "The Town Doctor." The articles discussed various phases of civic boosting.

In October of 1930, the Lions inaugurated "Business
Confidence Week." The occasion—you couldn't exactly
call it a celebration in the circumstances—produced observances limited only by the ingeniousness of the participating clubs. Little Rock, Arkansas, had a "Hot Dollar"
campaign. A dollar bill, mounted so that a log of its progress could be kept, was sent on its way by the club president, Will Terry. It returned to him in six days with a
record of 357 transactions, evidence of expenditure of that
many dollars. The Lions sponsored as many "make work"
and "pump-priming" devices as the next fellow during
those distressing years. But about the time the second
annual "Business Confidence Week" rolled around in 1931,
some Massachusetts Lions had fun invoking a "hex" which
may or may not have been inspired by that state's witch-
burning heritage.

"Arriving at the wake and funeral of 'Old Lady Depression' at Saugus, Massachusetts, we sat down to dinner
wearing top hats and black napkins," Reporter Ike Cowan
wrote in THE LION. "After a sumptuous dinner, the pall-
bearers, garbed in comic apparel, carried the deceased into

the room in a gray casket and placed it on the bier, which was covered with a grave rug of green.

"The undertaker, Attorney Lawrence Davis, placed flowers around and upon the casket. The mourners sat at the head of the casket and did a splendid job of weeping. After the minister, the Rev. Arthur W. Putnam, gave the eulogy, interrupted of course by the mourners, we all passed by the casket and read on a printed slip, passed to us as we stood in line: 'Good-by, Depression, no more breadlines . . .' The quartet sang a song and we all joined in the chorus, as follows:

> *Old Lady Depression, last night she died;*
> *Ring the bell for all is well,*
> *She's on the other side.*

> *Old Lady Depression, last night she died;*
> *Ring the bell, she's gone to—well,*
> *She's on the other side.*

"As the undertaker was about to adjust the lid his attention was attracted to the corpse (a wax figure). In great surprise he called for a doctor. The doctor examined the body with a stethoscope and asked for the surgeon, who entered, in hospital array, and after using the stethoscope pronounced life.

"The surgeon performed a caesarian operation and after the usual maneuvers by the doctor (with a large talking doll) the baby squealed and 'Prosperity' was born. The casket was then lowered in the grave, after which a flashlight picture was taken of the assembly and the party broke up by singing 'The Star-Spangled Banner.' "

In 1932, Melvin Jones became a member of the White House conference of business executives at the invitation of President Hoover and served as an advisor to Colonel Frank Knox, whom Hoover had deputized to develop the recommendations of the conference. In that year also, The International Association of Lions Clubs conducted an anti-hoarding campaign with the object of arresting the spread of jitters among the banks. Both in this move and in the inauguration of "Business Confidence Week," THE LION claimed in April, 1933, the Association was a full year ahead of the troubles which it foresaw.

"Both times it accomplished great good and both times it failed of full success because the whole country was not enrolled in Lions Clubs," THE LION editorialized. "Because these programs were not fully carried out, trouble came. These two great economic movements initiated by the Association would, if completely carried out by the people, have prevented the recent bank moratorium."

THE LION further asserted that: "A student of human affairs who is not a Lion but who knows the works of Lions said at a conference in International headquarters only a week ago that if the people of the United States had been guided by the principles of Lionism—if there had been enough Lions Clubs to influence the whole nation as they do their own communities—we would never have had the serious crisis from which we are just emerging."

Be that as it may, there is no gainsaying the accomplishment of energetic individual clubs, like the one in Shelbyville, Tennessee, of which it was written (THE LION, May, 1934):

"In a day when many localities are mourning the loss of business, vacant dwellings, empty store buildings, and lagging industry, Shelbyville, Tennessee, is actually promoting a building and loan association to build at least 100 houses to accommodate the families which are flocking there to work in the factories.

"This is not mere luck. It did not just happen. It was *done* by the Lions Club of Shelbyville. Two years or so ago, when a factory closed, it was the Shelbyville Lions who went after the U.S. Rubber Company to take over the building and establish a branch factory in it. The Lions helped to feed and clothe the workers until the factory could be got under way. It started with a pay roll of $5,000 a week, and has since increased.

"It was the Shelbyville Lions who secured another building for a canning factory, got a bank to finance the buying of machinery, sold stock to raise the money, arranged for the purchase of cans and the shipment of the product, went among the farmers and got them to sign contracts to supply fruit and vegetables.

"It was the Lions who put on a big dinner at which all the heads of all the twenty-five or thirty industries in Shelbyville were guests and showed them how the Lions Club and they could work together to their mutual benefit and got them all solidly back of the city.

"It is the Shelbyville Lions Club which is responsible for the high degree of prosperity the city is enjoying today. Without the Lions Club, Shelbyville would be just another little city trampled underfoot by the late depression. . . ."

22

NOR FLOOD NOR DROUGHT
NOR BOMBS SHALL STAY THEM

FROM their earliest begin-
ning, the Lions Clubs have been in the forefront of the
relief drives that follow in the wake of depression, disaster, and war. "Not so much for the money they have
given from their own pockets but because they always
organize the community and get everybody to work and
thus achieve immeasurably greater results, the Lions are
among the most important agencies for relief, especially
in the smaller communities," an astute observer once remarked.

The Association came into existence in time to participate in the tag end of the relief drives that accompanied
World War I, shipping shoes and clothing to Belgium and
the occupied areas of France, and then providing the same
relief when hard times came in the United States in the
early '20's. The clubs have been alerted in countless dis-
asters—tornadoes in the Mississippi Valley, hurricanes in

Florida, drought in the dust bowl, floods in the Ohio River Valley, the Texas City blast in 1947, and hundreds of other catastrophes more localized.

In all the areas where sections of the Friendship Train —which collected thousands of tons of foodstuffs for Europe in 1947—were assembled, the Lions Clubs spearheaded the collection drive. In some areas, Lions were the sole contributors. In others they performed an invaluable service in seeing that boxcars were loaded and waiting to be picked up in the various cities when the train passed through. Dismayed at being off the route of any Friendship Train section, Salinas, California, Lions hit on the idea of despatching the California training ship *Golden Bear* to Europe as a "good-will milk boat." In a week's time, they had collected 609 cases of tinned milk for their project. When the Texas Lions learned that the original Friendship Train was by-passing their state, they were instrumental in organizing a special section of the train from the Southwest.

Five members of the Texas City Lions Club lost their lives in the explosion there on April 16, 1947. An emergency fund that ultimately totaled $40,000 poured in from hundreds of Lions Clubs to the stricken city where everyone of prominence, it seemed, from the mayor and police chief to the principal bankers of the town, was a Lion. But not all of the relief money was earmarked by the Lions for their own. It was shared with "people outside the Lions Club, regardless of color, race, or creed," providing assistance to the unfortunates who did not have time to clear through other organized agencies. (Again is evident the Lions' policy of getting things done "fustest," whether or not with the "mostest.")

THE AMERICAN RED CROSS
CENTRALIA CHAPTER
CENTRALIA, ILLINOIS
April 4, 1947

Centralia Lion's Club
Centralia, Illinois

Gentlemen:

    A week ago last Thursday I appeared before your Club as Chairman of the Centralia Red Cross Chapter and asked your membership for volunteers to assist the Red Cross in performing the very necessary and vital service which Red Cross had been asked to perform in connection with the Centralia mine disaster which occurred on Tuesday, March 25 in which 111 miners lost their lives. It appeared that the bodies of the miners which were then being removed from the mine were in such a bad state of mutilation and decomposition that the only means by which identification could be established was by way of ascertainment from the families and next of kin of the deceased miners of the personal effects, etc. which the miners usually carried upon their person such as knives, pipes, cigarette cases, watches, etc. With this information the morticians would then be able to compare the data with the articles found on the bodies and thus establish identification. It was this task together with the additional duty of then returning to the homes of deceased miners after identification had been established and officially notifying the families which I explained to you and for which I asked volunteers.

    On behalf of the Centralia Red Cross Chapter I wish to express appreciation for the overwhelming response that was made to the request and for the work that was thereafter carried out by the members of your club. The task was by no means an easy one because in addition to performing the same under grief-stricken and calamitous circumstances it entailed persevering work both night and day until the last identifications were completed on Sunday, March 30, 1947. The work was all the more arduous by reason of the fact that a great many of the miners lived in homes which were remotely located and difficult to find, particularly during the night time when the greater part of this service was performed.

    The job was delicately, efficiently and capably handled by your club under the banner of the Red Cross and as I stated when I made my first appeal to you for help that since I was well acquainted with your club that I knew that when I accepted this responsibility in the name of the Red Cross that I could count on the Lion's Club to furnish the personnel to perform this service and that the Lion's Club is the type of organization and made up of the kind of men who are both eager to perform any possible service to mankind and also fully capable of performing that service. Since that time I have stated to you that I am sure that the service that you have performed will be to the everlasting credit of the Club. On behalf of the local Red Cross Chapter I therefore join with the bereaved families and friends of the miners, the mine officials, and the public in general in recording this note of thanks and appreciation of the great service you have performed.

                               Very truly yours,

                               Fred L. Wham, Jr., Chairman
                               Centralia Chapter

This letter pays tribute to the outstanding service given by the Centralia, Illinois, Lions Club for being on duty continuously until all identifications were completed and next of kin notified, following the Centralia mine disaster.

Revealing glimpses of the performance of Lions in time of emergency are scattered through the routine reports in the official magazine.

When tornadoes struck in Illinois, Tennessee, Indiana, and Missouri in 1925:

"Arriving at one of the disaster sites, the District Governor of Illinois and his committee found the immediate needs of the sufferers were being met by the American Red Cross with its powerful organization and immense staff of surgeons and nurses, its ability to get instant shipments of foodstuffs, and the backing of the U.S. Army in emergency. But there was one thing that nobody had thought of doing—a thing so close to the ideals of Lionism that the committee saw it at once—the need of getting all the children back into school. So the committee left in the capable hands of the Red Cross the direct care of the injured and took up the question of schools. The committee will spend $10,000 if necessary, in supplying every child with books, pencils, tablets, and all needed supplies. The books will become the permanent property of the children, but on the pages of each one will be stamped the legend that they were presented by the Lions."

When Long Beach, California, was ravaged by an earthquake in 1933:

"A bill was introduced in the United States Senate for an outright gift to the desolate and it was to Lions International that the Lions Club of Long Beach appealed to save them from the stigma of charity. The Long Beach Club urged that International Officers and Directors send telegrams to their senators and other government officials asking that no outright gift be made but that an RFC loan be granted the district, exactly as was being

done with banks and industries in distress. Telegrams to
this effect kept the wires busy for days and presently
news came that the government had changed its attitude
and that funds would be advanced as a loan."

When flood waters of twelve eastern rivers spread
disaster through New England, New York, and Pennsylvania in 1936:

"What of the Lions Clubs in this area? They are still
there, working harder than ever, with a story of heroic
action behind them and a rough path facing them. . . .
To the everlasting credit of Lions Clubs everywhere,
money, letters of sympathy, shipments of clothing, and
other supplies poured in to the secretary of the Johnstown
and other Lions Clubs in affected areas. . . . In Pennsylvania, District Governor Charles S. Smith was sick of flu
at the worst of the flood but, wishing to organize his clubs
for the emergency, he broadcast instructions to them over
the radio. Within two hours he had telephone calls from
sixteen clubs and before the worst of the flood was over
had reports from twenty-five. 'I certainly did feel good,'
he wrote, 'when they called back: "Bud, we heard your
broadcast and are on the job." ' "

Response of the Lions Clubs—then numbering about
4,200—to the declaration of war on December 8, 1941,
has been likened to "the dropping of a live coal into a
powder keg." From the International President's wire to
the White House to the action of the club of Harlan,
Kentucky, which promptly and personally declared war
on the three Axis nations, hell was a-poppin'. There was
even some thought of relaxing the International's sacred
no-assessment rule in order to facilitate the buying of
bombers by the clubs. But the ultimate decision favored

setting up a special "Bomber" or "Victory" fund for the accommodation of clubs and individuals wishing to make special gifts. Of course, like everyone else, Lions plunged into all the bond and bomber drives. By April of 1942, it was estimated that Lions were responsible for the purchase of $10,000,000 worth of war bonds. Chattanooga, Tennessee, Lions, a club of 63 members in a community of less than 200,000, put on a "Buy-a-Bomber" campaign, selling everything from a dime defense stamp to a $50,000 bond, that yielded the price of three bombers.

But it was the little unusual things that the clubs did in wartime as in peacetime that seem most arresting in retrospect. Under the laws of New Jersey, the Camden Lions incorporated a "Selectees Mothers Club" with the object of sending two mothers of servicemen each week to visit their sons in any camp within a thousand miles of Camden.

In those tense early days of the war, when the west coast was fully expecting to be invaded, Lions out there wanted to form guerrilla bands, under War Department supervision. The Board gave its okay if the authorities approved. In inland Riverside, California, a popular week-end leave center, men from the camps had no place to sleep. The Lions did what they could. They secured the co-operation of the manager of one local movie house and eventually two. At first only 150 men were handled on Saturday nights, bedded down on the loges and the over-stuffed lobby furniture. But presently 1,500 were coming, and the club put on a "pillow drive" to make the boys as comfortable as possible on the thickly carpeted floors. Club members stood watch throughout the night, attending to temperature and ventilation. Lions in the provinces

of Ontario and Quebec realized $103,000 for bombed-out
and orphaned British children through their "Mary Pickford" project. Miss Pickford, born in Toronto, donated a
piece of property in Toronto on which the Lions built a
bungalow. "Shares" were sold at a dollar each and the
bungalow went to the lucky "shareholder."

But over and above all, once more it was that personal
touch which Lions never have lost—even while their organization had expanded to a point where its community
and welfare projects are big business—that counted for
more in their war work than the records of eight-figure
bond drives ever will show, impressive as those records
may be. "What I am trying to say is rather hard to put
in words," a GI wrote from Marseilles to the Lions Club
of West Los Angeles in January of 1946. "It is something which words alone cannot express. You know that
I am speaking of your action and the wonderful results
of the operations on our youngest son, Terry Lee. My
wife and I, thousands of miles apart, together had kept
hope in our hearts and had prayed that the operations
might be a success. And they were.

"I know most of you fellows personally, and I feel
free to talk and tell a tale of myself. When my wife wrote
me of what you were doing I was so happy I cried like
a baby. I know it sounds funny that a fellow of my size
would burst out crying, but I did. You see, gentlemen,
you picked my son to help, when you might have chosen
any soldier's son. But you did choose my child, and gave
him an even chance in life.

"You would be surprised to know the number of men,
while the war was in progress, who voiced the question,
'What are we fighting for?' I tried to give the answer.

Among other things, I told them we were fighting to give our children a free country to live in, where they would have a decent chance at life. You fellows backed me up one hundred per cent.

"It is impossible for you to know how helpless a man feels when he is overseas and something is wrong at home. Then to receive word of the help you have given and are giving, takes a man's morale out of the dust and gives him the courage to face the future with a better outlook on life.

"As I said before, it is very hard to put into words, so I will just say THANK YOU from the bottom of my heart."

23

LIONS AND THE UNITED NATIONS

IT seems to me," Fred W. Smith, then International President, said in 1947, "that in all the thirty years of Lions' service our widest opportunity as an international organization has occurred within the past three years or since that time, in the fall of 1944, when Lions were accorded the privilege of participating in the off-the-record discussion of the Dumbarton Oaks proposals. Following closely upon this participation came the invitation to the Lions to have a consultant and two associate consultants to the United States delegation at the United Nations Conference in San Francisco. The Lions were represented at the Peace Conference in Paris in September, 1946, by D. A. Skeen and Clifford D. Pierce. Furthermore, ever since the opening days of the San Francisco Conference, the Lions have been active participants in the meetings of the 'nongovernmental groups' and early this year were recognized by the United Nations as an organization with special competence and ability to

The Lions Board of International Relations being received by His Excellency, Don Enrique Jiminez, President of the Republic of Panama, during the Board's Conference in Panama City in 1947

Secretary of State of the United States James F. Byrnes receiving from Clifford D. Pierce and D. A. Skeen a scroll of greetings from the Lions in Paris in 1946

represent peoples in many nations and thus were granted consultative status with the Economic and Social Council of the United Nations.

"This status, in my opinion, implies an obligation on the part of each Lion to develop a greater understanding of the multiplicity of the activities of the United Nations and particularly those relating to the Economic and Social Council. With this greater understanding by the individual Lion will come a greater opportunity for our Association to participate more fully in world affairs in the years ahead."

With that speech, Lionism had come a long way on a road where members once hesitated to set their feet. Service clubs generally had shied away from the World Court issue after World War I as being "partisan." The tinge of partisanship detected in a Lions Club meeting calls for prompt quarantine measures, the same as the appearance of measles. The reason for this caution is as obvious as the reason for the measles quarantine. You can't expect the members to attain that all-for-one-and-one-for-allness necessary to a going concern if they go around wearing their politics and their ideologies on their sleeves or on their shoulders. So Lions Club members always have been expected to check their deepest feelings in these matters with their hats before sitting down to the fruit cup.

But in recent years, the Lions have become acutely aware of the urgency of a world shrunk by A-bombs to altogether too cozy dimensions. How far the jolt will propel them as an organization into political action below the international level is a question that is still open. But they yield to no other group of comparable influence in all-out support of the United Nations.

As recently as 1937. the Lions, no more prophets than you or I or the prime ministers of Europe, conceived of international relations as something to be promoted by little visits back and forth and the exchange of postage stamps by school children. The club at Pawtucket, Rhode Island, received the commendation of the International Board that year for its "postage stamp mission" in which a packet of stamps was sent to "some Lion or influential man" in a foreign country. The latter was expected to give the stamps to his children who, in turn, would send fifty stamps to a Pawtucket Lion for his children, who in turn, etc., etc.

However, by 1943, the International was plugging hemispheric solidarity by seeing that Lions Clubs in Latin-American countries were supplied with material prepared by the OWI speakers' bureau.

At the International Convention held in Cleveland, in July of 1943, the Lions wholeheartedly endorsed a resolution advocating "the adoption of the Ball-Burton-Hatch-Hill Resolution, the Fullbright Resolution, or some other resolution similar in effect and purpose, at an early date, as a declaration of national policy." Both of these bills had to do with machinery for peace.

Late in 1944, the Lions were invited to send a representative to attend a meeting at the Department of State in Washington, D.C., for "off-the-record" discussions of the Dumbarton Oaks proposals, from which the Charter of the United Nations later came into being.

Reporting on these off-the-record discussions of the Dumbarton Oaks proposals, Past President Clifford D. Pierce of Memphis, Tennessee, then Second Vice-President and Lions International representative, told the Directors:

"I was quite impressed because we already had done the very things that the State Department hoped were being done. Our whole organization had developed means to get plans for the coming United Nations organizational conference before the people. I indicated that we thought we represented a cross section of business and professional thought in our Lions countries and that our program very definitely had been presented in such a way that we felt it was bringing results."

Thus began the years of Lions' participation in historic international strivings toward world peace.

In February, 1945, the Lions were again asked to send a representative to a meeting in Washington of national organizations, this time on the Bretton Woods agreement. Harold P. Nutter, Camden, N.J., and Secretary-General Melvin Jones represented the Lions at that meeting, which was conducted by Secretary of the Treasury Henry Morgenthau, Jr., and Assistant Secretary of State Archibald McLeish.

As a result of this particular meeting, Melvin Jones began to make plans for the Lions to take a more intensive part in the cause of world peace. Pamphlets containing the Dumbarton Oaks proposals had been mailed to all Lions Clubs, and on March 5, 1945, the Glenwood Springs, Colorado, Lions Club adopted a resolution which was to have far-reaching effect. The resolution in part said:

"We believe the President of the United States, the State Department, and the Senate should conclude, as soon as possible, agreements with our principal Allies providing for complete present and future demilitarization of Germany and Japan. . . . We believe that the framework and the details of a World Organization must be worked out by the chosen leaders of the nations; that the document on which it is based must be elastic enough to expand to meet the needs which the future will dictate; that the document must be given life, growth, and policies through the judgments of a final tribunal or assembly; and, finally, that such judgments, when the necessity arises, must be carried out by force of arms contributed by signatory nations. . . . We therefore endorse and urge a World Organization such as is indicated in the broad basic principles agreed upon at Dumbarton Oaks, notwithstanding the fact that it is neither perfect nor complete."

Things were happening fast. The opening session of the San Francisco Conference was still several weeks away when, on March 28, Secretary William R. Bird left Chicago for San Francisco to take charge of the Lions office to be opened there for the duration of the conference. Bird was also furnished press credentials to represent THE LION and EL LEON at the conference.

Early in April a letter went out from the International Office to all Lions Clubs asking them to celebrate the week of April 23-28 as United Nations Week and to hold a United Nations program in their club meeting during that opening week of the San Francisco Conference. With the letter went a program showing suggested procedure. The Glenwood Springs resolution was included in the program, as well as a suggestion that the clubs might wish to send a letter or a message of support to International President Skeen at Lions Conference Headquarters in the Sir Francis Drake Hotel, San Francisco.

On April 9, E. R. Stettinius, Jr.—who had only a short time before been named Secretary of State—sent this telegram to the International Office, addressed to International President Skeen:

> I AM HAPPY TO INVITE YOUR ORGANIZATION TO DESIGNATE A REPRESENTATIVE TO SERVE AS A CONSULTANT TO THE AMERICAN DELEGATION AT THE FORTHCOMING CONFERENCE ON INTERNATIONAL ORGANIZATION TO BE HELD AT SAN FRANCISCO BEGINNING APRIL 25. THE OFFICIAL AMERICAN DELEGATION CONSISTS OF THE EIGHT DELEGATES APPOINTED BY THE PRESIDENT, AND THEIR PROFESSIONAL AND TECHNICAL ADVISERS. CONSULTANTS REPRESENTING ORGANIZATIONS WILL BE AVAILABLE FOR CONSULTATION AT THE REQUEST OF THE DELEGATION AND WILL BE KEPT AS CLOSELY INFORMED OF THE WORK OF THE CONFERENCE AS POSSIBLE. IF YOU DESIRE TO APPOINT A CONSULTANT PLEASE WIRE THE NAME OF THE PERSON DESIGNATED.

The Board of Directors of Lions International immediately acted to name President Skeen as the official Lions consultant. Later when the Department of State authorized the appointment of associate consultants, the Board appointed Vice-President Fred W. Smith and Secretary-General Melvin Jones as associate consultants, and all three were at the opening session of the San Francisco Conference and participated from time to time in the consultants' meetings.

On April 24, the evening before the conference opened, 1,200 Lions and guests took part in a pre–United Nations Conference rally at a huge banquet sponsored by the Lions in the Scottish Rite Temple, in Oakland. Dr. Preston Bradley, pastor of the People's Church, Chicago,

was the principal speaker of the evening and, reported
THE LION:

"The audience was deeply moved by his eloquent and
thrilling address. He took as his subject 'The World of
Tomorrow' and his plea was for the success of the conference about to open. The size of the gathering, the deep
—almost reverent—earnestness of the members, and the
character and high standing of the participants made a
deep impression. The *Oakland Tribune* the following day
ran a cut five columns wide showing part of the banquet
scene, as well as a running story and other pictures of
prominent Lions and interviews with some of them. It
was made clear that Lions are backing to the full the endeavors of the conference to work out a plan for harmony
among nations."

Bradley's talk, which was broadcasted, was so well received that the station which put it on the air rebroadcasted it the following evening and again on April 27.

The Lions had made their presence felt at the conference. They were to do so on more than one occasion in
the days ahead. On May 8, President Skeen addressed a
letter to the Secretary of State, assuring him the Lions
were solidly in favor of what had been done in the conference to date, and telling him about the several thousands of messages which had poured into the Lions Conference Headquarters from Lions Clubs in many countries.
All of these without exception indicated the enthusiasm
which these Lions felt because their organization had a
place in the work of the conference. These messages of
support came from every state in the United States, and
from Puerto Rico, Alaska, and Hawaii; also from practically every province of Canada, from Cuba, Venezuela,

Nicaragua, El Salvador, Guatemala, and Honduras.

On May 1, the first of a series of Newsletters went out to the Lions Clubs from Conference Headquarters, to acquaint Lions everywhere with happenings of interest at San Francisco. In the second of these letters, dated May 10, Fred W. Smith reported: "In our consultant meetings we have accomplished many worth-while things. We had been meeting at odd times, occasioned largely by the difficulty of determining when the American delegates could meet with us. It occurred to me that in view of this it might be well to arrange for regular meetings each day, to be addressed by some of the consultants or other officials of the Department of State, in addition to the special meetings called. Yesterday I presented a resolution to that effect, with the result that the plan has been adopted, but on a twice-a-week basis instead of daily."

It was well that Fred W. Smith had started this new plan because some of the consultants, all busy men and women, were commencing to feel that they could not afford to stay in San Francisco for only occasional meetings with the American delegation. But with the new plan in effect, it was possible to hold a meeting of the consultants with only one of the delegates present, which worked out very satisfactorily.

The Lions, however, sensing the still restive outlook of some of the consultant group, sent informal invitations to all of them to attend a get-together dinner on the evening of May 22. Many of the consultants were preparing to leave for home, and the invitation stressed the opportunity the dinner would afford to have all consultants get together informally before they left. Seventy-eight of the consultant group responded.

Nearly everyone present at the dinner was either at the head or near the head of organizations having great influence on American life. Upon arriving, the guests were seated in typical Lions fashion and well mixed— businessmen and labor leaders, farmers and industrialists, religious leaders and educators, representatives of organizations of business and professional men and women, all from the forty-two consultant groups. Speeches were limited and brief. During the course of the evening each guest was asked to introduce the man or woman seated on his left. Out of this grew much fun and fellowship, and the reserve and aloofness noticed in the earlier meetings of the consultant group disappeared; and complete unanimity, mutual understanding, good fellowship, and cooperation became predominant in the month of consultants' meetings which followed. The U.S. Department of State was greatly elated over the new vigor attained by the consultants.

But before the conclusion of the conference, the Lions Board of Directors, in order to stimulate further the work of their consultants in connection with the United Nations, held a Board meeting in San Francisco. The Honorable Tom Connally, a leading member of the U.S. delegation and chairman of the United States Senate Foreign Relations Committee, was the principal speaker at a banquet tendered the Board during its sessions there. This meeting was also attended by a number of State Department representatives.

At the conclusion of the San Francisco Conference, the consultants were made happy by the remarks (which were also included in his official report) of the U.S. Secretary of State, Edward R. Stettinius:

"I am delighted with the way in which the relationship with the consultants has worked out. There is no question but that there are many things that you have helped us on of great importance and I think you will find that many specific things will have found their way into the United Nations charter as a result of this activity that might otherwise not have been in the final expression."

There is no doubt that the Lions delegation left San Francisco inspired with zeal for its mission of keeping the country sold on the United Nations as the only feasible approach to world peace. At a subsequent Board meeting, Skeen told the Directors the way to serve the cause of peace was to look toward the United Nations with faith and confidence rather than mere tolerance or, worse still, encouragement of a search for a substitute organization. He bitterly criticized "people traveling throughout the country talking to high-school and university groups, boards of county commissioners, city councils, etc., to the detriment of the United Nations."

In November, 1945, the Lions International Headquarters asked all Lions Clubs to observe the week of December 2–8 as another LIONS–UNITED NATIONS Week, and to study and discuss the Organization Plan of the UN and the purposes and functions of the United Nations Organization, so that all Lions might be familiar with some of the matters which it was expected would come before the General Assembly and the Security Council when these two bodies met in London early in 1946.

Many clubs which had participated in the first United Nations Week during April 23–28, 1945, and which had formed special committees in their clubs for that purpose, had continued their committees. Many other clubs had also added similar committees which came to be known as United Nations committees until today nearly every Lions Club in the Association has a United Nations committee.

The United Nations committees in the local clubs keep abreast of United Nations happenings. They see to it, also, that members are supplied with copies of the UN charter and that a reasonable number of regular club meetings are devoted to United Nations discussion. They also arrange for community observance of United Nations Day on October 24 of each year.

It was the Lions, incidentally, who first conceived the idea of this world-wide celebration. Back in February, 1946, the Lions Board of Directors, meeting in Havana, Cuba, adopted a resolution proposing that one day be set aside each year as a day of universal observance of peace.

In many communities, this observance of United Nations Day has taken the form of a model Security Council meeting, or a panel discussion of the UN charter, to acquaint the community with the workings of the United Nations organization.

Much of the success and interest in this type of meeting is due to the efforts of Fred W. Smith, who, in 1947, as chairman of a committee of Non-Governmental Organizations Affiliated with the United Nations, drew up a model UN program. This program was sent to all Lions Clubs as well as to nongovernmental organizations all over the world. As late as May, 1949, requests for additional copies were still coming into the Lions International headquarters along with reports from faraway places of meetings in which the program was used.

As International President and Past President, respectively, Lions Pierce and Skeen flew to Paris for the Peace

Conference there in September of 1946. They arrived in Paris at a time when encouragement to the cause of peace was greatly needed, when the outlook for harmony and conference success appeared discouraging and the situation critical. The fact that the Lions were at hand at just the right time to express their support personally, helped immeasurably in dispelling uncertainties, reassuring the statesmen, and strengthening their position in their labors for peace.

That the support brought by the Lion spokesmen was welcomed was evidenced by the warm reception accorded them from the moment their plane landed in Paris. They were immediately received by the highest American officials in Paris and within two days of their arrival they had accomplished that part of their mission involving the presenting to the Secretary of State of the United States, the Honorable James F. Byrnes, a magnificent parchment scroll of greetings in which the Lions expressed confidence in the efforts being made by the delegates to the conference to achieve a firm basis for a lasting world peace. Signed by Pierce, Skeen, and Melvin Jones, this scroll carried the following message: "WE THE LIONS, members of The International Association of Lions Clubs, represented in eighteen countries, whose primary object is 'to create and foster a spirit of generous consideration among the peoples of the world through a study of the problems of international relationships,' do hereby extend greetings to the DELEGATES OF THE NATIONS AT THE PARIS PEACE CONFERENCE, and make manifest our endorsement and wholehearted approval of the efforts made by them to formulate treaties, which we feel confident will ensure equitable treatment and justice to all

peoples, and a certain and lasting peace for the world."
(It is understood that a copper gavel which the Lions
presented at the same time as a personal gift to Secretary
Byrnes was put to effective use in subsequent sessions of
the conference.)

It was a happy and cordial Secretary Byrnes who
accepted the scroll and who undertook to present it in
turn, on behalf of the Lions, to the conference during
one of its plenary sessions. The results of the Lions' expression of confidence were immediately perceived. "They
demonstrated to the world," recalls Melvin Jones, "that
the Lions are unflinchingly united in a strong stand for a
peace that ensures freedom and justice for all peoples and
nations; that appeasement has been irrevocably discarded;
that there can be no temporizing where human values and
rights are concerned. There was a quick change for the
better in the outlook for harmony in the peace councils,
greater willingness to discuss knotty problems and to compromise, more reasonable attitudes, and less talk of threats
of war."

In January of 1947, Lions International staged a world
conference of its own and literally brought the United
Nations to Central and South America, when Herbert C.
Petry, Jr., Chairman of the Board of International Relations called a meeting of this Board to be held in Panama,
the "crossroads of the world," to discuss intra-Lions
international policy, with particular relation to the United
Nations.

Present at this meeting were members of the Board
from each country where the Lions are represented in the
Western Hemisphere. Present also were Trygve Lie, Secretary-General of the United Nations, Benjamin Cohen

(a native of Chile), UN Assistant Secretary-General, and other high UN officials who had accepted the Lions' invitation to participate in this conference.

The Union Club in Panama City glittered with jeweled orders as the Panamanian cabinet and diplomatic corps gathered with the Lions at a dinner tendered by the Lions of Panama to their own Minister of Foreign Relations and former President of the Republic, Don Ricardo J. Alfaro, and the visiting Lions and delegates.

In an address to the Board of International Relations, UN Assistant Secretary-General Cohen commended the Lions on their work with the United Nations and asked for their continued co-operation.

"I have a very sincere request to make," he concluded. "No international organization can realize its objectives if it does not have support. It is impossible for it to fulfill its program if the states which compose the organization do not fulfill their duties toward it. And in order that the states may fulfill these duties, it is necessary to have a vigilant and well-informed public, conscious of the international situation and of the responsibility that rests on each individual to work for the maintenance of peace and for international good will and co-operation.

"If we wish that the United Nations, which many believe to be the last hope which remains for us, may become successful and make it possible for our sons and grandsons to live without terror of war hanging over them, without the constant worry that their homes and lives be endangered by an aggressor, it is necessary that you, men of good will and men of action, devote to this cause the same fervor that fills us in the United Nations organization, who have dedicated our lives to the realization of this hope for peace and international amity."

Lions International had been granted consultative status in the United Nations Economic and Social Council in March, 1947. At the meeting of the Lions Board of Directors in July of that year, President Pierce was urging that:

"Wherever you are able to speak to Lions or to others, this important status should be brought to public notice for the further advancement of our own interest in the development of the peace movement."

Then he added:

"Of course there are many things that have happened nationally and internationally that have affected world affairs and have caused some skepticism. But I do feel that we, in our position and with our objectives, should very definitely keep going onward and upward in connection with this important objective of the Association as a whole."

In October, 1947, New York City was the scene of one of the most outstanding events in Lionism's dynamic history, as well as one of the most noteworthy even in such a world's gathering place as the metropolitan Home of the United Nations. The occasion was the celebration of the 30th anniversary of the founding of the Lions Association, the holding of an International Board meeting, and a meeting of the members of the Board of International Relations to which the officials of the United Nations were invited. The meeting was specifically held in New York to enable the Lions officials to enter into close contact with officials and leaders of the United Nations Secretariat, General Assembly, and Security Council and, vice versa, to give both groups opportunity to acquaint themselves more intimately with each other's viewpoints, procedures, and objectives.

The climax of the event was an elaborate banquet at the Waldorf-Astoria Hotel. It was a distinguished gathering. In addition to the officers and Directors and Board of International Relations there were Lions from all parts of New York State and neighboring states and from many countries. The Lions had as their guests many high public officials, delegates to the General Assembly, members of the United Nations Secretariat, ambassadors, consuls general, and other eminent personages from many nations. Among the evening's speakers were: Clark M. Eichelberger, Director, American Association for the United Nations; Chester S. Williams, Public Liaison Officer, U.S. Delegation to the United Nations; and J. B. Orrick, Chief, Section for Non-Governmental Organizations of the United Nations.

The principal speaker of the occasion was the Honorable Andrew W. Cordier, Executive Assistant to the Secretary-General of the United Nations, who paid glowing tribute to the Lions for the energetic and vital part they had played from the very beginning in the support of the United Nations and in the cause of international understanding and co-operation, lasting world peace, and human welfare.

Melvin Jones was still urging faith in the United Nations in 1948 when a harried populace was being made bitterly aware of their own frustration and inadequacy in a crisis. The intent was that the United Nations organization should grow and gain in strength, Jones pointed out at the spring meeting of the Board. It had not been considered a perfect, finished job. The United Nations had no military arm, and miracles were not to be expected. On the other hand, Jones added, he couldn't conceive of an atom-bomb war because that wasn't the Soviet way. Their way was to take over ideologically, through advance of propaganda columns. Jones cited Czechoslovakia as a case in point.

"They are working here," he went on. "They are hiring people. They are organizing. They are in South America. They are in Cuba. . . .

"But the Lions are doing a good job in hewing to the United Nations. Give the United Nations a chance to grow! Civilization has been seven or eight thousand years attaining its present state and this most revolutionary step toward world government isn't going to be taken overnight.

"Let's all get out and back the United Nations and keep backing it and keep all the nations we can in the United Nations together, so we can ward off war," he proposed.

In the latter part of 1948, Fred W. Smith, while attending the Third Plenary Sessions of the United Nations General Assembly at Paris, was asked, with eleven other representatives from among the 60-odd Non-Governmental Organizations there, to make a five-day inspection tour of the American Zone in Germany and the American sector of Berlin, as guest of General Lucius B. Clay and the American Military Government. Lions International was the only service-club organization participating in this tour.

Then on June 26, 1949, Smith, embarked on an around-the-world tour under the auspices of Town Hall. This tour included visits to fourteen capitals of the world with radiobroadcasts being made from each one. These transcribed broadcasts, edited and trimmed to size for a one-hour program on Town Hall, were flown back each week to the United States, where they were rebroadcasted coast to coast. In addition to being heard over the air from these world-famous cities, the members on the tour—representatives of twenty leading national and international organizations—had an opportunity to confer with the peoples of the countries visited, and to obtain firsthand a clearer understanding of their problems.

International peace, a world forever free of war or the threat of war, is a condition devoutly to be desired. It is the hope of every Lion; indeed, the hope of all men of good will everywhere. But peace will not manifest itself unaided. It must be striven for with earnestness and zeal. As Melvin Jones puts it:

"The Lions are doing a good work. When we were in war, we worked assiduously for victory in war. We must work just as hard to win victory in peace. And not only should we work, but we should pray also. We should be calm in the face of emergencies, because only from calmness springs intelligent thought, courage, and inspiration. Trials faced with confidence and a cheerful outlook are more than half won. We should have less doubt and more faith, less pessimism and more mental clarity."

24

LIONS INTERNATIONAL CITY

"And once again the scene was changed,
New earth there seem'd to be,
I saw the Holy City
Beside the tideless sea;
The light of God was on its streets,
The gates were open wide,
And all who would might enter,
And no one was denied.
No need of moon or stars by night,
Or sun to shine by day,
It was the new Jerusalem
That would not pass away. . ." *

"A great city is that which has the greatest men and women." ("Song of the Broad-Axe," Walt Whitman.)

For one who by no possible twist of the definition could be called a visionary, Melvin Jones has had a remarkable success looking into

*From "The Holy City" by F. E. Weatherly, published by Boosey & Company.

the future and translating dreams into tangible practicality.

"Dreams," he says, "are the fool ideas of day before yesterday that have become the commonplace miracles of today."

So it was hardly a surprise to anybody when the Lions entered upon a postwar era of prosperity and expansion with the announcement that they intended to have a city of their own . . . a real city with offices, homes, churches, memorials, and transportation terminals all in the best traditions of Lionism and exemplifying its philosophy.

"This city isn't any vision," stated Mr. Jones when somebody referred to it as a "dream city." "It got out of the dream stage long ago, and it was always something more than a gleam in an architect's eye. The site has been selected by a committee of Lions and now belongs to the International. The plans have been completed in minute detail. And the building of the physical city now depends only on the force and initiative of the Lions, who have never been lacking in either."

So the enormous energies of the organization are now directed toward the development of a community in the rolling woodlands just south of Chicago on U.S. Highway 30 (Lincoln Highway)—beginning at U.S. Highway 54, and extending east and south of the Illinois Central Railroad right of way to the Michigan Central Railroad. This site is served by the main line of the Illinois Central Railroad and its suburban electric trains, with stations at 211th Street (Lincoln Highway), and 216th Street (Matteson). Such a community will certainly be without precedent in the archives of service clubs, if not in the history of the world. Its idea spans not only the time since Secretary-General Jones's first luncheon with The Busi-

ness Circle more than thirty years ago, but the whole
gamut of human relationships.

"The whole purpose of Lionism," says Jones, "has
been to teach people the importance of the brotherhood
of man. The Lions have demonstrated that unselfishness
can be the greatest force for good in any neighborhood
no matter what size or in what country. Lions have
broken bread with one another and have worked with one
another for one another. In Lions International City, sym-
bolically at least, they may have the opportunity of living
together in a community devoted to service.

"What is a city anyway? Primarily a group of men
banded together for a common purpose. That some cities
are filled with dissension and bickering doesn't alter the
fact that unity was in the minds of the founders whether
they wanted to promote the worship of Apollo or improve
the trade with Phoenicia or only to provide a solid front
against the Sioux Indians.

"In the old countries cities first sprang into being as
fortresses in man's eternal waging of combat against his
fellow man. Later, becoming places of trade, they were
still in the primary sense fortresses. As time passed, a
civilization came to the ancient cities of the old world, but
it remained for the new world to set the fashion in cities
of peace.

"Mighty American metropolises have sprung up from
the prairies, the riverbanks, and even the desert for what
would seem to be the most trivial of reasons: there was a
water hole, or the channel of the stream, as nature had it,
was a trifle deeper; a miner with his pick struck a vein of
silver; a geologist felt rather than saw crude oil; a stubborn
farmer refused a railroad right of way through his land,

so the road went to another section owner; a man opened a roadside trading post at what he thought rightly was about the end of a day's trek on the way to the western gold fields. These became giant marts of commerce and industry

"Many cities," continued Jones, "characterized by the purposes of the men who built them, have been famous through the years, some of them even in their ashes. . . . The Holy City, which was Jerusalem; Rome, the Eternal City; Paris, the City of Light; Petra, the 'rose-red city half as old as time'; Philadelphia, the city of brotherly love; Damascus, city of hammers; Athens, city of learning; Angkor, city of imperishable might; Butte, Montana, city of fallen stars. . . . Less poetically we have the cities of industry and commerce and recreation—rubber city, steel city, sunshine city, mountain city, lake city, motor city, coal city, silver city—cities of churches, cities of homes, cities of mines, power plants, electrical plants, factories. . . . Some of them are already more famous for the wares they have to show than for the men and women who make up the census. Their status with posterity is something nobody would care to predict."

The Secretary-General makes his point with a quotation from "The City's Crown," by William Dudley Foulke:

What makes a city great? Huge piles of stone
Heaped heavenwards? Vast multitudes who dwell
Within wide circling walls?

True glory dwells where glorious deeds are done,
Where great men rise whose names, athwart the dusk
Of misty centuries, gleam like the sun!

> *So may the city that I love be great*
> *Till every stone shall be articulate.*

It is easy for Melvin Jones to find ancestral voices prophesying the need for a city such as he can see already taking shape.

"Vachel Lindsay had something to say on the subject in his poem 'The Building of Springfield,'" he says. "He knew that no matter how high you push up the office buildings, you don't have a city until you have the right kind of people in it:

> *. . . Record it for the grandson of your son—*
> *A City is not builded in a day;*
> *Our little town cannot complete her soul*
> *Till countless generations pass away.*

"And he was only echoing the thought of Edwin Markham:

> *Why build these cities glorious*
> *If man unbuilded goes?*
> *In vain we build the world unless*
> *The builder also grows.*

"And Thucydides, who would have made a great Lion, antedated all of them:

"'And when Athens shall appear great to you,' he said, 'consider, then, that her glories were purchased by valiant men and by men that learned their duty, by men that were sensible of dishonor when they came to act; by such men as, though they failed in their attempt, yet would not be wanting to the city with their virtue, but made unto it a most honorable contribution.'

"So we are building a city on a principle and our

materials will be men and ideals as well as bricks and mortar."

The sort of city it is going to be is set forth in the petition that gave it being:

Lions International City

TO provide a permanent home for Lions International, buildings and other equipment necessary to take care of the headquarters' staff, which is constantly increasing in size, and to make available homes for employees and other Lions who may want homes within the City, together with all other facilities that come within the natural scope of a city;

TO provide for the erection of a printing plant and storehouses for paper, supplies, and other necessary material;

TO provide for the printing of all publications issued by Lions International and for the distribution of supplies and material to the thousands of Lions Clubs in the Association;

TO provide for the installation of a post office, express and freight offices for dispatching the thousands of pieces of mail which go out of the International offices each day, and switch tracks for loading and unloading;

TO make provision for a hotel and parking facilities for visiting Lions and guests;

TO make available facilities for the hospitalization and care of retired employees;

TO provide for the establishment of a library, a house of worship, a Lions museum, a memorial where busts or statues may permanently commemorate·some of

the eminent leaders of Lionism, a mausoleum, a
chapel, and a tower as a shrine to those Lions who
have passed on, where visitors may offer up a prayer
for those whom they wish to memorialize;

TO provide for the establishment of schools and colleges,
not only for educational purposes but also for the
purpose of creating and fostering a spirit of generous
consideration among the peoples of the world, to the
end that through intelligence, forbearance, understanding, patience, and diplomacy, statesmen of the
world may "beat their swords into plowshares, and
their spears into pruning hooks; nation shall not lift
up sword against nation, neither shall they learn
war any more"; to promote the theory and practice of the principles of good government and
good citizenship; to hold friendship as an end and
not as a means; and "to be careful with my criticism
and liberal with my praise; to be true to myself."

25

DEMONSTRATION OF THE JONES LAW

IT becomes pretty obvious at this point that the Lions are the fastest growing and most influential group of their kind in the world. And since Lionism grew out of the simple philosophy of "Melvin Jones's Law"—*you can't get very far without doing something for somebody else*—it follows that the truth of the law has been fairly well established. Melvin Jones, himself, is more than a little surprised at the results.

It was never his intention to set himself up as a spiritual leader or to make a religion out of the realistic creed that decency in business as well as in one's personal life brings a considerable return this side of the grave. He had been interested in friendship. He had abhorred loneliness. He had tried to bring kindred spirits together for the personal motive that he liked to meet people himself and in the instinctive realization that all men are gregarious. He would probably have liked to go through life as a sort of permanent entertainment committee, leading the band, giving verve to the choruses, lending most of his time to the promotion of gaiety. But his philosophy—his personal application of the golden rule—took him far into other fields. Whether he wanted to be or not, he had become a great spiritual force in the order he had founded.

He has been led to preach on a number of texts during the years—an interest in good government, aid to underprivileged children, pride in one's community, support of educational projects, and active participation in all programs for the common good. . . . But he never got very far from his fundamental idea of how human beings ought to behave. In all his public pronouncements the keynote has been unselfishness. He speaks now with complete confidence—not that he ever lacked it—and the inspiriting knowledge that the Jones Law has become more than a theory.

Edwin Markham has expressed the essence of the Jones Law in his celebrated quatrain:

> *There is a destiny that makes us brothers;*
> *None goes his way alone;*
> *All that we send into the lives of others*
> *Comes back into our own.*

David Lawrence, in an article, "I Saw America," in the *Saturday Evening Post*, gave wholehearted support to a proposition that Melvin Jones has been dingdonging into the ears of the world for better than thirty years:

"Are we developing leaders? I am sure that we are. . . . I am more and more impressed, for example, with the work the service clubs are doing in the United States. . . . I have attended service-club luncheons from coast to coast in my journeys during the past quarter of a century. I find them the best instrument for the development of an awakened social responsibility that we have ever devised."

Mr. Lawrence was a little late in announcing his discovery, but Jones accepted his support uncritically.

"It doesn't make any difference who discovers truth so long as he discovers it," he once said. "Truth has been in existence longer than anybody who goes out looking for it."

He was quick to point out the immediate application of Lawrence's remarks.

"In this case," he said, "he has struck directly to the very core of Lionism. Lions Clubs build leaders. Lions Clubs serve their communities.

"It is not given to a great many men in the ordinary conduct of their lives to exercise leadership within a group; yet every member of a Lions Club has this opportunity. Group action, the ability to live with others, is the basis of our civilization. By giving the business and professional men of the community the opportunity to lead their fellow businessmen toward accomplishments that redound to the good of the entire community, Lionism is broadening and strengthening this base.

"It is not an uncommon thing for a Lions Club to accomplish the complete transformation of a man from a misanthropic, selfish individual to a community benefactor. . . . It is not uncommon for a Lions Club to effect the renovation of an entire community. I have been in more than one town where suspicion, personal ambition, and greed were so dominant, so much the motivating factors in the public life, that they were obvious in the face of every businessman you met along the Main street. Nobody would speak well of a neighbor. Nobody cared a hoot for anybody else. Yet in a few years a Lions Club brought an entirely new atmosphere to the place. Lionism had demonstrated once more that what you give to humanity you get back, that bread cast upon the waters is something different from pie in the sky when you die. . . .

"There is a great need, as David Lawrence saw, of trained community leaders whose vision is not confined to their own doorsteps but is as broad as the world itself. Lions Clubs are schooling such men."

An obvious corollary to the proposition that one should help his fellow man in general, is the rule of Lions to help one another not for material gain but for the perfection of the selfless unity that has been Lionism's chief asset and sole guarantee of continuing existence.

"Who owns this club?" inquired Melvin Jones in one of his pastoral letters. "Well I thought it was mine as much as anybody else's. . . . But from the way John has been carrying on you'd think he owned it all by himself. . . . He's the first to greet distinguished visitors. . . . He's the first to criticize all suggestions but his own. . . . And then you've heard about Frank, 'Frank thinks he owns this club. He wants to make all the motions and do all the speaking all of the time.' . . . Or maybe somebody laments in your ear that Tom or Bob or Frank or Jim has been hogging all the club honors for himself. . . . Well, who owns this club?

"In one of the suburbs of Chicago I own, at least I bought and pay taxes on, a strip of land of approximately four acres. I call it my home. One rather warm Sunday last April I strolled out to look things over. Coming to a warm, southern slope, I saw close to each other, two

garter snakes sunning themselves. Nonpoisonous snakes
are not killed on this place. The fact that they apparently
had no intentions of moving caused me to wish to drive
them to cover; so I threw my glove at them. They immediately attacked the glove, and when I tried to recover
my glove they attacked the stick; the battle they put up
indicated that they thought they owned the place. I left
them and went on to a sunny knoll. A ground squirrel
chattered defiantly in an attempt to drive me away from
his place. I chased him in his hole and mussed it up, but
had not gone far when he was out again, telling me in
his own language that this spot was his and to stay away
from it. As I came to the birdhouses I found that a fight
over ownership was going on there. The bluebirds and
the sparrows were having it out over the right to a bird
box. I arrived just in time to see Mr. Bluebird ruff a sparrow across the back, knocking him down, and as the
sparrow started to arise, Mrs. Bluebird gave him the same
sort of treatment. They, too, owned the place. Later in
the season the robins came. With the authority of ownership they built their nest under our window, and, with the
same independence, sang at their pleasure, reared back,
stuck out their breasts, and hopped happily over the lawn.
Toward summer Mr. Wren came. He picked out a box
with a small hole in it, and this impudent, saucy little
fellow drove away everyone who came near; he darted
here and there, and he owned the place. Then the bees
disputed the rights of ownership of the flowers. My wife,
who says she owns the place herself, told me to get rid
of them, but I didn't own the bees; I didn't buy them;
they came from miles around and lived there the whole
day through. But if you want to know who really owns

the place, just come prowling around and let our dog see you. Yes, the dog, the birds, the bees, *all* claim ownership of my home—the place *I* bought and on which *I* pay taxes. . . .

"It is wintertime now; snow covers the ground—there are no bees, no flowers, no birds. The bees are in their hives; the birds have gone to their winter retreats; my wife and my dog are in the South—nothing here but lifeless shrubbery and trees—yet it is the place I bought and on which I am paying taxes, but I realize now that it takes more than a piece of ground and a few trees to make a home. So I raise my sad eyes to the direction of the southern wind, and say, 'Hurry, hurry, southern breeze; bring back spring; bring back summer; bring back the flowers, the bees, the birds, my wife, my dog, and say to them that the place I thought was mine is theirs, too. I bought it. I pay taxes on it, but it is lifeless without them. Say to them that what is mine is theirs; what is theirs is mine, and together it is ours. It is our home, and our home is my home.'

"Now who owns this club — Tom? Jim? Frank? John? John likes to shake hands with everyone. Tom likes to sing. Harry likes to propose resolutions. Jim likes to be toastmaster. Frank likes to put on the boiled shirt and do the highbrow stuff. It's their club. I like to sit back and feel that I own the club too. So *my* club is *their* club and *their* club is *my* club and all together it is *our* club. And *our* club belongs to the community in which we live just as much as it belongs to us. Otherwise it could have no purpose in existence."

This, of course, is pure Jones Law given some practical application. That it should be accepted as a basis for social intercourse among business and professional men may have been remarkable in the early days when the Lions were breaking away from the luncheon-club tradition, but it's established doctrine now, one of the accepted canons of the Lions.

The concomitant of unselfishness is, of course, friendship—a fact which Melvin Jones, apparently, foresaw from the very beginning. He may never have put into words his belief that friendship is the logical and unavoidable result of mutual association in the service of somebody else. But a complete understanding of that principle of psychology has motivated all his work for Lionism.

He writes:

"I have often said that the Lions Club is a corporation of friends and has for its capital stock 'friendship.' Every member in a Lions Club is a friend of every other member, and as the members of a club are linked together, so, also, are the clubs linked together in the Association. This means that every member in a club has approximately 400,000 friends. From another point of view, every member in a club is a partner of every other member. So there are approximately 400,000 partners in this great Association of friends.

"Members of the Association place a very high value on friendship, for they have incorporated in the Lions Code of Ethics the following:

" 'To hold friendship as an end and not as a means. To hold that true friendship exists not on account of the service performed by one to another, but that true friendship demands nothing, but accepts service in the spirit in which it is given.'

"In other words, as a friend, I serve you. I demand

nothing from you. It is my privilege and my pleasure to do so, because you are my friend. You, knowing that I am your friend, knowing as a friend that I demand nothing for my service, and knowing that you cannot afford to accept service for which you cannot pay, other than from a friend, accept my service. I demand nothing; you owe nothing: I give; you accept in the spirit in which the service is rendered—the spirit of friendship.

"There is a great deal of practical wisdom in old Omar Khayyám. He knew men and he knew the world, neither of which have changed in their essentials from his day to now. And one of his observations will be with me till the day I die.

" 'He who has a thousand friends,' said Omar, 'has not a friend to spare.'

"No one could express more beautifully or more effectively the reason for our being. . . . We are primarily friends, friends to our Club, friends to our Association, friends to one another. . . . Approximately 400,000 loyal Lions, 400,000 friends, and yet not one to spare."

The words are the words of Jones, but the thought is that of all the Lions in the world.

Vincent C. Hascall
Omaha, Neb.

Richard J. Osenbaugh
Denver, Colo.

Edwin R. Kingsley
Parkersburg, W. Va.

Frank V. Birch
Milwaukee, Wis.

Walter F. Dexter
Sacramento, Calif.

Alexander T. Wells
Long Island City, N.Y.

Karl M. Sorrick
Jackson, Mich.

George R. Jordan
Dallas, Tex.

Edward H. Paine
Michigan City, Ind.

Dr. E. G. Gill
Roanoke, Va.

D. A. Skeen
Salt Lake City, Utah

Dr. Ramiro Collazo
Havana, Cuba

Clifford D. Pierce
Memphis, Tenn.

Fred W. Smith
Ventura, Calif.

Eugene S. Briggs
Enid, Okla.

L. H. Lewis
Dallas, Tex.

Dr. C. C. Reid
Denver, Colo.

Ewen W. Cameron
Minneapolis, Minn.

Ed. S. Vaught
Oklahoma City, Okla.

John S. Noel
Grand Rapids, Mich.

Harry A. Newman
Toronto, Ontario, Can.

Benjamin F. Jones
Newark, N.J.

William A. Westfall
Mason City, Iowa

Irving L. Camp
Johnstown, Pa.

Ben A. Ruffin
Richmond, Va.

Ray L. Riley
Sacramento, Calif.

Earle W. Hodges
New York, N.Y.

Julien C. Hyer
Fort Worth, Tex.

Charles H. Hatton
Wichita, Kan.

Roderick Beddow
Birmingham, Ala.

APPENDIX

PAST PRESIDENTS OF LIONS INTERNATIONAL

Perhaps some would call it luck; others might call it fate. But whatever appellation you give it, it is apparent that the Lions have always been fortunate in having just the right men as leaders of their Association. In the beginning there was L. H. Lewis, an extremely conscientious man who always did exactly what he thought was best for the Association. Highly religious, he would go to any extent to keep a friend.

Succeeding Presidents, each imbued with an earnest conviction for the necessity of establishing a firm foundation for the Association, laid their personal contributions of wisdom, energy, time, and self upon the altar of service to humanity—lawyers, businessmen, educators, doctors, all sacrificing unselfishly to firmly implant the roots of the ever-expanding tree of Lionism.

Paragraphs could be written about each of these stalwart leaders, for without them the Association's history could never have been so glorious. There is Dr. C. C. Reid, the senior Past International President still living, who so ably helped guide the Association through its formative years. Then came Ewen W. Cameron and Ed. S. Vaught, both contributing vastly to the development of the constitution, the slogan, the objects, and the code of ethics. John S. Noel, the financial wizard, was instrumental in placing the Association on a sound fiscal footing. And then there was Harry A. Newman from Toronto, Ontario, Canada, the first President of Lions International to be elected from a country other than the United States.

Throughout the history of the Association, as each new condition or situation has arisen, the right man for the job seems, happily, to have been at hand. "I have always believed it advisable," says Melvin Jones, "to have a good bookkeeper, a good salesman, and a good lawyer." And there certainly has been no dearth of good lawyers on the roster of the Association's leaders. Among the first, in the early days when the convention delegates seemed to be making an annual pastime of completely revamping the constitution, came two capable, efficient attorneys—Benjamin F. Jones and William A. Westfall—whose legal prowess lent great stability to the Association's affairs. As successive chairmen of the constitution and by-laws committee, they were instrumental in the initial establishment of a practical, working version of the constitution. For many years, Past President Westfall continued as the Association's chief adviser on legal matters, and it is only recently that this task was shifted to the able shoulders of Past President D. A. Skeen and later to those of Clifford D. Pierce.

In keeping with the optimistic business outlook of the booming late '20's, the Lions chose as their leader Irving L. Camp, truly a businessman's President, who insisted that the Association be run on a rigid business basis. Then, in close order, followed three Presidents whose outstanding abilities as public speakers are well remembered. These silver-throated orators, Ben A. Ruffin, Earle W. Hodges, and Julien C. Hyer, who thought beautiful thoughts and expressed them eloquently, were always favorite speakers among Lions Clubs everywhere.

The depth of the depression found Charles H. Hatton at the Association's helm. A banker and financier of acknowledged ability, his prudence in economic matters helped maintain a steadfast course for the Association through the perilous early '30's. Through many other pairs of competent hands passed successively the task of guiding the Association's destiny. There was Roderick Beddow, the Southern gentleman whose poise and grace lent great dignity to the Presidency; and Frank V. Birch, vigorous and aggressive, who carried the name Lions to the corners of the globe; and many others, each adding in his own way his own particular contribution. Ray L. Riley, the political-minded, stressed the importance of selecting the right leaders for the right years. Richard J. Osenbaugh did much to develop mutual understanding and good-fellowship among the members of each Lions Club. Edwin R. Kingsley, stanch and upright, with his dignified appearance and lordly bearing, was rigidly insistent that every job be well done. Lionism meant so much to him that he has made it his life's work. Walter F. Dexter, scholar and educator, opened new vistas of the work being done by all Lions Clubs throughout the world, and did much to cement inter-American relationships.

In 1940, while Hitler's war machine rolled unhampered over a startled Europe, the Lions chose as their highest officer calm, efficient Karl M. Sorrick, whose firm leadership and capable administrative ability were great stabilizing forces for the Lions as they began to prepare for the inevitable conflict. When war actually came, in December, 1941, George R. Jordan, who was then President, was the man to unite the Lions Clubs everywhere in gearing their activities to the support of the all-out effort which ultimately proved victorious for the freedom-loving peoples of the world. Carrying on and co-ordinating the work of the Lions during those dark war years were two other capable leaders, Edward H. Paine—the indefatigable traveler, lecturer, and authority on world history—and Dr. E. G. Gill—internationally famous surgeon—each advocating extensive indoctrination in the philosophy of Lionism as a panacea for the world's ills.

Even before the close of World War II, the Lions were laying the foundation for their participation in the establishment of a lasting peace. The intervening years have brought to the Association's highest office such earnest seekers-after-world-peace as D. A. Skeen, Ramiro Collazo, Clifford D. Pierce, Fred W. Smith, and Eugene S. Briggs, all of whom have ably represented the Lions in their work with the United Nations. For the leadership of these men, laboring tirelessly to establish international amity and good will among men of all nations, the Association and the world will be forever grateful.

The Lions will long remember all the great leaders of their Association. Through the years as the Association has grown, the Lions have never forgotten their fellow members who have served and passed on. Many years ago there was instituted as one of the most important parts of their annual International Convention program, a Necrology Ceremony paying solemn tribute to deceased fellow Lions. The presentation of this impressive ceremony has always been pretty much the province of the Past International Presidents, and, since the Pittsburgh Convention in 1939, has largely been handled by Vincent C. Hascall and Alexander T. Wells, and since Hascall's death in 1946, exclusively by Wells.

Here, then, for posterity, is the list of Past Presidents of The International Association of Lions Clubs, whom the Lions look upon as the elder statesmen of their great Association. Some have passed through "the old door, set in a garden wall," but those who are still living have never ceased to contribute their counsel and guidance for the welfare of the Association they love and to which they have rendered the full measure of devotion.

*L. H. Lewis	Dallas, Texas
Dr. C. C. Reid	Denver, Colorado
Ewen W. Cameron	Minneapolis, Minnesota
Ed. S. Vaught	Oklahoma City, Oklahoma
*John S. Noel	Grand Rapids, Michigan
Harry A. Newman	Toronto, Ontario, Canada
*Benjamin F. Jones	Newark, New Jersey
William A. Westfall	Mason City, Iowa
*Irving L. Camp	Johnstown, Pennsylvania
*Ben A. Ruffin	Richmond, Virginia
Ray L. Riley	Sacramento, California
*Earle W. Hodges	New York, New York
Julien C. Hyer	Fort Worth, Texas
*Charles H. Hatton	Wichita, Kansas
Roderick Beddow	Birmingham, Alabama
*Vincent C. Hascall	Omaha, Nebraska
Richard J. Osenbaugh	Denver, Colorado
Edwin R. Kingsley	Parkersburg, West Virginia
Frank V. Birch	Milwaukee, Wisconsin
*Walter F. Dexter	Sacramento, California
Alexander T. Wells	Long Island City, New York
Karl M. Sorrick	Jackson, Michigan
George R. Jordan	Dallas, Texas
Edward H. Paine	Michigan City, Indiana
Dr. E. G. Gill	Roanoke, Virginia

*Deceased

D. A. Skeen	Salt Lake City, Utah
Dr. Ramiro Collazo	Havana, Cuba
Clifford D. Pierce	Memphis, Tennessee
Fred W. Smith	Ventura, California
Eugene S. Briggs	Enid, Oklahoma

LIONS CLUBS ABROAD

The countries or geographic divisions in which Lions Clubs have been established as of June 30, 1949, are: Australia, Bermuda, Bolivia, British Honduras, Canada, Chile, China, Colombia, Costa Rica, Cuba, Ecuador, El Salvador, France, Guatemala, Honduras, Mexico, Netherlands West Indies, Nicaragua, Norway, Panama, Peru, Philippine Islands, Sweden, Switzerland, United States (including Alaska, Hawaii, and Puerto Rico), and Venezuela.

Clubs and members were distributed in this territory as follows:

UNITED STATES

STATES AND TERRITORIES	CLUBS	MEMBERS
Alabama	107	4,914
Alaska	6	394
Arizona	37	1,621
Arkansas	108	5,326
California	450	25,209
Colorado	100	5,337
Connecticut	47	2,614
Delaware	29	1,566
District of Columbia	11	807
Florida	131	6,385
Georgia	155	7,034

STATES AND TERRITORIES	CLUBS	MEMBERS
Hawaii	24	1,484
Idaho	54	2,628
Illinois	329	17,562
Indiana	289	15,244
Iowa	139	7,089
Kansas	155	7,772
Kentucky	171	6,712
Louisiana	120	6,076
Maine	54	2,702
Maryland	115	6,040
Massachusetts	108	5,484
Michigan	226	11,164
Minnesota	85	4,651
Mississippi	111	4,503
Missouri	157	8,485
Montana	51	2,645
Nebraska	105	4,420
Nevada	18	1,118
New Hampshire	25	1,271
New Jersey	149	7,114
New Mexico	47	2,863
New York	257	12,702
North Carolina	186	9,604
North Dakota	32	1,657
Ohio	260	13,347
Oklahoma	137	7,503
Oregon	94	4,887
Pennsylvania	487	26,482
Puerto Rico	30	1,816
Rhode Island	18	1,526
South Carolina	92	4,860
South Dakota	18	1,059
Tennessee	123	5,808
Texas	552	32,602
Utah	97	4,392
Vermont	9	505
Virginia	139	7,749
Washington	123	6,578
West Virginia	126	5,672
Wisconsin	137	6,393
Wyoming	34	2,247
Totals	6,664	345,623

CANADA

PROVINCES	CLUBS	MEMBERS
Alberta	45	1,863
British Columbia	29	1,358
Manitoba	9	524
New Brunswick	7	225
Newfoundland	4	207
Nova Scotia	14	488
Ontario	184	9,831
Quebec	17	909
Saskatchewan	20	948
Totals	329	16,353

ALL LION COUNTRIES

	CLUBS	MEMBERS
Australia	2	56
Bermuda	1	70
Bolivia	4	62
British Honduras	1	2
Canada	329	16,353
Chile	12	441
China	2	70
Colombia	44	1,841
Costa Rica	4	169
Cuba	95	6,340
Ecuador	10	374
El Salvador	5	374
France	1	36
Guatemala	5	325
Honduras	9	383
Mexico	170	5,020
Netherlands West Indies	2	96
Nicaragua	5	239
Norway	1	20
Panama	11	479
Peru	14	770
Philippine Islands	4	122
Sweden	6	256
Switzerland	2	54
United States	6,664	345,623
Venezuela	24	1,851
Totals	7,427	381,426

A negative estimate is simpler than a positive one in bringing out the point that, in practically every state, province, or country where Lionism has been established, Lions have outdistanced other service-club groups in accumulating members. The only exceptions, according to the Secretary-General's compilation on June 30, 1949, are the states of South Dakota, Connecticut, New Hampshire, and Vermont, the territory of Alaska, the provinces of British Columbia, Quebec, Nova Scotia, and New Brunswick, the Commonwealth of Australia, and the countries of Ecuador, Peru, Norway, Nicaragua, France, China, Philippine Islands, Chile, Bolivia, Sweden, and Switzerland. In the countries where Lions are less numerous than the other groups, they generally are Johnny-come-latelies.

THE EXTENSION OF LIONISM

COUNTRY	FIRST CLUB ESTABLISHED	DATE
1. United States		June 7, 1917
a. Hawaii	Honolulu	Sept. 30, 1926
b. Puerto Rico	San Juan	Dec. 22, 1936
c. Alaska	Anchorage	June 6, 1944
2. Canada	Windsor, Ontario	March 12, 1920
3. Mexico	Nuevo Laredo	March 15, 1925
4. China	Tientsin	Oct. 1, 1926
5. Cuba	Havana	June 23, 1927
6. Panama	Cristobal-Colón	Aug. 6, 1935
7. Costa Rica	San Jose	Oct. 22, 1935
8. Colombia	Barranquilla	Jan. 20, 1936
9. Guatemala	Guatemala City	Oct. 29, 1941
10. El Salvador	San Salvador	Feb. 4, 1942
11. Honduras	Tegucigalpa	April 18, 1942
12. Nicaragua	Managua	Dec. 4, 1942
13. Venezuela	Barquisimeto	Jan. 17, 1943
14. British Honduras	Belize	March 17, 1943
15. Peru	Lima	Feb. 18, 1945
16. Neth. West Indies	Curaçao	Jan. 10, 1946
17. Bermuda	Hamilton	May 12, 1946
18. Ecuador	Quito	June 17, 1946
19. Australia	Lismore, N.S.W.	July 1, 1947
20. Sweden	Stockholm	March 24, 1948
21. Switzerland	Geneva	April 16, 1948
22. Chile	Santiago	April 24, 1948
23. France	Paris	July 26, 1948
24. Bolivia	La Paz	Oct. 15, 1948
25. Philippine Islands	Manila	March 23, 1949
26. Norway	Oslo	May 11, 1949

ANNUAL CONVENTIONS OF
THE INTERNATIONAL ASSOCIATION OF
LIONS CLUBS

FIRST ANNUAL CONVENTION

Dallas, Texas, October 8–10, 1917

The First Annual Convention was held at the Adolphus Hotel, Dallas, Texas, on October 8, 9, and 10, 1917, with delegates attending from clubs located in the following 23 cities:

TEXAS	*Abilene*	OKLAHOMA	*Ardmore*
	Austin		*Chickasha*
	Beaumont		*Muskogee*
	Dallas		*Oklahoma City*
	Fort Worth		*Tulsa*
	Houston	COLORADO	*Colorado Springs*
	Paris		*Denver*
	Port Arthur	ILLINOIS	*Chicago*
	Texarkana	ARKANSAS	*Little Rock*
	Waco	TENNESSEE	*Memphis*
	Wichita Falls	LOUISIANA	*Shreveport*
MISSOURI	*St. Louis*		

At this first convention, the name "The International Association of Lions Clubs" was officially adopted; the

Constitution was written, in which there was embodied
the wording that "no club shall hold out as one of its
objects financial benefits to its members"; the colors of
purple and gold were adopted as the official colors; and
the next convention city of St. Louis, Missouri, was selected.

The following officers were elected:

L. H. Lewis	Dallas, Texas
E. N. Kaercher	St. Louis, Missouri
Harry Meyers	Denver, Colorado

Directors elected to serve one year were:

R. A. Kleinschmidt	Oklahoma City, Oklahoma
J. L. McRee	Memphis, Tennessee
H. F. Endsley	Texarkana, Texas
R. E. Wheles	Shreveport, Louisiana
Charles J. Kirk	Houston, Texas
A. V. Davenport	Tulsa, Oklahoma

*Melvin Jones, Chicago, Illinois, was elected Secretary-
Treasurer.*

SECOND ANNUAL CONVENTION

St. Louis, Missouri, August 19–21, 1918

The Second Annual Convention was held at the Mar-
quette Hotel, St. Louis, Missouri, on August 19, 20, and
21, 1918.

The name "The International Association of Lions
Clubs" was readopted; the Lions Code of Ethics was
adopted; and Chicago, Illinois, was selected as the next
convention city.

The following officers were elected:

L. H. Lewis	Dallas, Texas
Dr. C. C. Reid	Denver, Colorado
F. C. Brinkman, Jr.	Shreveport, Louisiana

Directors elected were:

Two-year terms:	A. V. Davenport	Tulsa, Oklahoma
	Ewen W. Cameron	Minneapolis, Minnesota
One-year term:	J. J. Boyle	Houston, Texas

Melvin Jones, Chicago, Illinois, was re-elected Secretary-Treasurer.

THIRD ANNUAL CONVENTION

Chicago, Illinois, July 9–11, 1919

The Third Annual Convention was held at the Hotel LaSalle, Chicago, Illinois, on July 9, 10, and 11, 1919.

The Lions' slogan, "Liberty, Intelligence, Our Nation's Safety," was adopted; the Lions Club Objects were adopted; the Constitution was revised; and Denver, Colorado, was selected as the next convention city.

The following officers were elected:

Dr. C. C. Reid	Denver, Colorado
F. C. Brinkman, Jr.	Shreveport, Louisiana
O. C. Lasher	Ardmore, Oklahoma

Director elected was:

Three-year term:	J. J. Boyle	Houston, Texas

Melvin Jones, Chicago, Illinois, was re-elected Secretary-Treasurer.

The Board of Directors for the year was comprised of the above-named men plus the following:

A. V. Davenport	elected Director in 1918 and serving his second year
Ewen W. Cameron	elected Director in 1918 and serving his second year

FOURTH ANNUAL CONVENTION

Denver, Colorado, July 14–16, 1920

The Fourth Annual Convention was held at the Albany Hotel, Denver, Colorado, on July 14, 15, and 16, 1920. The Constitution was revised, and Oakland, California, was selected as the next convention city.

The following officers were elected:

Dr. C. C. Reid	Denver, Colorado
Ewen W. Cameron	Minneapolis, Minnesota
Harry A. Newman	Toronto, Ontario
O. C. Lasher	Ardmore, Oklahoma

Directors elected were:

Three-year terms:	Judge John F. Garner	Quincy, Illinois
	John S. Noel	Grand Rapids, Michigan
Two-year terms:	A. V. Davenport	Tulsa, Oklahoma
	Dr. J. L. Weber	Paducah, Kentucky
One-year terms:	Dr. Max Emmert	Omaha, Nebraska
	Avery Haggard	Cheyenne, Wyoming
	Skipwith W. Adams	Helena, Arkansas

Melvin Jones, Chicago, Illinois, was re-elected Secretary-Treasurer.

The Board of Directors for the year consisted of the above-named men plus the following:

J. J. Boyle	elected Director in 1919 and serving his second year

FIFTH ANNUAL CONVENTION

Oakland, California, July 19–21, 1921

The Fifth Annual Convention was held at the Hotel Oakland, Oakland, California, on July 19, 20, and 21, 1921.

The Constitution and By-Laws were revised, and Hot Springs, Arkansas, was selected as the next convention city.

The following officers were elected:

Ewen W. Cameron	Minneapolis, Minnesota
Harry A. Newman	Toronto, Ontario
W. G. Higgins	San Antonio, Texas
Dr. B. W. Beatty	Dayton, Ohio

Directors elected to serve three years were:

John Burlanek, Jr.	Cedar Rapids, Iowa
Wayland P. Cramer	Camden, New Jersey
John S. Fabling	Denver, Colorado

Melvin Jones, Chicago, Illinois, was re-elected Secretary-Treasurer.

The Board of Directors for the year consisted of the above-named men plus the following:

J. J. Boyle	elected Director in 1919 and serving his third year
Judge John F. Garner	elected Director in 1920 and serving his second year
John S. Noel	elected Director in 1920 and serving his second year
A. V. Davenport	elected Director in 1920 and serving his second year
Dr. J. L. Weber	elected Director in 1920 and serving his second year

SIXTH ANNUAL CONVENTION

Hot Springs, Arkansas, June 20–23, 1922

The Sixth Annual Convention was held at the Eastman Hotel, Hot Springs, Arkansas, on June 20, 21, 22, and 23, 1922.

The Constitution and By-Laws were revised, and Atlantic City, New Jersey, was selected as the next convention city.

The following officers were elected:

Ed. S. Vaught	Oklahoma City, Oklahoma
John S. Noel	Grand Rapids, Michigan
W. G. Higgins	San Antonio, Texas
Ray E. Bigelow	Seattle, Washington

Directors elected to serve three-year terms were:

Harry A. Newman	Toronto, Ontario
John H. Boys	Wichita, Kansas
B. A. Ruffin	Richmond, Virginia

Director elected for one year to fill unexpired term of John S Noel:

Julien C. Hyer	Fort Worth, Texas

Melvin Jones, Chicago, Illinois, was· re-elected Secretary-Treasurer.

The Board of Directors for the year consisted of the above-named men plus the following:

Judge John F. Garner	elected Director in 1920 and serving his third year
Wayland P. Cramer	elected Director in 1921 and serving his second year
John S. Fabling	elected Director in 1921 and serving his second year
John Burianek, Jr.	elected Director in 1921 and serving his second year

SEVENTH ANNUAL CONVENTION

Atlantic City, New Jersey, June 27–29, 1923

The Seventh Annual Convention was held at the Steel Pier, Atlantic City, New Jersey, on June 27, 28, and 29, 1923.

The Constitution and By-Laws were revised to provide, among other things, for (1) the election at the annual convention of all officers of the International Association except the district governors (who are elected at district conventions) and the Secretary-General and Treasurer (appointed by the Board of Directors); (2) the setting up of a Board of Governors consisting of the district governors elected in the various districts; and (3) the inclusion of the Immediate Past President as a member of the Board of Directors. Omaha, Nebraska, was selected as the next convention city.

The following officers were elected:

John S. Noel	Grand Rapids, Michigan
W. G. Higgins	San Antonio, Texas
Benjamin F. Jones	Newark, New Jersey
Ray E. Bigelow	Seattle, Washington

Directors elected to serve three-year terms were:

Ray L. Riley	Sacramento, California
Howard M. Bird	Harrisburg, Pennsylvania
Julien C. Hyer	Fort Worth, Texas

The Board of Directors for the year consisted of the above-named men plus the following:

Ed. S. Vaught	Immediate Past President
Wayland P. Cramer	elected Director in 1921 and serving his third year
John S. Fabling	elected Director in 1921 and serving his third year

John Burianek, Jr.	elected Director in 1921 and serving his third year
Harry A. Newman	elected Director in 1922 and serving his second year
John H. Boys	elected Director in 1922 and serving his second year
B. A. Ruffin	elected Director in 1922 and serving his second year

EIGHTH ANNUAL CONVENTION

Omaha, Nebraska, June 24–26, 1924

The Eighth Annual Convention was held at the City Auditorium, Omaha, Nebraska, on June 24, 25, and 26, 1924.

The Constitution and By-Laws were revised, and Cedar Point, Ohio, was selected as the next convention city.

The following officers were elected:

Harry A. Newman	Toronto, Ontario
Benjamin F. Jones	Newark, New Jersey
William A. Westfall	Mason City, Iowa
Irving L. Camp	Johnstown, Pennsylvania

Directors elected for three-year terms were:

Dr. M. M. Nielson	Salt Lake City, Utah
Fred N. Redheffer	Kansas City, Missouri
Mason M. Forbes	Duluth, Minnesota

Director elected for one year to fill the unexpired term of Harry A. Newman:

Thomas H. Halliburton   Macon, Georgia

The Board of Directors for the year consisted of the above-named men plus the following:

| John S. Noel | Immediate Past President |
| B. A. Ruffin | elected Director in 1922 and serving his third year |

John H. Boys	elected Director in 1922 and serving his third year
Ray L. Riley	elected Director in 1923 and serving his second year
Howard M. Bird	elected Director in 1923 and serving his second year
Julien C. Hyer	elected Director in 1923 and serving his second year

NINTH ANNUAL CONVENTION

Cedar Point, Ohio, June 30–July 2, 1925

The Ninth Annual Convention was held at the Breakers Hotel, Cedar Point, Ohio, on June 30 and July 1 and 2, 1925.

The Constitution and By-Laws were revised to provide, among other things, (1) that not more than one director or officer of the International Association should come from any one district; (2) that in order for a delegate to vote or a club to cast its voting strength in a district convention the delegates of the club had to be present in person at the convention; (3) that the Board of Directors of the International Association should gather data on possible convention cities and certify to the convention those cities which met convention requirements; and (4) that the Board of Directors shall manage each International convention. The convention approved the selection of San Francisco, California, as the convention city for 1926.

The following officers were elected:

Benjamin F. Jones	Newark, New Jersey
William A. Westfall	Mason City, Iowa
Irving L. Camp	Johnstown, Pennsylvania
Ben A. Ruffin	Richmond, Virginia

Directors elected for three-year terms were:

Thomas H. Halliburton	Macon, Georgia
Earle W. Hodges	Little Rock, Arkansas
Charles M. Bakewell	New Haven, Connecticut

The Board of Directors for the year consisted of the above-named men plus the following:

Harry A. Newman	Immediate Past President
Ray L. Riley	elected Director in 1923 and serving his third year
Howard M. Bird	elected Director in 1923 and serving his third year
Julien C. Hyer	elected Director in 1923 and serving his third year
Dr. M. M. Nielson	elected Director in 1924 and serving his second year
Fred N. Redheffer	elected Director in 1924 and serving his second year
Mason M. Forbes	elected Director in 1924 and serving his second year
Edward H. Ellis	Greybull, Wyoming, Chairman of Board of Governors (Director, ex officio)

TENTH ANNUAL CONVENTION

San Francisco, California, July 21–24, 1926

The Tenth Annual Convention was held at the Exposition Auditorium, San Francisco, California, on July 21, 22, 23, and 24, 1926.

The Constitution and By-Laws were revised, and the selection of Miami, Florida, as the convention city for 1927 was approved by unanimous vote.

The following officers were elected:

William A. Westfall	Mason City, Iowa
Irving L. Camp	Johnstown, Pennsylvania
Ben A. Ruffin	Richmond, Virginia
Ray L. Riley	Sacramento, California

Directors elected for three-year terms were:

Arthur C. Call	Anderson, Indiana
Carl E. Croson	Seattle, Washington
Julien C. Hyer	Fort Worth, Texas

The Board of Directors for the year consisted of the above-named men plus the following:

Benjamin F. Jones	Immediate Past President
Dr. M. M. Nielson	elected Director in 1924 and serving his third year
Fred N. Redheffer	elected Director in 1924 and serving his third year
Mason M. Forbes	elected Director in 1924 and serving his third year
Thomas H. Halliburton	elected Director in 1925 and serving his second year
Earle W. Hodges	elected Director in 1925 and serving his second year
Charles M. Bakewell	elected Director in 1925 and serving his second year
Edward H. Ellis	Chairman of Board of Governors (Director, ex officio)

ELEVENTH ANNUAL CONVENTION

Miami, Florida, June 15–18, 1927

The Eleventh Annual Convention was held at Cinderella Hall, Miami, Florida, on June 15, 16, 17, and 18, 1927.

The Constitution and By-Laws were revised to provide, among other things, that any chartered Lions Club which violated any provision of the Constitution and By-Laws and which had said violation called to its attention by the International Office might be suspended or have its charter annulled. The selection of Des Moines, Iowa, as the convention city for 1928 was approved by unanimous vote.

The following officers were elected:

Irving L. Camp	Johnstown, Pennsylvania
Ben A. Ruffin	Richmond, Virginia
Ray L. Riley	Sacramento, California
Earle W. Hodges	New York, New York

Directors elected for three-year terms were:

Judge G. H. Hastings	Winston-Salem, North Carolina
Horace S. Kerr	Columbus, Ohio
Dr. M. M. Nielson	Salt Lake City, Utah

Director elected for one year to fill the unexpired term of Earle W. Hodges:

Charles Hatton	Wichita, Kansas

The Board of Directors for the year consisted of the above-named men plus the following:

William A. Westfall	Immediate Past President
Thomas H. Halliburton	elected Director in 1925 and serving his third year
Charles M. Bakewell	elected Director in 1925 and serving his third year
Arthur C. Call	elected Director in 1926 and serving his second year
Carl E. Croson	elected Director in 1926 and serving his second year
Julien C. Hyer	elected Director in 1926 and serving his second year
Vincent C. Hascall	Omaha, Nebraska, Chairman of the Board of Governors (Director, ex officio)

TWELFTH ANNUAL CONVENTION

Des Moines, Iowa, July 10–13, 1928

The Twelfth Annual Convention was held at the Shrine Temple, Des Moines, Iowa, on July 10, 11, 12, and 13, 1928.

The Constitution and By-Laws were revised to provide, among other things, (1) that any director having served a full term of three years should be ineligible for re-election to succeed himself; and (2) that, instead of the International conventions being financed by registration fees paid by delegates or alternates, a special semiannual convention fund tax of 25¢ was to be levied upon each member and paid in advance by each club on January 1 and July 1 of each year. The selection of Louisville, Kentucky, as the convention city for 1929 was approved by unanimous vote.

The following officers were elected:

Ben A. Ruffin	Richmond, Virginia
Ray L. Riley	Johnstown, Pennsylvania
Earle W. Hodges	New York, New York
Julien C. Hyer	Fort Worth, Texas

Directors elected for three-year terms were:

Vincent C. Hascall	Omaha, Nebraska
Charles H. Hatton	Wichita, Kansas
C. H. Jameson	Tulsa, Oklahoma

Director elected for one year to fill the unexpired term of Julien C. Hyer:

Albert Thornton	Tampa, Florida

The Board of Directors for the year consisted of the above-named men plus the following:

Irving L. Camp	Immediate Past President
Arthur C. Call	elected Director in 1926 and serving his third year
Carl E. Croson	elected Director in 1926 and serving his third year

Judge G. H. Hastings	elected Director in 1927 and serving his second year
Horace S. Kerr	elected Director in 1927 and serving his second year
Dr. M. M. Nielson	elected Director in 1927 and serving his second year
N. N. Rosenquest	Eastland, Texas, Chairman of the Board of Governors (Director, ex officio)

THIRTEENTH ANNUAL CONVENTION

Louisville, Kentucky, June 18–21, 1929

The Thirteenth Annual Convention was held at the Jefferson County Armory, Louisville, Kentucky, on June 18, 19, 20, and 21, 1929.

The Constitution and By-Laws were revised to provide, among other things, (1) that the Board of Directors should have power to appoint an ex-officio member of the Board from a country other than the United States, such member to be selected by clubs in such country under such rules and regulations as might be adopted by the country's clubs; (2) that the district governors and ex-officio members of the Board of Directors should be accredited delegates to the International convention; (3) that the Chairman of the Board of Governors and all ex-officio members of the Board of Directors should be invited to all meetings of the Board with the same privileges as members of the Board except the right to vote; and (4) that the following paragraph be added to Article II, Section 1, of the Constitution as a further Lions Club Object:

*"To create and foster a spirit of generous con-
sideration among the peoples of the world through a
study of the problems of international relationships
from the standpoint of business and professional
ethics."*

The selection of Denver, Colorado, as the convention
city for 1930 was approved by unanimous vote.

The following officers were elected:

Ray L. Riley	Sacramento, California
Earle W. Hodges	New York, New York
Julien C. Hyer	Fort Worth, Texas
Robert L. McKeever	Washington, D.C.

Directors elected for three-year terms were:

Joseph R. Adams	Chicago, Illinois
Roderick Beddow	Birmingham, Alabama
A. William Yungstrom	Elmira, New York

*The Board of Directors for the year consisted of the above-
named men plus the following:*

Ben A. Ruffin	Immediate Past President
Judge G. H. Hastings	elected Director in 1927 and serving his third year
Horace S. Kerr	elected Director in 1927 and serving his third year
Dr. M. M. Nielson	elected Director in 1927 and serving his third year
Vincent C. Hascall	elected Director in 1928 and serving his second year
Charles H. Hatton	elected Director in 1928 and serving his second year
C. H. Jameson	elected Director in 1928 and serving his second year
William S. Hewlett	Bridgeport, Connecticut, Chairman of the Board of Governors (Director, ex officio)
Jack W. Connell	Toronto, Ontario, Director (ex officio), representing Canada for one year

FOURTEENTH ANNUAL CONVENTION

Denver, Colorado, July 15–18, 1930

The Fourteenth Annual Convention was held at the Municipal Auditorium, Denver, Colorado, on July 15, 16, 17, and 18, 1930.

The Constitution and By-Laws were revised to provide, among other things, (1) that the election of honorary Lion members should be made only upon the proposal by the local club and approval of the International Board of Directors; (2) that district governors should be considered officers of the International Association; (3) that the Board of Directors should be increased from nine to ten, that the full term of a Director should be shortened to two years, that no one should be eligible, when elected for a full term, to succeed himself, and that five Directors should be elected at each annual convention for a term of two years; and (4) that any district having more than 50 clubs should be entitled to an additional district governor for each additional 50 clubs or major fraction thereof, the division of districts for the purpose of election of district governors to be made by the respective district conventions and approved by the International Board of Directors.

The selection of Toronto, Ontario, Canada, as the convention city for 1931 was approved by a unanimous vote.

The following officers were elected:

Earle W. Hodges	New York, New York
Julien C. Hyer	Sacramento, California
Robert L. McKeever	Washington, D.C.
Charles H. Hatton	Wichita, Kansas

Directors elected for two-year terms were:

Richard J. Osenbaugh	Denver, Colorado
Edwin R. Kingsley	Parkersburg, West Virginia

Directors elected for one-year terms were:

Julius J. Wuerthner	Great Falls, Montana
Robert L. Phillips	Lafayette, Indiana
Jack W. Connell	Toronto, Ontario

Director elected for one year to fill unexpired term of Charles H. Hatton:

William S. Hewlett	Bridgeport, Connecticut

Director elected for one year to fill unexpired term of C. H. Jameson:

Russell B. Brown	Ardmore, Oklahoma

The Board of Directors for the year consisted of the above-named men plus the following:

Ray L. Riley	Immediate Past President
Vincent C. Hascall	elected Director in 1928 and serving his third year
Roderick Beddow	elected Director in 1929 and serving his second year
Joseph Adams	elected Director in 1929 and serving his second year
A. William Yungstrom	elected Director in 1929 and serving his second year
Dr. C. F. Starr	Mason City, Iowa, Chairman of the Board of Governors (Director, ex officio)

FIFTEENTH ANNUAL CONVENTION

Toronto, Ontario, Canada, July 14–17, 1931

The Fifteenth Annual Convention was held at the Automotive Building, Toronto, Ontario, Canada, on July 14, 15, 16, and 17, 1931.

The Constitution and By-Laws were revised to provide, among other things, (1) that one director or officer might be elected from each country other than the United States having at least 45 Lions Clubs; and (2) that the Board of Directors should have the right to appoint other and additional district governors, but that any district having 50 clubs or major fraction thereof should be entitled to have that district subdivided, the Board of Directors being required to recognize that division if the district convention so recommended.

The selection of Los Angeles, California, as the convention city for 1932 was approved by unanimous vote.

The following officers were elected:

Julien C. Hyer	Fort Worth, Texas
Charles H. Hatton	Wichita, Kansas
Roderick Beddow	Birmingham, Alabama
Vincent C. Hascall	Omaha, Nebraska

Directors elected for two-year terms were:

Jack W. Connell	Toronto, Ontario
William A. G. Fox	Philadelphia, Pennsylvania
William S. Hewlett	Bridgeport, Connecticut
Frank V. Birch	Milwaukee, Wisconsin
Dr. C. F. Starr	Mason City, Iowa
Robert L. Phillips	Lafayette, Indiana

Director elected for one year to fill unexpired term of Roderick Beddow:

Julius J. Wuerthner	Great Falls, Montana

The Board of Directors for the year consisted of the above-named men plus the following:

Earle W. Hodges	Immediate Past President
Joseph Adams	elected Director in 1929 and serving his third year

A. William Yungstrom	elected Director in 1929 and serving his third year
Richard J. Osenbaugh	elected Director in 1930 and serving his second year
Edwin R. Kingsley	elected Director in 1930 and serving his second year
Robert A. Clark	Paducah, Kentucky, Chairman of the Board of Governors (Director, ex officio)

SIXTEENTH ANNUAL CONVENTION

Los Angeles, California, July 19–22, 1932

The Sixteenth Annual Convention was held at the Biltmore Hotel, Los Angeles, California, on July 19, 20, 21, and 22, 1932.

The selection of St. Louis, Missouri, as the convention city for 1933 was approved by unanimous vote.

The following officers were elected:

Charles H. Hatton	Wichita, Kansas
Roderick Beddow	Birmingham, Alabama
Vincent C. Hascall	Omaha, Nebraska
Richard J. Osenbaugh	Denver, Colorado

Directors elected for two-year terms were:

Sam M. Braswell	Clarendon, Texas
John A. Lloyd	Portsmouth, Ohio
M. B. Mitchell	Seattle, Washington
Dr. Elliott H. Rowland	Santa Ana, California
Will Terry	Little Rock, Arkansas

The Board of Directors for the year consisted of the above-named men plus the following:

| Julien C. Hyer | Immediate Past President |
| Jack W. Connell | elected Director in 1931 and serving his second year |

William A. G. Fox	elected Director in 1931 and serving his second year
William S. Hewlett	elected Director in 1931 and serving his second year
Frank V. Birch	elected Director in 1931 and serving his second year
Dr. C. F. Starr	elected Director in 1931 and serving his second year
Robert L. Phillips	elected Director in 1931 and serving his second year
W. K. Charles	Greenwood, South Carolina, Chairman of the Board of Governors (Director, ex officio)

SEVENTEENTH ANNUAL CONVENTION

St. Louis, Missouri, July 11–14, 1933

The Seventeenth Annual Convention was held at the Jefferson Hotel, St. Louis, Missouri, on July 11, 12, 13, and 14, 1933.

The selection of Grand Rapids, Michigan, as the convention city for 1934 was approved by unanimous vote.

The following officers were elected:

Roderick Beddow	Birmingham, Alabama
Vincent C. Hascall	Omaha, Nebraska
Richard J. Osenbaugh	Denver, Colorado
Edwin R. Kingsley	Parkersburg, West Virginia

Directors elected for two-year terms were:

W. K. Charles	Greenwood, South Carolina
Harold A. Crane	Manchester, New Hampshire
Dr. E. G. Gill	Roanoke, Virginia
Alexander T. Wells	New York, New York
W. H. McClelland	Chicago, Illinois
Dr. H. Irvine Wiley	Windsor, Ontario, Canada

The Board of Directors for the year consisted of the above-named men plus the following:

Charles H. Hatton	Immediate Past President
Sam M. Braswell	elected Director in 1932 and serving his second year
John A. Lloyd	elected Director in 1932 and serving his second year
M. B. Mitchell	elected Director in 1932 and serving his second year
Dr. Elliott H. Rowland	elected Director in 1932 and serving his second year
Will Terry	elected Director in 1932 and serving his second year
Rev. W. Murray Allan	Grand Forks, North Dakota, Chairman of the Board of Governors (Director, ex officio)

EIGHTEENTH ANNUAL CONVENTION

Grand Rapids, Michigan, July 17–20, 1934

The Eighteenth Annual Convention was held at the Civic Auditorium, Grand Rapids, Michigan, on July 17, 18, 19, and 20, 1934.

Several minor changes were made in the Constitution, and the selection of Mexico City, D.F., Mexico, as the convention city for 1935 was approved by unanimous vote.

The following officers were elected:

Vincent C. Hascall	Omaha, Nebraska
Richard J. Osenbaugh	Denver, Colorado
Edwin R. Kingsley	Parkersburg, West Virginia
Frank V. Birch	Milwaukee, Wisconsin

Directors elected for two-year terms were:

Rev. W. Murray Allan	Grand Forks, North Dakota
Walter F. Dexter	Whittier, California
Fred O. Grimes	Hillsboro, Texas

| Ed H. Shea | Portland, Oregon |
| Karl M. Sorrick | Springport, Michigan |

The Board of Directors for the year consisted of the above-named men plus the following:

Roderick Beddow	Immediate Past President
W. K. Charles	elected Director in 1933 and serving his second year
Harold A. Crane	elected Director in 1933 and serving his second year
Dr. E. G. Gill	elected Director in 1933 and serving his second year
W. H. McClelland	elected Director in 1933 and serving his second year
Alexander T. Wells	elected Director in 1933 and serving his second year
Dr. H. Irvine Wiley	elected Director in 1933 and serving his second year
Wilbur J. Dixon	New Canaan, Connecticut, Chairman of the Board of Governors (Director, ex officio)

NINETEENTH ANNUAL CONVENTION

Mexico City, D.F., Mexico, July 23–25, 1935

The Nineteenth Annual Convention was held at the Palace of Fine Arts, Mexico City, D.F., Mexico, on July 23, 24, and 25, 1935.

The Constitution was revised, to clarify certain items in Article II, and the selection of Providence, Rhode Island, as the convention city for 1936 was approved by unanimous vote.

The following officers were elected:

Richard J. Osenbaugh	Denver, Colorado
Edwin R. Kingsley	Parkersburg, West Virginia
Frank V. Birch	Milwaukee, Wisconsin
Walter F. Dexter	Whittier, California

Directors elected for two-year terms were:

William P. Allen	Bartow, Florida
W. W. French	Mishawaka, Indiana
Dr. S. J. Hooper	Jackson, Mississippi
Dr. C. W. A. Spies	Jefferson Barracks, Missouri
J. Earl Tanner	Eldorado, Kansas
Thomas H. Wiley	St. Catharines, Ontario, Canada

Director elected for one year to fill the unexpired term of Walter F. Dexter:

John A. Lloyd	Portsmouth, Ohio

The Board of Directors for the year consisted of the above-named men plus the following:

Vincent C. Hascall	Immediate Past President
Rev. W. Murray Allan	elected Director in 1934 and serving his second year
Fred O. Grimes	elected Director in 1934 and serving his second year
Ed H. Shea	elected Director in 1934 and serving his second year
Karl M. Sorrick	elected Director in 1934 and serving his second year
Rodolfo M. Fernandez	Mexico City, D.F., Mexico, appointed Director (ex officio) for one year to represent Mexico
William T. Ray	Athens, Georgia, Chairman of the Board of Governors (Director, ex officio)

TWENTIETH ANNUAL CONVENTION

Providence, Rhode Island, July 21–24, 1936

The Twentieth Annual Convention was held at the Metropolitan Theatre, Providence, Rhode Island, on July 21, 22, 23, and 24, 1936.

The Constitution was revised to provide, among other

things, for an International Council composed of a representative from each country represented in or affiliated with the International Association of Lions Clubs.

The selection of Chicago, Illinois, as the convention city for 1937 was approved by unanimous vote.

The following officers were elected:

Edwin R. Kingsley	Parkersburg, West Virginia
Frank V. Birch	Milwaukee, Wisconsin
Walter F. Dexter	Whittier, California
Alexander T. Wells	New York, New York

Directors elected for two-year terms were:

J. Nelson Alexander	Providence, Rhode Island
William H. Coleman	Lewisburg, Pennsylvania
Bob J. Lyles	Austin, Texas
D. A. Skeen	Salt Lake City, Utah
George B. Timmerman	Batesburg, South Carolina

The Board of Directors for the year consisted of the above-named men plus the following:

Richard J. Osenbaugh	Immediate Past President
William P. Allen	elected Director in 1935 and serving his second year
W. W. French	elected Director in 1935 and serving his second year
Dr. S. J. Hooper	elected Director in 1935 and serving his second year
J. Earl Tanner	elected Director in 1935 and serving his second year
Thomas H. Wiley	elected Director in 1935 and serving his second year
Dr. C. W. A. Spies	elected Director in 1935 and serving his second year
Rodolfo M. Fernandez	appointed Director (ex officio) for one year to represent Mexico
Jack Minton	Nashville, Tennessee, Chairman of the Board of Governors (Director, ex officio)

TWENTY-FIRST ANNUAL CONVENTION

Chicago, Illinois, July 20–23, 1937

The Twenty-first Annual Convention was held at the Civic Opera Auditorium, Chicago, Illinois, on July 20, 21, 22, and 23, 1937.

Section 2 of Article IV of the Constitution was amended. The selection of Oakland, California, as the convention city for 1938 was approved by unanimous vote.

The following officers were elected:

Frank V. Birch	Milwaukee, Wisconsin
Walter F. Dexter	Whittier, California
Alexander T. Wells	New York, New York
Karl M. Sorrick	Jackson, Michigan

Directors elected for two-year terms were:

Rev. W. Murray Allan	Grand Forks, North Dakota
Dr. E. G. Gill	Roanoke, Virginia
Murray S. Hanes	Springfield, Illinois
Jack L. Minton	Nashville, Tennessee
Edward H. Paine	Michigan City, Indiana
R. Reid Murdock	Toronto, Ontario, Canada

The Board of Directors for the year consisted of the above-named men plus the following:

Edwin R. Kingsley	Immediate Past President
J. Nelson Alexander	elected Director in 1936 and serving his second year
William H. Coleman	elected Director in 1936 and serving his second year
Bob J. Lyles	elected Director in 1936 and serving his second year
D. A. Skeen	elected Director in 1936 and serving his second year
George B. Timmerman	elected Director in 1936 and serving his second year

Rodolfo M. Fernandez	appointed Director (ex officio) for one year to represent Mexico
Henry T. Bowers	Toledo, Ohio, Chairman of the Board of Governors (Director, ex officio)

TWENTY-SECOND ANNUAL CONVENTION

Oakland, California, July 19–22, 1938

The Twenty-second Annual Convention was held at the Civic Auditorium, Oakland, California, on July 19, 20, 21, and 22, 1938.

Section 8 of Article VIII of the Constitution was revised to provide that each Lions Club in good standing should be entitled in the district convention to one voting delegate and one alternate for each ten members of said club, or major fraction thereof.

Pittsburgh, Pennsylvania, was selected as the convention city for 1939.

The following officers were elected:

Walter F. Dexter	Sacramento, California
Alexander T. Wells	New York, New York
Karl M. Sorrick	Springport, Michigan
George R. Jordan	Dallas, Texas

Directors elected for two-year terms were:

W. H. Baxter	Seattle, Washington
Henry T. Bowers	Toledo, Ohio
Dale E. Carrell	Keokuk, Iowa
Millard B. Conklin	Daytona Beach, Florida
Bert W. Kelly	Denver, Colorado

The Board of Directors for the year consisted of the above-named men plus the following:

Frank V. Birch	Immediate Past President
Rev. W. Murray Allan	elected Director in 1937 and serving his second year

Dr. E. G. Gill	elected Director in 1937 and serving his second year
Murray S. Hanes	elected Director in 1937 and serving his second year
Jack L. Minton	elected Director in 1937 and serving his second year
Edward H. Paine	elected Director in 1937 and serving his second year
R. Reid Murdock	elected Director in 1937 and serving his second year
Rodolfo M. Fernandez	appointed Director (ex officio) for one year to represent Mexico
Carbis A. Walker	Winston - Salem, North Carolina, Chairman of the Board of Governors (Director, ex officio)

TWENTY-THIRD ANNUAL CONVENTION

Pittsburgh, Pennsylvania, July 18–21, 1939

The Twenty-third Annual Convention was held at Duquesne Garden, Pittsburgh, Pennsylvania, on July 18, 19, 20, and 21, 1939.

Havana, Cuba, was selected as the convention city for 1940.

The following officers were elected:

Alexander T. Wells	New York, New York
Karl M. Sorrick	Springport, Michigan
George R. Jordan	Dallas, Texas
Edward H. Paine	Michigan City, Indiana

Directors elected for two-year terms were:

Fred H. Gabbi	Portland, Maine
Jesse W. Kayser	Chickasha, Oklahoma
Lossie E. Morris	Collinsville, Illinois
Dr. Arthur T. Spankie	Calgary, Alberta, Canada
Henry W. Sweet	Birmingham, Alabama
Carbis A. Walker	Winston-Salem, North Carolina

The Board of Directors for the year consisted of the above-named men plus the following:

Walter F. Dexter	Immediate Past President
W. H. Baxter	elected Director in 1938 and serving his second year
Henry T. Bowers	elected Director in 1938 and serving his second year
Dale E. Carrell	elected Director in 1938 and serving his second year
Millard B. Conklin	elected Director in 1938 and serving his second year
Bert W. Kelly	elected Director in 1938 and serving his second year
Rodolfo M. Fernandez	appointed Director (ex officio) for one year to represent Mexico
Dr. Carl L. Kennedy	Montgomery, West Virginia, Chairman of the Board of Governors (Director, ex officio)

TWENTY-FOURTH ANNUAL CONVENTION

Havana, Cuba, July 23–25, 1940

The Twenty-fourth Annual Convention was held in Havana, Cuba, on July 23, 24, and 25, 1940.

New Orleans, Louisiana, was selected as the convention city for 1941.

The following officers were elected:

Karl M. Sorrick	Springport, Michigan
George R. Jordan	Dallas, Texas
Edward H. Paine	Michigan City, Indiana
Dr. E. G. Gill	Roanoke, Virginia

Directors elected for two-year terms were:

George H. Dobbins	Weyauwega, Wisconsin
George S. Johnson	La Grange, Georgia

Dr. Carl L. Kennedy	Montgomery, West Virginia
H. L. Loreman, Jr.	Salisbury, Maryland
Fred W. Smith	Ventura, California

The Board of Directors for the year consisted of the above-named men plus the following:

Alexander T. Wells	Immediate Past President
Fred H. Gabbi	elected Director in 1939 and serving his second year
Jesse W. Kayser	elected Director in 1939 and serving his second year
Lossie E. Morris	elected Director in 1939 and serving his second year
Dr. Arthur T. Spankie	elected Director in 1939 and serving his second year
Henry W. Sweet	elected Director in 1939 and serving his second year
Carbis A. Walker	elected Director in 1939 and serving his second year
Dr. Ramiro Collazo	Havana, Cuba, appointed Director (ex officio) for one year to represent Cuba
L. Russell McKee	Joplin, Missouri, Chairman of the Board of Governors (Director, ex officio)

TWENTY-FIFTH ANNUAL CONVENTION

New Orleans, Louisiana, July 22–25, 1941

The Twenty-fifth Annual Convention was held at the Municipal Auditorium, New Orleans, Louisiana, on July 22, 23, 24, and 25, 1941.

The Constitution was revised to provide that the district governors themselves, and not the district conventions, should select the district secretaries.

Toronto, Ontario, Canada, was selected as the convention city for 1942.

The following officers were elected:

George R. Jordan	Dallas, Texas
Edward H. Paine	Michigan City, Indiana
Dr. E. G. Gill	Roanoke, Virginia
D. A. Skeen	Salt Lake City, Utah

Directors elected for two-year terms were:

Dr. Harry J. Hoerner	Elgin, Illinois
G. Garland Lyell	Jackson, Mississippi
L. Russell McKee	Joplin, Missouri
L. W. Peterson	Windsor, Ontario, Canada
Kenneth F. Taylor	New Milford, Connecticut
V. Royal Vergades	Clay Center, Kansas
Dr. Ramiro Collazo	Havana, Cuba

The Board of Directors for the year consisted of the above-named men plus the following:

Karl M. Sorrick	Immediate Past President
George H. Dobbins	elected Director in 1940 and serving his second year
George S. Johnson	elected Director in 1940 and serving his second year
Dr. Carl L. Kennedy	elected Director in 1940 and serving his second year
H. L. Loreman, Jr.	elected Director in 1940 and serving his second year
Fred W. Smith	elected Director in 1940 and serving his second year
C. Arthur Johnson	Sioux City, Iowa, Chairman of the Board of Governors (Director, ex officio)

TWENTY-SIXTH ANNUAL CONVENTION

Toronto, Ontario, Canada, July 21–24, 1942

The Twenty-sixth Annual Convention was held at the Maple Leaf Gardens, Toronto, Ontario, Canada, on July 21, 22, 23, and 24, 1942.

The Constitution was revised to provide for a new membership classification, that of "pioneer members." On account of war conditions, no convention city for 1943 was selected, but it was decided that the Board of Directors would designate the time and place of holding the 1943 International convention at a later date.

The following officers were elected:

Edward H. Paine	Michigan City, Indiana
Dr. E. G. Gill	Roanoke, Virginia
D. A. Skeen	Salt Lake City, Utah
Dr. Ramiro Collazo	Havana, Cuba

Directors elected for two-year terms were:

Ernest C. Gibson	Monroe, Louisiana
Dr. Arthur S. Haines	Wilkinsburg, Pennsylvania
Thomas S. Neilson	Berkeley, California
Clifford D. Pierce	Memphis, Tennessee
Charles J. Stevenson	Cambridge, New York

The Board of Directors for the year consisted of the above-named men plus the following:

George R. Jordan	Immediate Past President
Dr. Harry J. Hoerner	elected Director in 1941 and serving his second year
G. Garland Lyell	elected Director in 1941 and serving his second year
L. Russell McKee	elected Director in 1941 and serving his second year
L. W. Peterson	elected Director in 1941 and serving his second year
Kenneth F. Taylor	elected Director in 1941 and serving his second year
V. Royal Vergades	elected Director in 1941 and serving his second year
Harold P. Nutter	Camden, New Jersey, Chairman of the Board of Governors (Director, ex officio)

TWENTY-SEVENTH ANNUAL CONVENTION

Cleveland, Ohio, July 20–22, 1943

The Twenty-seventh Annual Convention was held at the Cleveland Public Auditorium, Cleveland, Ohio, on July 20, 21, and 22, 1943.

The Constitution was revised (1) to change the name of the "International Council" to the "Board of International Relations," and (2) to provide that the Board of Directors might appoint an ex-officio member to the Executive Council of the Board of Governors from the Eastern or the Western section of Canada, whichever section did not have direct representation on the International Board of Directors or the Executive Council of the Board of Governors.

There was no voting on the 1944 convention city because of war conditions, but it was determined that the Board of Directors would designate the time and place of holding it at a later date.

The following officers were elected:

Dr. E. G. Gill	Roanoke, Virginia
D. A. Skeen	Salt Lake City, Utah
Dr. Ramiro Collazo	Havana, Cuba
Clifford D. Pierce	Memphis, Tennessee

Directors elected for two-year terms were:

C. P. Dodson	Decatur, Texas
Edgar M. Elbert	Maywood, Illinois
Dr. Charles O. Lennox	New Toronto, Ontario, Canada
Harold P. Nutter	Camden, New Jersey
Chris D. Russell	Maysville, Kentucky
Howard R. Sisson	St. Joseph, Missouri

*Director elected for one year to fill unexpired term of Clif-
ford D. Pierce:*

    Thomas N. Fowler   Seattle, Washington

*The Board of Directors for the year consisted of the above-
named men plus the following:*

Edward H. Paine	Immediate Past President
Ernest O. Gibson	elected Director in 1942 and serving his second year
Dr. Arthur S. Haines	elected Director in 1942 and serving his second year
Thomas S. Neilson	elected Director in 1942 and serving his second year
Charles J. Stevenson	elected Director in 1942 and serving his second year
W. Russell Porter	New Bedford, Massachusetts, Chairman of the Board of Governors (Director, ex officio)

TWENTY-EIGHTH ANNUAL CONVENTION

Chicago, Illinois, August 1–3, 1944

The Twenty-eighth Annual Convention was held at
the Chicago Civic Opera House, Chicago, Illinois, on
August 1, 2, and 3, 1944.

The Constitution was revised to provide, among other
things, that the time and place of meeting of the International convention should be determined by the Board
of Directors instead of having the selection made by the
convention.

The following officers were elected:

D. A. Skeen	Salt Lake City, Utah
Dr. Ramiro Collazo	Havana, Cuba
Clifford D. Pierce	Memphis, Tennessee
Fred W. Smith	Ventura, California

Directors elected for two-year terms were:

E. B. Brant	St. Petersburg, Florida
Eugene S. Briggs	Enid, Oklahoma
Thomas N. Fowler	Seattle, Washington
W. Russell Porter	New Bedford, Massachusetts
Ralph M. Sheehan	Marquette, Michigan

Director elected for a one-year term was:

Joaquin Garza y Garza	Monterrey, Mexico

The Board of Directors for the year consisted of the above-named men plus the following:

Dr. E. G. Gill	Immediate Past President
C. P. Dodson	elected Director in 1943 and serving his second year
Edgar M. Elbert	elected Director in 1943 and serving his second year
Dr. Charles O. Lennox	elected Director in 1943 and serving his second year
Harold P. Nutter	elected Director in 1943 and serving his second year
Chris D. Russell	elected Director in 1943 and serving his second year
Howard R. Sisson	elected Director in 1943 and serving his second year
Ronald B. Laing	Abilene, Kansas, Chairman of the Board of Governors (Director, ex officio)

1945—No Convention Held

The Board of Directors of Lions International, in session at San Francisco, California, on June 5, 1945, passed a resolution directing the International President to call an annual convention of the Association for September 10, 1945, at St. Louis, Missouri. The call was issued as directed, but due to restrictions on transportation imposed by the Office of Defense Transportation and other circumstances beyond the Association's control, the Board found it necessary to postpone the 1945 International convention so as to have it called and held in conjunction with the 1946 convention, and the President declared it postponed.

The Board of Directors did meet on September 10, 1945, however, and received resignations from those whose terms were expiring and proceeded to fill the vacancies thus created.

The following officers were elected:

Dr. Ramiro Collazo	Havana, Cuba
Clifford D. Pierce	Memphis, Tennessee
Fred W. Smith	Ventura, California
Eugene S. Briggs	Enid, Oklahoma

Directors elected for two-year terms were:

Ronald B. Laing	Abilene, Kansas
G. W. Brentlinger	Lima, Ohio
Ralph F. Lesemann	East St. Louis, Illinois
John W. Mentzer	McConnellsburg, Pennsylvania
H. C. Petry, Jr.	Carrizo Springs, Texas
Walter C. Fisher	Queenston, Ontario, Canada

Director elected for one-year term was:

Francisco Doria-Paz	Mexico City, D.F., Mexico

Director elected for one year to fill unexpired term of Eugene S. Briggs:

Ellis Loveless	Norfolk, Virginia

The Board of Directors for the year consisted of the above-named men plus the following:

E. B. Brant	elected Director in 1944 and serving his second year
Thomas N. Fowler	elected Director in 1944 and serving his second year

W. Russell Porter	elected Director in 1944 and serving his second year
Ralph M. Sheehan	elected Director in 1944 and serving his second year
Teodoro Mendez	Caracas, Venezuela, appointed Director (ex officio) for one year to represent Venezuela
John H. Kalte	High Point, North Carolina, Chairman of the Board of Governors (Director, ex officio)

TWENTY-NINTH ANNUAL CONVENTION

Philadelphia, Pennsylvania, July 16–19, 1946

The Twenty-ninth Annual Convention was held at the Municipal Auditorium, Philadelphia, Pennsylvania, on July 16, 17, 18, and 19, 1946.

The Constitution and By-Laws were revised to provide, among other things, (1) that the words "from the standpoint of business and professional ethics" be deleted following the word "relationships" in the Objects of the Association so that this would read, "To create and foster a spirit of 'generous consideration' among the peoples of the world through a study of the problems of international relationships"; (2) that a new club in a city having two or more Lions Clubs could obtain members only within the territory in which they met; (3) that there should be a new membership classification of "father and son"; (4) that all Lions Clubs should be under the jurisdiction of the Board of Directors; and (5) that the International Association should have new officers of Assistant Secretary-General, Secretary, and Assistant Secretaries, and that the number of Directors on the International Board from the United States should be increased from 10 to 16. The

Board of International Relations, and what it might do, was also defined.

The following officers were elected:

Clifford D. Pierce	Memphis, Tennessee
Fred W. Smith	Ventura, California
Eugene S. Briggs	Enid, Oklahoma
Walter C. Fisher	Queenston, Ontario, Canada

Directors elected for two-year terms were:

Francisco Doria-Paz	Mexico City, D.F., Mexico
James F. Daniel, Jr.	Greenville, South Carolina
A. E. Hukle	Lexington, Kentucky
H. E. Johnson	Davenport, Iowa
John H. Kalte	High Point, North Carolina
Howard K. Lewis	Indianapolis, Indiana
Ellis Loveless	Norfolk, Virginia
Harold P. Nutter	Camden, New Jersey
Dr. L. A. Rademaker	Salisbury, Maryland

Directors elected for one-year terms were:

Parke T. Gilbert	Casa Grande, Arizona
Arthur Hinman	Portland, Maine
Sidney T. Roebuck	Newton, Mississippi

The Board of Directors for the year consisted of the above-named men plus the following:

Dr. Ramiro Collazo	Immediate Past President
Ronald B. Laing	elected Director in 1945 and serving his second year
Ralph F. Lesemann	elected Director in 1945 and serving his second year
John W. Mentzer	elected Director in 1945 and serving his second year
H. C. Petry, Jr.	elected Director in 1945 and serving his second year
Teodoro Mendez	appointed Director (ex officio) for one year to represent Venezuela
Roy P. Herold	Wheeling, West Virginia, Chairman of the Board of Governors (Director, ex officio)

THIRTIETH ANNUAL CONVENTION

San Francisco, California, July 28–31, 1947

The Thirtieth Annual Convention was held at the Civic Auditorium, San Francisco, California, on July 28, 29, 30, and 31, 1947.

The following officers were elected:

Fred W. Smith	Ventura, California
Eugene S. Briggs	Enid, Oklahoma
Walter C. Fisher	Queenston, Ontario, Canada
H. C. Petry, Jr.	Carrizo Springs, Texas

Directors elected for two-year terms were:

Richard C. Bell	White Hall, Illinois
Harold E. Curran	Syracuse, New York
Dr. Rene de La Valette	Guanabacoa, Cuba
Parke T. Gilbert	Casa Grande, Arizona
S. A. Dodge	Detroit, Michigan
Roy P. Herold	Wheeling, West Virginia
C. H. McNulty	Melbourne, Florida
Caye A. Nelson	Baton Rouge, Louisiana
Monroe L. Nute	Kennett Square, Pennsylvania

The Board of Directors for the year consisted of the above-named men plus the following:

Clifford D. Pierce	Immediate Past President
James F. Daniel, Jr.	elected Director in 1946 and serving his second year
Francisco Doria-Paz	elected Director in 1946 and serving his second year
A. E. Hukle	elected Director in 1946 and serving his second year
H. E. Johnson	elected Director in 1946 and serving his second year
John H. Kalte	elected Director in 1946 and serving his second year
Ellis Loveless	elected Director in 1946 and serving his second year

Howard K. Lewis	elected Director in 1946 and serving his second year
Harold P. Nutter	elected Director in 1946 and serving his second year
Dr. L. A. Rademaker	elected Director in 1946 and serving his second year
Dr. Manuel A. Rueda V.	Bogotá, Colombia, appointed Director (ex officio) to represent Gran Colombia for one year
Jesus Maria Sosa D.	Panama, R.P., appointed Director (ex officio) for one year to represent Central America
Jack Peddycord	Seattle, Washington, Chairman of the Board of Governors (Director, ex officio)

THIRTY-FIRST ANNUAL CONVENTION

New York, New York, July 26–29, 1948

The Thirty-first Annual Convention was held at Madison Square Garden, New York, New York, on July 26, 27, 28, and 29, 1948.

The following officers were elected:

Eugene S. Briggs	Enid, Oklahoma
Walter C. Fisher	Queenston, Ontario, Canada
H. C. Petry, Jr.	Carrizo Springs, Texas
Harold P. Nutter	Camden, New Jersey

Directors elected for two-year terms were:

Harold A. Ashley	Waterbury, Connecticut
A. B. Dredge	Springfield, Ohio
Salvador Franco-Urias	Mexico City, D.F., Mexico
Edward H. McMahan	Brevard, North Carolina
Verne Miller	Dyer, Indiana
Jack Peddycord	Seattle, Washington
Jules C. Ricker	Washington, D.C.
James A. Sherrill	Chattanooga, Tennessee
Clarence L. Sturm	Manawa, Wisconsin

The Board of Directors for the year consisted of the above-named men plus the following:

Fred W. Smith	Immediate Past President
Richard C. Bell	elected Director in 1947 and serving his second year
Harold E. Curran	elected Director in 1947 and serving his second year
Dr. Rene de La Valette	elected Director in 1947 and serving his second year
S. A. Dodge	elected Director in 1947 and serving his second year
Parke T. Gilbert	elected Director in 1947 and serving his second year
Roy P. Herold	elected Director in 1947 and serving his second year
C. H. McNulty	elected Director in 1947 and serving his second year
Caye A. Nelson	elected Director in 1947 and serving his second year
Monroe L. Nute	elected Director in 1947 and serving his second year
Dr. Jose R. Chiriboga	Quito, Ecuador, appointed Director (ex officio) for one year to represent Gran Colombia
Jesus Maria Sosa D.	Panama, R.P., appointed Director (ex officio) for one year to represent Central America
Melvin B. Wright	Salt Lake City, Utah, Chairman of the Board of Governors (Director, ex officio)

INDEX

Aberdeen, S. Dak., 172
Abilene, Tex., 121
Adams, Joseph R., 131
Addison, 149
Aigner, George, 131
Akeley, Carl, 29
Alfaro, Ricardo J., 225
Algonquin Round Table, 13
Allan, the Rev. W. M., 72
Allison, Walter, 108
Amarillo, Tex., 115
American Mercury, The, 41, 42, 43
American Medical Association, 15
American Red Cross, 159, 206
Ames, Iowa, 72
Ancaster, Ontario, 168
Andalusia, Ala., 188
Androcles, 32
Angkor, 233
Annapolis, Md., 108
Apollo Club, 110
Ardmore, Okla., 121, 141-42
Armstrong, H. R., 77
Atchison, Kans., 199-200
Athens, Greece, 233, 234
Atlantic City, N.J., 80, 94, 167
Austin, Tex., 121, 131

Baedecker, 42
Ball-Burton-Hatch-Hill Resolution, 214
Baltimore, Md., 43, 121
Batesville, Ark., 171
Beatty, Clyde, 30, 36
Beaumont, Tex., 121, 138
Beddow, Roderick, 249, 251
Belle Fourche, S. Dak., 75
Benson, Phil, 118
Berkeley, Calif., 185
Bessemer, Ala., 170
Binghamton, N.Y., 107
Birch, Frank V., 249, 251
Bird, William R., 216
Blink, Maury, 22, 25, 35, 131
Bliven, Bruce, 42, 143
Bonheur, Rosa, 34, 129

Bonham, George A., 183
Boulder, Colo., 199
Bradley, Dr. Preston, 217
Braille, 131, 184-85
Brandt, Harold, 118
Bretton Woods, 215
Bridgeport, Conn., 178
Briggs, Eugene S., 250, 252
Broomtown, 186
Brown, Russell B., 134
Buck, Frank, 30
Buffalo Bill's grave, 76
Burlingame, Calif., 196
Burrows. Bob, 145
Business Circle, The, 2-9, 10, 11, 14, 16, 17, 20, 21, 22, 23, 24, 26, 27, 74, 131, 231
Business Confidence Week, 200-202
Business Man's Prayer, 27
Butler, Ellis Parker, 101
Butte, Mont., 233
Byrd, Admiral Richard, 81
Byrnes, James F., 223

Calipatria, Calif., 118
Camden, N.J., 185, 209
Cameron, Ewen W., 102, 114, 247, 251
Camp, Irving L, 181, 248, 251
Caracas, Venezuela, 121
Carlson, C. W., 154
Cedar Point, Ohio, 78
Central Club, 131, 133
Centralia (Ill.) mine disaster, 206
Century of Progress, 108-9
Chattanooga, Tenn., 157, 209
Cheshire Cheese, London, 13
Chicago (Auburn Park), Ill., 139
Chicago (Central), Ill., 131, 133
Chicago, Ill., 4, 5, 16, 34, 35, 37, 59, 64, 68, 69, 80, 100, 108, 111, 121, 240
Chicago Civic Opera, 123
Chickasha, Okla., 121
Cibicu Creek, 4
Cincinnati, Ohio, 183

301

Cincinnati (Price Hill), Ohio, 173
Cirgonians, 25
Citizenship and Patriotism Code, 71-73
Civil Club, London, 13, 20
Clay, General Lucius B., 228
Clearwater, Fla., 179-80
Clemens, Charles B., 21
Cleveland, Ohio, 214
Clovernook Home, 183
Cobb, Irvin S., 101
Cohen, Benjamin, 225
Collazo, Dr. Ramiro, 123, 124, 250, 252
Collier's magazine, 190
Colorado Springs, Colo., 121
Columbus, Ohio, 121
Comstock, Andy, 131
Conings, Denis, 124
Connally, Senator Tom, 220
Cook County Lions Clubs, 128
Coral Sea (battle), 51
Cordier, Andrew W., 227
Cordova, Ala., 175
Corley, Mary, 188
Cothan, Judge C. T., 44, 45
Cowan, Ike, 200
Cripe, Arlie J., 60
Crook, Colo., 49
Cuba, 122, 123
Cumberland, Md., 145
Cunningham, G. M., 59
Curwood, James Oliver, 101
Custer, S. Dak., 45
Cut Bank, Mont., 118

Dallas, Tex., 54, 57, 59, 92, 121, 127
Davenport, A. V., 48
Davis, Lawrence, 201
Declaration of Independence, 70
de Laderbis, E., 124-25
Denver, Colo., 64, 69, 76-77, 78, 116, 121
Department of State, 214, 215, 220
Detroit, Mich., 122
Detroit (East Side), Mich., 186
de Vry, Cy, 30

Dexter, Dr. Walter F., 64, 249, 251
Dillon, John J., 175
Dix, Dorothy, 105
Douglas, John C., 153
Downer's Grove, Ill., 196
Dumbarton Oaks, 212, 214, 215

Eagles, the, 134
East Liberty, Pa., 121, 179
Edinburgh University, 72
Eichelberger, Clark M., 227
Elbert, Edgar, 38
Elks, the, 134
EL LEON (magazine), 89, 105-6, 216
El Paso (Texas) *Times*, 174
El Reno, Okla., 121
Emmitsburg, Md., 175
Endsley, H. F., 60

Farley, Jim, 10
Fellows, Esther, 184
F.F.V.'s, 53
Florida, 192
Fort Thomas, Ariz., 4
Fort Worth, Tex., 121
Forum, 42
Founders Day, 127-28, 131, 133
Foulke, William Dudley, 233
Fredericksburg, Tex., 50
Fredonia, Pa., 174
Friendship Train, 205
Fry, Frank, 131
Fullbright Resolution, 214
Fullmer, F. W., 131

Galland, Jean-Paul, 125-26
Galli-Curci, 123
Garden, Mary, 123
"Garner, Jack," 37-38
Gary, Ind., 114
Geneva, Switzerland, 126, 170
Germany, Gene, 37

Geronimo, 4
Gila River, 4
Gill, Dr. E. G., 250, 251
Glaydes, Dr. J. E., 186
Glenwood Springs, Colo., 215
"God Bless America," 113-14
Grand Forks, N. Dak., 72
Grand Rapids, Mich., 121
Green, Al, 114-15
Greenville, Tex., 121
Guines, Cuba, 122, 138
Gullett, George, 118

Hallenbeck, F. M., 24
Halsey, Admiral William, 108
Hamilton, Bermuda, 170
Hamilton, J. Ed, 142
Harlan, Ky., 208
Hartford, Conn., 112
Hascall, Vincent C., 51, 251
Hatton, Charles H., 189, 249, 251
Havana (Guines), Cuba, 122, 138
Havana, Cuba, 121, 122, 222
Hays, Dr. Powell L., 179
Hertig, Captain, 4
Hewer, John, 123
Hickory Ridge, Ark., 196
Higgins, Colonel W. G., 37, 123
Hines, Edward, 3
Hirsch, August J., 60
Hodges, Earle W., 249, 251
Holmes, Burton, 81
Honolulu, 125
Hooker, E. C., 3
Hot Springs, Ark., 60
Houston, Tex., 59, 121
Howick, Ontario, 169
Huerta, President, 1
Hugo, Okla., 154
Hundt, Walter, 153
Hurst, E. F., 60
Hyer, Julien C., 249, 251

Illinois Central Railroad, 231

Insurance Exchange Building, Chicago, 92, 99
I.W.W., 69

Jacksonville, Ill., 196
Jerusalem, 233
Jewel Cave National Monument, 196
Johnson, Dr., 149
Johnson & Higgins, 5
Johnson, Martin, 29, 31
Johnstown, Pa., 181
Jones, Benjamin F., 114, 248, 251
Jones, Captain John C., 4
Jones's Law, 13, 20, 39, 40, 237, 238
Jones, Melvin, 1, 2, 3, 4, 6, 7, 9,
  10, 11, 12, 16, 17, 18, 19, 21,
  24, 25, 28, 30, 31, 34, 35, 36,
  37, 38, 39, 43, 45, 47, 53, 54,
  56, 57, 59, 60, 62, 65, 66, 68,
  71, 72, 74, 75, 78, 79, 81, 85,
  86, 87, 91, 92, 93, 94, 95, 96,
  97, 98, 99, 100, 101, 103, 110,
  115, 117, 118, 124, 127, 128,
  130, 131, 140, 150, 151, 157,
  158, 167, 184, 202, 215, 217,
  224, 227, 228, 229, 230, 231,
  233, 234, 238, 240, 243, 244
Jones, Rose Amanda Freeman, 16,
  18, 74, 86, 133
Jonesville, Ark., 199
Jordan, George R., 250, 251
Justinian Codex, 60

Kalamazoo, Mich., 36
Kalaupapa, T. H., 125
Kearcher, E. N., 26
Keaton, R. Roy, 83
Keller, Helen, 78
Kellogg, Robert, 112
Khayyám, Omar, 244
Kingsley, Edwin R., 249, 251
Kirkland Lake, Ontario, 179
Kleinschmidt, R. E., 59, 76
Knox, Frank, 202

Kurtz, Oscar C., 103, 104
Kyne, Peter B., 101

Laderbis, E. de, 124-25
Ladies' Nights, 145, 146, 149
La Guardia, Fiorello, 109
Lake Charles, La., 121
Lakeview, Ill., 154
Lake Zurich, Ill., 196
La Porte, Ind., 173
Lark, Utah, 196
Lasher, C. C., 141-43
Lawrence, David, 238, 239, 24ᵣ
Lawrenceville, Ga., 175
Leaside, Ontario, 169
Lewis, L. H., 247, 251
Lewis, Sinclair, 31, 41
Lie, Trygve, 224
Life Magazine, 107
Lima, Peru, 121
Lindsay, Vachel, 234
Lion of Judah, 29
LION, THE (magazine), 51, 53, 89,
    99, 101, 104, 110, 125, 129, 134,
    155, 157, 181, 200, 202, 216, 218
Lions Board of Governors, 79
Lions Board of International Re-
    lations, 79, 82, 83
Lions Club Objects, 63-68, 76, 195
Lions Clubs (an Indiana corpora-
    tion), 25
Lions Code of Ethics, 56, 60, 62,
    76, 195
Lions District Organization plan,
    81
Lions, International Association,
    2, 9, 16, 35, 39, 43, 47, 48,
    49, 50, 57, 62, 63, 65, 72, 74,
    112, 116, 127, 177, 202, 224, 228
Lions International City, 230-36
Lions International Convention,
    36, 214
Lions International Counsellors, 83
Lions International Office, 86-87
Lion Tamer, 140, 151
Lismore, Australia, 169
"Little Beaver," 139
Little Rock, Ark., 44, 121, 200

Livingston, Bill, 22, 24, 131
London, England, 41, 221
Long Beach, Calif., 184, 199, 206
Lookout Mountain, 77
Lord, Frank, 30
Los Angeles, Calif., 178
Louisville, Ky., 79
Lubbock, Tex., 121
Lumpkin, Ga., 188
Lybrand, Walter, 59, 76
Lyles, Bob, 131

Manila, Ark., 171
Markham, Edwin, 234, 238
Marseilles, France, 210
Mason City, Iowa, 179
Matteson, Ill., 231
Maury, Dr., 188
McCarthy, Dr. M. F., 167, 183, 184,
    189
McCormick Building, Chicago, 86,
    87, 90, 93, 130
McLeish, Archibald, 215
Mel Chico, 37
Memphis, Tenn., 121
Mencken, H. L., 31, 41, 42
Menke, Anthony, 122
Mermaid Tavern, London, 13
Messing, Gust, 26
Metairie, La., 121
Metro-Goldwyn-Mayer, 35-36
Mexico City, Mexico, 121
Meyer, Gus, 131
Miami, Fla., 78
Michigan Central Railroad, 231
Midway (battle), 51
Miles, Major General, 4
Milwaukee, Wis., 184
Minneapolis, Minn., 93
Minute Men, 70
Mobile, Ala., 188
Monroe, Utah, 174
Montgomery, Ala., 170
Monticello, Ark., 171
Montrose, Colo., 108
Moose, the, 134
"Moral Code for Youth," 189, 194
Morgan, J. Pierpont, Sr., 1

Morgenthau, Henry, Jr., 215
Mosaic commandments, 60
Muratore, 123
Muskogee, Okla., 121

Napoleon, 60
Nathan, George J., 31, 41, 42
Newcastle, Wyo., 195
Newman, Harry A., 248, 251
New York, N.Y., 109, 121, 183
Nimitz, Admiral Chester W., 51
Noel, John S., 102, 248, 251
Norfolk, Va., 172
North, E. C., 3
North Little Rock, Ark., 121
Nuevo Laredo, Mexico, 123
Nutter, Harold P., 215
Nutter, Louis, 131
Nyack, N.Y., 139

Oakland, Calif., 53, 121, 135, 199, 217
Oakland (Elmhurst), Calif., 175
Oakland Tribune, 218
Ogden, Utah, 59
Oklahoma City, Okla., 34, 59, 121
Okmulgee, Okla., 121
Old Monarchs, 129, 130
Omaha (Concord Club), Nebr., 25
Optimists, 25, 26
Orange, Tex., 121
Orrock, J. B., 227
Osenbaugh, Richard J., 249, 251
Ottawa, Ontario, 169
Owensville, Mo., 154
OWI speakers bureau, 214

Page, Milton, 131
Paine, Edward H., 105, 250, 251
Panama City, 224, 225
Pan-Pacific Club, 125
Paris, France, 222, 223, 228, 233
Paris Peace Conference, 212
Paris, Tex., 121
Parry Sound, Ontario, 169

Pawtucket, R.I., 214
Pearl Harbor, 133
People's Church, Chicago, 217
Peoria, Ill., 182, 183
Peoria Star, 182
Petra, 233
Petry, Herbert C., Jr., 224
Philadelphia, Pa., 77, 233
Phoenix, Ariz., 170
Pickford, Mary, 210
Pierce, Clifford D., 212, 214, 222, 226, 250, 252
Pittsburgh, Pa., 36, 37, 181
Pittsburgh (East Liberty), Pa., 121, 179
Planters Hotel, Chicago, 8
Port Arthur, Tex., 121, 199
Power, W. J., 27
Powers, Oreg., 176
Prince, C. R., 118
Providence, R.I., 82
P.T.A., 194
Pueblo, Colo., 121
Puerto Rico, 123
Putnam, the Rev. Arthur, 201

Quincy, Ill., 4

Raber, Edwin J., 22, 24, 131
Raleigh, N.C., 121
Reader's Digest, The, 105
Reciprocity Clubs, 25
Reconstruction Finance Corporation, 206
Redheaded Men's League, 15
Redland City, Calif., 179
Reid, C. C., 77, 116, 247, 251
Reynolds, S. J., 131
Richard III, 29
Riley, Ray L., 64, 103, 151, 249, 251
Rinehart, Mary Roberts, 101
Ringling Brothers, 81
Rio Piedras, Puerto Rico, 121
Ritter, Halsted, 69, 71, 167
Riverside, Calif., 209

Romney, W. Va., 186
Roosevelt, Theodore, 31
Ruffin, Ben A., 249, 251

Sacramento, Calif., 175
St. Louis, Mo., 4, 58, 63, 75, 92, 100, 121, 179
St. Paul, Minn., 25, 26, 121
Salinas, Calif., 205
San Angelo, Tex., 121
San Antonio, Tex., 121, 123
San Francisco, Calif., 53, 77, 109
San Francisco Conference, 212, 216
San Juan, Puerto Rico, 121
San Salvador, El Salvador, 121
Santa Claus, 179
Sattler, Dennis S., 3, 24, 131
Saturday Evening Post, 238
Saugus, Mass., 200
Scottsbluff, Nebr., 172
Sekhet (goddess), 29
Shaw, A. D., 150
Shaw, George Bernard, 41
Shelbyville, Ind., 171
Shelbyville, Tenn., 202, 203
Shreveport, La., 121
Shu (goddess), 29
Siegfried, André, 41
Simmang, Theodore J., 123
Skeen, D. A., 212, 216, 217, 218, 221, 222, 250, 252
Smalley, George, 131
Smith, Chas. S., 208
Smith, Fred W., 115, 212, 217, 219, 222, 228, 250, 252
Smith, Ned H., 186
Songs for Lions, 114
Soquel-Capitola, California, 176
Sorrick, Karl M., 249, 251
Southport, N.C., 196
Southwest Harbor Lions Club, 128
Springfield, Colo., 145, 174
Steele, 149
Stettinius, Edward R., Jr., 217, 220
Stevens, Charles, 3, 5, 6
Stevenson, Charles J., 104
Stewart, Ernst A., 106
Stockholm, Sweden, 170

Stockton, Calif., 121
Streutker, Otto, 174
"Studies in Conduct," 189, 192
Sweetwater, Tex., 176

Tygart Valley, W. Va., 139
Tail Twister, 141, 148-53
Tarentum, Pa., 180
Taylor, Larry, 152
Temple, Tex., 121
Terry, Will, 200
Texarkana, Tex., 121
Texas City, Tex., 205
Texas State College for Women, 176
Thucydides, 234
Thurston, Joseph W., 112
Tientsin, China, 123, 124, 125, 185
Tokyo, Japan, 108
Torgney, Bruce, 108
Toronto, Ontario, Canada, 78, 79, 93, 128, 210
Toronto (Danforth), Ontario, 168
Torres, Fidel, 106
Towaoc, Colorado, 108
Towne, William, 1, 2, 4, 6, 16
Trienens, Joseph, 22, 26, 131
Tsingtao, China, 124
Tularosa, N.M., 174
Tulsa, Okla., 121, 186
Tuskegee, Ala., 170

United Nations, 212, 213, 214, 216, 221, 222, 226
United States Senate Foreign Relations Committee, 220
Utterbach, Judge Hubert, 166, 167

Vaught, Judge Edgar S., 166, 167, 247, 251
Victoria, Tex., 176
Vinita, Okla., 179
Vortex Clubs, 25, 57, 58

Waco, Texas, 121
Waldorf-Astoria Hotel, N.Y., 227

Wallbrun, Maurice, 131
Warren, K. H., 60
Warrilow, Thomas, 114, 115
Washington, D.C., 152, 154
Watson, Thomas J., 185
Waycross, Ga., 136
Webster, Daniel, 69
Wells, Alexander T., 167, 251
West, James, 78
Westfall, William A., 248, 251
West Los Angeles, Calif., 210
West Virginia School for the Blind, 186
Whelan, Grover, 109
White cane, 182
White House, the, 208

Wichita Falls, Tex., 121
Wilkinsburg, Pa., 181
Williams, Chester, 227
Wilson, Wilburn L., 96
Wilson, Woodrow, 1
Windsor, Ontario, Canada, 122
Wood River, Ill., 154
Woodson, Marle, 179
World War I, 120, 204, 213
World War II, 208, 250
Wright, Melvin B., 132

Youngstown, Ohio, 131
Yukon River, 70

CPSIA information can be obtained at www.ICGtesting.com
Printed in the USA
BVOW011419150713

325986BV00008B/232/P